MW01049718

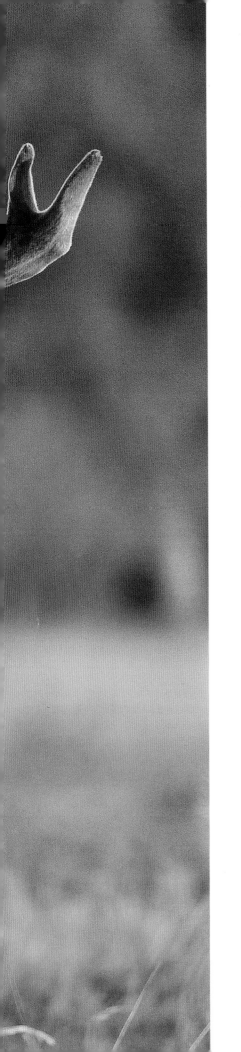

THE BIG BOOK OF
Whitetail

STRATEGIES, TECHNIQUES, AND TACTICS

MVP
BOOKS

First published in 2013 by MVP Books, an imprint of MBI Publishing Company, 400 First Avenue North, Suite 400, Minneapolis, MN 55401 USA

© 2013 MVP Books

Text and photography © 2013 Editors of MVP Books

All photographs are from the author's collection unless noted otherwise.

All rights reserved. With the exception of quoting brief passages for the purposes of review, no part of this publication may be reproduced without prior written permission from the Publisher.

The information in this book is true and complete to the best of our knowledge. All recommendations are made without any guarantee on the part of the author or Publisher, who also disclaims any liability incurred in connection with the use of this data or specific details.

We recognize, further, that some words, model names, and designations mentioned herein are the property of the trademark holder. We use them for identification purposes only.

MVP titles are also available at discounts in bulk quantity for industrial or sales-promotional use. For details write to Special Sales Manager at MBI Publishing Company, 400 First Avenue North, Suite 400, Minneapolis, MN 55401 USA.

To find out more about our books, visit us online at www.voyageurpress.com.

Cataloging-in-Publishing data on file with the Library of Congress

ISBN-13: 978-0-7603-4373-9

10 9 8 7 6 5 4 3 2 1

Printed in China

Editor: Jordan Wiklund
Design Manager: Brad Springer
Designer: Simon Larkin
Layout: John Sticha
Cover designer: Simon Larkin

Sections of this book appear in previous Quayside titles, including *500 Deer Hunting Tips*, *Advanced Whitetail Hunting*, *The Complete Guide to Hunting, Dressing & Cooking Wild Game*, *Whitetail Hunting*, and *Whitetail Tactics & Techniques*.

Contributing writers include Gerald Almy, Scott Bestul, Mike Bleech, Philip Bourjaily, Monte Burch, Jay Cassell, Peter J. Fiduccia, Michael Furtman, Grits Gresham, Tom Gresham, Tom McIntyre, Don Oster, Aaron Fraser Pass, Shawn Perich, Clair Rees, Dwight Schuh, Bill Vaznis, and Wayne van Zwoll.

Photo Credits
On the front cover: A hunter poses with a 10-point trophy. *Ron Spomer, Windigoimages.com*

On the back cover: Top: A bowhunter poised to strike at sundown. Right top: A buck in the rut follows a doe in estrus. Right middle: A buck uses his sensitive nose to sniff out nearby danger. Right bottom: A buck snorts to warn others away. *Shutterstock.*

On the frontispiece: A midwest whitetail walks through a field of tall grass and alfalfa. *Shutterstock.*

On the title page: A southern late-season buck's velvety antlers are just about ready to fall. *Shutterstock.*

Contributing photographer credits: Charles Alsheimer, 27, 32, 76 (top left, middle left, bottom right); Mike Barlow, 151 (middle right, bottom center); John Ford, 151 (top right, bottom left); CPi, 199, 215-218, 221-225

Images on 111, 173, 190 (bottom), 192, and 213 courtesy of iStockphoto.

All other images courtesy of Shutterstock.

CONTENTS

THE WHITETAIL ERA

Theodore Roosevelt felt that "the finding and killing of the game is after all but a part of the whole." He extolled the virtues of hunting in rugged wilderness, and of adventuring into new territory. Hunting built character, pitting man versus nature in an ancient test of patience, guile, wits, speed, strength, and skill. And no other animal so embodies these virtues than the white-tailed deer.

The white-tailed deer is America's most popular big game animal. Remarkably adaptable, it survives—and often thrives—in northern forests, midwestern farmlands, southern swamps, western scrub, and even suburban backyards. Wherever it is found, the whitetail is an elusive quarry that challenges even the most experienced hunters. You can spend a lifetime honing your deer-hunting skills and still never see a buck during the season—they are more than worthy adversaries.

Today's deer hunting is better than it's ever been before. In recent decades, scientific wildlife management has greatly increased both the range and abundance of whitetails, providing close-to-home hunting opportunities for millions of hunters. This truly is the Whitetail Era, a golden age for growing numbers of devoted deer hunters.

But there can be too much of a good thing. Without predation or adequate hunter harvest, whitetails proliferate to nuisance levels. Hungry deer destroy vegetation in farm fields, forests, and backyards. From car-deer collisions to Lyme disease, human health

risks increase when deer are overabundant. Recent discoveries of chronic wasting disease (CWD) in wild deer populations may indicate that high deer densities can lead to starvation, winter loss, and disease.

Wildlife managers use regulated hunting to keep deer populations in check. Extra antlerless-only permits, special hunts, and extended seasons are used as incentives to encourage hunters to kill more deer. Many hunters are aware of their individual role in deer management. They practice local management by selectively harvesting deer to maintain a balanced herd.

Deer hunting has become more sophisticated during the Whitetail Era, but the basic challenge remains the same. The white-tailed deer is a wary animal that relies on a keen sense of smell, excellent hearing, and eyesight to detect and avoid danger. To beat a deer's sensory defenses, you must stay quiet, be patient, and keep the wind in your face. Within these ground rules, you have many ways to play the game. Traditional tactics— driving, standing, and still-hunting—are effective wherever whitetails roam. Newer strategies—calling,

Whitetail hunting is a rewarding experience one can enjoy for life.

scents, rattling, and decoys—have also entered the hunting mainstream.

While firearms seasons are the most popular, archery and "black powder" hunts attract hunters who enjoy longer seasons and less hunting pressure. Many hunters take up bowhunting or muzzleloading so they can enjoy the challenges of these methods and spend more time afield. Archers are frequently used by wildlife managers to harvest deer in suburban situations. In some metropolitan areas, experienced bowhunters have formed organizations that specialize in safe removal of problem deer.

For many hunters, however, deer hunting is simply an enjoyable time spent outdoors with family and friends.

You don't need to be an expert hunter to have fun—a good beginning is to read this book. We've supplied you with the basic information you need to understand whitetail behavior, find a place to hunt, select the right equipment, and choose a proven hunting strategy. What you learn in the following pages will give you the confidence necessary to become a successful hunter.

For the responsible hunter, the learning process never stops. There are always more tactics to know, more advantages to gain, more deer habits to understand and analyze. And make no mistake, the whitetail deer is not stupid—its ability to thwart the best hunters continues to fuel late night bull sessions around the campfire. It has adapted to man and his encroachment upon the

For many hunters, the onset of winter near the end of November signals the end of the season. The rewards of whitetail hunting last all year, however.

wilderness. In fact, deer are absolutely thriving—as of this writing, there are an estimated 27 million whitetail deer in North America, many more than were here when European settlers first set foot upon the continent. Each year, almost 10 million people hunt them, and perhaps 2 million are successful. It's not easy.

Your enjoyment of whitetail hunting doesn't have to end when the season closes. There are many ways to extend it. For example, successful hunters bring home venison, a lean, mild-flavored meat you can prepare in many ways. You can visit your hunting area in winter and early spring to scout, learn more about

deer, and look for discarded antlers. Attend hunting shows and seminars. Get involved in a hunting or conservation organization.

Where to start? Well, this book is here to help you out. We can't guarantee that reading this book will help bag you a Boone & Crockett–class buck this coming season, but we can say with confidence that if you follow the advice found in these pages, you will become a better deer hunter. We guarantee that.

When you step into the world of the whitetail, hunting becomes a way of life!

Whitetails are challenging quarry, equipped with keen vision and supernatural senses of smell and hearing.

CHAPTER ONE

WORLD OF THE WHITETAIL

No hunter succeeds without complete knowledge of the animal he or she pursues.

If that's true, then it is doubly true for the deer hunter, for the white-tailed deer is a complex animal, physically and behaviorally. You simply can't get close enough to one of these secretive animals without knowing how it behaves, and why it does so.

As with all animals, two primary urges control the whitetail's behavior. Food is first, for without that, there is no health. Sex is second, for once adequate food is acquired, the majority of a healthy, well-fed whitetail's behavior revolves around reproduction.

Few creatures are as wary and sly as whitetail deer. The more you know, the more you'll enjoy the hunt.

Not just the actual sex act, mind you, but the whole cycle of reproducing. For the buck, that means acquiring the size and antler configuration to "out compete" his rivals and to attract does. For the doe, it means being healthy enough to carry a fetus through the long winter, to give birth in spring and to ensure her fawns grow large enough to survive their first winter.

Ensuring success in these energy-intensive endeavors requires physical skills and finely tuned senses. Whitetails have all of that, the result of eons of evolution, during which they've been repeatedly tested by weather, predators, and disease. The weak were found lacking, and the strong were not. The hunter must pit himself or herself against the result of natural selection over thousands of generations—quite a daunting task.

Many hunters scour their hunting areas for antlers and signs of trophy bucks, and sometimes they even stumble upon skulls.

DEER ANATOMY

It may seem strange to begin a discussion on the whitetail's physiology by looking first at its stomach, but it really is the stomach that in many ways influences the shape of everything else.

Digestive System

So how does a stomach influence a species? Consider this: If a deer must stand long enough in one spot to thoroughly chew its food until it is digestible, it also exposes itself to predators for long periods. The whitetail's compound stomach is comprised of four chambers: rumen, reticulum, omasum, and abomasum. When it has consumed a sufficient quantity of food, it travels to a secure hiding area, brings the food back up, and chews its cud in relative leisure and safety. By being able to digest and chew food at a later time, a deer can browse and move, making it a more difficult target to find.

The white-tailed deer selectively chooses more digestible plants, or the most digestible parts of plants, rather than consuming large quantities of less-digestible food. Deer rarely stand in one place for long, but prefer to nip and move. Once they've temporarily eaten their fill and stored the food in the rumen (the stomach's first chamber), white-tailed deer move to an area in their territory they consider safe. Here they bed down,

and once they are confident that no danger awaits them, they regurgitate a ball, or bolus, of food for further chewing.

White-tailed deer have a highly specialized digestive system that permits both this feeding behavior and the ability to eat a variety of plant foods. Although they are, like cattle, considered ruminants, they are not true grazers as are cows. Cattle can eat grass or other ruffage. This involves considerable "head down" grazing in order to consume the large volume of less-nutritious forage needed. A cow or bison with its head down all the time isn't being particularly alert to threats. Herding behavior offsets this because as some animals graze, others stand by, chewing their cuds, and act as guards.

Whitetails can afford to be selective; the forest and its edge hold a wide variety of succulent plants, browse, fruits, and nuts. True grazers, like cattle and bison, are animals of the plains where they feed on varieties of less-nutritious and less-digestible grasses.

The fact that deer can be choosy means they have a slightly different digestive system than other ruminants. The whitetails' rumen is smaller than that of other deer, and their salivary glands are larger.

After carefully selecting their food, whitetails nip it from the main plant. Whitetails lack incisors on the upper jaw (and have no true canine teeth), so they shred food from the plant stem by grasping it between the lower incisors and the tough, bony roof of the upper jaw. If you study browsed plants carefully, you'll soon be able to distinguish those slightly shredded twig tips left

Competition for does among healthy bucks is fierce, and groups of does can often be found together during the rut.

Due to their sophisticated digestive system, whitetails are able to eat a wide variety of foods, like acorns and corn.

Their angular faces allow whitetails to reach food in hard-to-get places and to pinpoint the exact plants they'd like to eat.

by browsing whitetails from the cleanly cut tips made by other animals, like rabbits.

The whitetail's selective feeding behavior is aided by its nimble lips and narrow face, which have evolved to allow them to "insert" their face and mouth into trees and shrubs, or among various ground plants, to select not only the species of choice, but the portion of the plant they desire. After tearing off a mouthful, whitetails chew the food very briefly—only enough to swallow it—which is aided by the abundance of saliva whitetails can manufacture. Then, as stated earlier, they move off to their bedding area to further chew and digest their food.

Knowing where deer bed, then, is an important bit of knowledge for the hunter. Deer repeatedly use the same bedding areas, and routes to them. Once bedded, they are nearly impossible to find, so the hunter's best chance is to waylay the deer on its way from a feeding area to the bedding grounds.

With its stomach dictating that it be fed, almost everything else about the deer's body is designed to facilitate that. Feet, legs, joints, bones; all are designed

Deer usually retire to a secluded location to bed and further chew their food.

to get a deer quietly around the forest so that it can find the food its stomach demands, and to get it out of trouble should trouble find it. Its fine array of senses evolved to provide it with an early-warning system, and to utilize the chemical messages left by its glandular system.

Speed and stealth for whitetails begin "where the rubber meets the road"—in their case where the keratin meets the detritus (OK—in lay terms, where the outer hoof meets the decaying material that makes up the Earth).

Hooves and Legs

The whitetail's narrow, tapered hooves are specialized to allow minimal contact with the ground. That serves deer well in two ways: Minimal contact reduces friction, which increases speed; and narrow hooves are easier to place quietly amidst the forest floor's noisy leaves and sticks. In addition, whitetails are "perfect walkers," which simply means that while walking at normal speed, the rear hooves fall exactly into the tracks of the front hooves. The advantage of this seems fairly obvious: Once the front hooves have been safely and quietly placed, the deer knows that its rear steps will be equally well placed.

The track of a whitetail hoof is like that of paired commas. Looking at a whitetail's tracks, one would easily assume that it only has two toes per leg. If you guessed that, you'd be exactly half right, since there are two other vestigial toes farther up the back of the leg, known as dewclaws. The front legs' dewclaws are nearer to the hoof than those of the rear. Usually dewclaws don't show in tracks unless the deer has been walking in snow or mud, or running at high speed.

When walking, the closed, rounded point of the track faces forward. However, at full gallop, or braking down a steep embankment, deer splay their hooves wide at the front, reversing the impression. Since whitetails carry more weight on their front hooves, these are slightly larger than those of the rear, and the hooves of bucks are larger than those of same-age does. Some research indicates that buck hooves are slightly more rounded at the tip than those of does, perhaps because the extra weight carried by mature bucks causes additional wear. Some also believe, although studies have never proven it, that drag marks appearing between tracks in snow

less than 6 inches in depth indicate the passing of a buck. In snow deeper than 6 inches, however, it is impossible for deer not to leave drag marks, so their presence reveals little about age or sex.

The hoof itself is comprised of the outer, tough horn made of keratin (our fingernails are made of the same material) and a spongy surface on the sole that provides some shock absorption and traction. Deer hooves wear constantly and, like our own nails, are replaced as they wear, although the rate of growth varies with the season.

Deer have two vestigial claws known as dew claws above and behind their hooves.

Their narrow feet and legs are designed for speed and maneuverability. The rear legs provide the greatest thrust, while the front legs steer with great precision. Unlike humans, the whitetail's front shoulders lack a collarbone assembly and are free-floating—their front legs can pivot independently of each other, allowing for those "on the dime" turns at which we marvel.

A powerful rear leg structure allows whitetails to leap over tall obstructions, even from a standing start. From a dead stop, they can clear a fence or windfall of up to 7 feet; once running, that vertical height increases to over 8 feet.

Coat

Bundling all this together is a mass of muscle and a coat of dense, hollow hair—not fur. The whitetail's coat is a shade of color that blends in well with many surroundings. That the darkest hair is on the top, especially along the spine, is no accident. It gives the impression of a shadow cast from above. Grayish hairs scattered through the winter coat's shoulders and haunches also tend to act as a shadow effect, as well as serving to blend into the trunks of trees. White patches beneath the chin and along the entire underside help to break up the deer's own natural shadow, making it look less than three dimensional to passing predators.

Deer are swift runners, silent and fast. As the rut approaches, they become ever more jumpy.

But beyond just camouflage, the whitetail's coat is designed to protect. Since it must do so both in warm weather and extreme cold, whitetails evolved two specialized coats and therefore must molt twice a year. The spring molt occurs in May in the North, and as early as March in Texas and is marked by the shedding of the long winter hair. Winter coats are usually fully grown-in by mating season.

Their winter coat, the one most hunters encounter, is comprised of darker, sun-absorbing guard hairs and a second layer of woolly underfur. Unlike the summer coat, the winter coat's individual guard hairs are hollow,

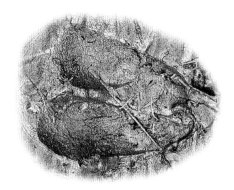

A deer track can reveal many aspects about the speed and size of the animal.

At full run, deer can reach nearly 40 mph, and they are agile jumpers—they often escape predators and hunters by leaping fences at full speed.

increasing the amount of dead air space and insulation. So little heat escapes that snow falling on a deer doesn't melt.

Tail

Considering that whitetails have evolved a coat that—besides keeping them protected from the elements—is designed to "protect" them from predators through camouflage, one might wonder why they have such a conspicuous white tail for which they are named.

This "flag" serves an important purpose. Its evolution was no accident. Although deer survival depends largely upon being unseen in the forest, they are social animals that need to keep track of each other. Thus they evolved a tail that meets both needs.

When lowered, the tail presents only minimal white to the searching eyes of a predator, and so doesn't

A deer's winter coat turns more grayish and dull, and looks much more shaggy.

The summer coat is smooth and lighter.

adversely impact camouflage. Raised, however, it becomes a white beacon to other deer, serving as a warning that danger is present, allowing fleeing deer to easily follow each other. Since the tail is raised only when danger is imminent, and only when the whitetail is exercising its speed and agility in an escape (which are its last, best defense), it is probably no disadvantage that predators can also see the flag. However, whitetails don't always raise this flag when escaping. A deer that is trying to sneak away often pins its tail tightly to its rump.

The tail also serves as a silent early-warning system. When a whitetail is suspicious of a noise or object, it erects its rump hair and pumps its tail up and down. Since deer usually turn to face the possible threat, this silent warning is usually only viewed by other deer to its rear. Once the danger is identified and located, the tail becomes fully erect. Now every deer within eyesight is silently warned. If the noise or intruder is eventually deemed to be nonthreatening, the cautious whitetail will flick its tail side-to-side once, relax, and go on about its business. This flick lets other deer know that the "coast is clear."

While at rest or investigating a new food source or area, the proverbial white tail is usually low and loose.

SENSES

When you live life as food for something else, much of what you do is designed to avoid ending up on something else's menu while you find something to put on yours. To that end, white-tailed deer have evolved remarkably acute senses.

Smell

The whitetail's sense of smell may just be the most important when it comes to avoiding predators and communicating with other deer. Although studies have never quantified just how much better the whitetail's sense of smell is than our own, there is unanimous agreement among scientists and hunters that it far outstrips our own meager scenting abilities. Not only can deer differentiate between species through just the use of scent (even the best of us would have a hard time scenting a wolf, but even if we did catch a whiff, would you know what it is you're smelling?), they seem to be able to determine the age of an odor. In other words, wolf scent that is old, though it registers on the deer's "smell-o-meter," causes a far different behavioral reaction than one that is fresh.

When it comes to warning deer of danger, the sense of smell is the ultimate judge. Hearing a noise, the deer will look in that direction. Seeing what is making that noise may cause the deer to stare intently. But even when taken together, the deer still may not be able to identify the intruder or be inclined to flee. One good whiff, however, is enough to finally pass judgment. And, of course, a deer needn't see a human, wolf, or cougar to know that it needs to disappear. Seeing a predator simply isn't required when you can smell it.

Scent is also an important communication tool, especially for fawns and does trying to keep track of each other, as a means of finding a prospective mate, and for detecting invisible, chemical signposts that tell bucks about each other's rank and territory. And as mentioned earlier, deer can scent-track each other, a useful tool in following other deer to safety or food.

Finally, like us, deer follow their noses to food. Whitetails do one thing that especially enhances their sense of smell. They wet their nose with their tongue so

Scent Control

Of a buck's three primary senses, there's no doubt that his sniffer is the most powerful. When an unsuspecting buck sees something out of place or hears an unusual sound, he will most likely investigate the commotion from a safe distance before skulking back into the shadows. But let him get a fresh whiff of his age-old enemy—the autumn hunter—and he could disappear for the rest of the season. Here are a few tips to help avoid that scenario.

- When it's time to hunt, take a shower with a scent-free soap, and don't put on any outer clothing until you reach your hunting area. Of course, this is easier said than done when temperatures dip.

- Hunting boots stink—no way around it. To eliminate unwanted odors, spray the inside with a good over-the-counter foot powder, and then store them in a clear, scent-free plastic bag until it's time to hunt. Do not wear your boots while pumping gas or around camp where they can pick up strange odors.

- Wash all your hunting clothing with a scent-free detergent and then store them in a scent-free plastic container with leaves, twigs, weeds, and dirt from your hunting area. This helps reduce human odors.

- Get rid of your old hats—they soak up human odors like a sponge. Spray a new hat with a good scent eliminator, and then only wear it in the field. Change hats at least once a week.

- When handling buck lures, urines, attractant scents, decoys, or climbing pegs, be aware that deer will walk right up and smell the canisters, the decoys, and metal steps without hesitation. Always wear rubber gloves sprayed with scent eliminators to avoid leaving a human odor.

- Be more concerned with the scent you leave on the ground than any airborne odor; the latter dissipates rather quickly into the wind, but ground scent can linger for hours, spooking deer long after you've gone home and to bed.

- To keep ground scent to a minimum, be careful where you walk, what you touch, and avoid rubbing up against any waist-high weeds or underbrush. Rubber-bottomed boots sprayed liberally with a good scent eliminator can help, as can foot pads and drag rags soaked in fox, skunk, raccoon, or coyote urine.

- Despite all precautions, there is no cover-up scent that can handle human odors all the time. Remember to play the wind despite all scent precautions.

While trotting or running, the tail is often held high as a sign of danger to other deer. This is often the last thing hunters see if they're too slow or sloppy!

that scent molecules increase in dampness as they enter the nostrils. Molecules so humidified tend to cling better to olfactory cells.

It makes great evolutionary sense that an animal that lives in the woods, where the distance one can see is limited, would develop other means of interpreting signals. The sense of smell fills that role. But deer have at least one other tool that aides them when visibility is limited—an acute sense of hearing.

Hearing

Humans have eyesight that perceives depth of field, or distance. Our hearing, however, does not, built as we are with immobile ears set on either side of our head.

The whitetail's ears sit atop the head and can move independently of each other. It isn't uncommon to see a deer with one of these large "audible scoops" facing one direction, with the other pointing off somewhere else. Whitetails may even keep one ear forward and another rearward while at full gallop, so that they might hear if they're being pursued from behind, while they simultaneously listen for trouble ahead. By being able to direct their ears, whitetails not only hear better than we do, they can determine the direction and distance from which a sound emanates. If it reaches the left ear first, then whatever made the sound is nearer to that side, and through comparing the minute difference in time it takes the sound to reach the other ear, deer can effectively triangulate to get a fix on the source.

While humans tend to turn toward a sound, deer may just turn an ear toward it. By doing so, they can amplify the noise. For gathering sound waves, whitetails have four times more ear surface area than humans. In addition, they can hear sounds that we can't, particularly at the higher frequencies. White-tailed deer can hear sounds in the 20 to 20,000 Hertz range; humans, from 500 to 12,000 Hz. The deer's hearing isn't supreme in the animal world, though. Dogs can hear better, able to discern sounds in a range that begins lower (15 Hz) and ends higher (44,000 Hz).

Despite excellent hearing, sudden loud noises may confuse the whitetail's ability to detect the source or direction of the sound. As some hunters can attest, deer sometimes stand around even after a loud gunshot, apparently unable to find the source. Most research

A whitetail that has detected a predator stares in the direction the odor came from to pick up any movement. Many hunters are familiar with the stare-down game.

indicates that deer move around less, or are more nervous, on windy days, most likely because they are uncomfortable with their diminished hearing.

Vision

The third major sense, vision, is the whitetail's least acute. It isn't that their eyesight is poor. It just isn't quite as superb as are their hearing and scenting abilities.

White-tailed deer eyes are adapted to see well both in low light (even in darkness) as well as under the bright light of day. Their pupils contract into a narrow slit, unlike ours, which form a circular opening. This slit concentrates light in a narrow band against the back of the eye, or retina, which contains the light-sensing receptors clustered in a horizontal band. Combined with the actual placement in the skull, deer have a remarkable 270-degree field of view. The only place they can't see is behind them. Our field of view is limited to 180 degrees.

Inside their eyes, whitetails (and other animals designed to see in low light) have a membrane that humans lack—the tapetum lucidum. It is this membrane

Deer can pinpoint the source of a sound hundreds of yards away, particularly low frequencies, such as other deer (or hunters) grunting.

Not only do deer have a wider radius of vision than humans (deer field of vision in red; human in yellow), their pupils gather about nine times more light than human eyes. Deer also have better peripheral vision.

that reflects the light of a car's headlights. It also allows light to reflect through their eyes light receptors twice, increasing their ability to see in the dark.

Do whitetails see color? That debate still rages. In order to see color as we know it, an animal must have the right kind of photoreceptors. Our eyes have two kinds; cones, which give us daylight and color vision, and rods, which enable vision in low light, but in shades of gray, like a black-and-white movie. Deer definitely have rods, but studies conflict on whether or not they have cones. Two studies insist that there are cones on the whitetail's retina, and seem to indicate that whitetails see some color, especially in the yellow and blue ranges. These studies also indicate that if deer do see color, they are

least sensitive to long wavelengths—those in the red-orange range. However, another study that used electron microscopes found that whitetails do not have color-sensing cones. Some studies also indicate that whitetails see well in the ultraviolet range, which is invisible to humans.

Whatever the case, deer are remarkably adept at seeing motion. The slightest movement by a hunter or other whitetail will focus the deer's unwavering attention. Deer can stand unblinking for what seems like an eternity, trying to get you to move again. Often they'll lower their head for a second, trying to fool you into thinking that they are no longer observing you. Within seconds, however, they snap their head back up. If you've

Both bucks and does make a wide variety of calls. They can snort, bleat, whine, and more, and distinguishing between calls is challenging, even for the veteran hunter.

moved so much as an inch, they'll note the difference and vanish in a flurry of bounds and snorts.

The whitetail's array of senses is imposing. It is very difficult for any living thing to sneak up on them, although obviously this occurs or predators would have vanished long ago, and human hunters would have long since given up. And although we've discussed their senses separately, they work in concert. A deer may hear a sound first, then turn to watch for movement. If it can't see it, it may move downwind to see if it can catch a whiff. One or another of the senses will eventually determine whether or not the deer can remain safely, or warn it to move off.

COMMUNICATION

Whitetails spend most of their lives in groups, a habit that improves their chances of survival. With many eyes and ears on alert, the deer can easily detect an approaching intruder. When one deer senses trouble, it quickly communicates alarm to other group members. Understanding how whitetails communicate can help you predict their behavior—upping your odds of taking a deer.

Whitetails spend most of their lives in groups, and are highly sensitive to the slightest interruption of their space. Predators and even loud noises often cause the group to flee.

A casual tail is a sign of safety, even when other competing bucks are in the area.

Sounds Made by Deer

Compared to other animals, white-tailed deer aren't particularly vocal. That shouldn't be surprising, since sound doesn't carry well in the woods, and animals that are prey species are better off not advertising their presence by making a lot of noise.

That said, whitetails do make an array of sounds, all of which are designed to communicate with each other. Sounds are made by both sexes and at all ages.

Of course, females and fawns regularly communicate through a series of grunts, whines, and bleats. Doe-fawn calls are seldom useful to hunters, although a fawn bleat or bawl can sometimes lure a doe into view.

Of most importance to hunters are the sounds deer make during the autumn mating season. Both bucks and does emit agonistic calls—sounds designed to imply aggressiveness. A single low grunt is used by both sexes year-round to let other deer know that they aren't at all happy about sharing food, or that the other deer is too near or unwelcome. As the encounter becomes more intense, the aggressor deer may add a series of snorts. This "grunt-snort" call is most fully developed in rutting bucks, particularly between mature bucks that are of near-equal stature physically and socially. The most threatening sound a rutting, dominant buck can make is the "grunt-snort-wheeze" designed to let his rival know

Although not a widely used warning system, deer stomping their feet is effective enough to be used occasionally.

Forehead gland

Preorbital gland

Tarsal gland

Interdigital gland

Metatarsal gland

Glands secrete scents called pheromones that are important signals for other deer. The scent from each of these glands can send important messages, from the urgency to breed to the need to flee.

that he won't tolerate his presence. If the competitor doesn't respond to this call by leaving, a dominance battle may erupt.

Although not often heard by hunters, another whitetail call made during the autumn, especially during the rut, is the "tending grunt." This low, guttural sound is emitted by a buck courting a doe in heat, or while he is tracking her.

Some hunters confuse this mating grunting with the whitetail's alarm call. Often called a "buck snort," this wheezing whistle is actually made by both bucks and does. Caused by the sudden expelling of air through the nasal passage, it serves as a warning to all other deer nearby that danger lurks. When deer are suddenly startled, this sound is singular and explosive; when they have detected trouble from a distance, warning is often given in a series of lengthier snorts.

Body Language

Sometimes just a barely perceptible movement of an ear is all a deer needs to communicate. Other times it's just a twitch of a muscle—and danger is understood. Deer in groups may stomp their feet when alarmed to warn others. But foot-stomping can be heard for only a short distance.

The most-used communication tool may be a deer's tail. A casual side-to-side motion—wagging similar to that of horses or cattle—with no hair standing erect signals no danger. If the tail begins a sharp side-to-side motion with the tail horizontal or upright and hairs are erect, you know that the deer is sending out signals of mild alarm. If nothing else confirms that feeling, the deer may go back to what it was doing and not take flight. But once the deer is convinced the danger is real, it will hold the tail upright, waving it back and forth, exposing the white hair underneath. This signals a high state of alarm, and any deer within sight of it will quickly leave the area.

Other Silent Messages

Glands—those mysterious chemical-producing organs found in the oddest of locations—exert tremendous control over the seasonal routine of the whitetail.

Located primarily in, or just below, the skin, glands serve as generators of chemical communication for whitetails, enhancing the role of the deer's already important sense of smell. Each gland emits its own unique scent, known as a "pheromone." Think of pheromones as the alphabet of an olfactory language, a language that allows deer to tell each other things about their readiness to mate, to recognize each other, to establish dominance or territory, and to warn others of impending danger. All of these important signals are transmitted without a sound, and are readable by passing deer long after the messenger has disappeared. In a forest environment, where sound carries poorly and members of the species rarely congregate in large numbers, an eloquent language of odors seems like an immense advantage. It is.

Deer use several glands to mark territory and attract females. This buck is rubbing his forehead gland to mark an overhead twig.

The roles of some glands aren't fully understood because they have only recently been discovered. However, we do know, or suspect, that the following glands function in certain ways.

- Found just in front of the eye, the preorbital gland is a hairless, shallow slit-like pocket. Witnessing a deer scent-mark a twig with this gland brings on an involuntary twinge in the human observer, for it almost appears that the deer is poking a stick into its eye. Bucks frequently rub the preorbital gland on twigs that overhang buck scrapes. Researchers don't know what message is conveyed by the scent emitted from this gland, but it certainly is of importance to whitetails, for passing whitetails definitely stop to check the odor left at these sites. Not only do rutting bucks frequently use this gland on overhead twigs, they flare it during displays of dominance, as do does when they are nursing their fawns.

- Forehead glands are thought to be used for scent marking. During autumn, whitetails of both sexes rub their foreheads on branches, depositing this gland's scent.

- Interdigital glands are found on all four feet in folds between the whitetail's toes. Although the purpose of this scent-making gland is unknown, it must, at the very least, serve as a means of leaving a scent trail. Such a trail would alert deer to the passing of one of their kind, an important message year-round, but especially during breeding season.

- Located about 6 inches above the hoof, the metatarsal gland is marked by a white tuft of hair on the outside of both rear legs. Interestingly, this gland is far larger in northern subspecies of whitetails. In black-tailed deer this gland has been proven to emit an odor that warns other deer of danger. Studies have failed to confirm that the whitetail uses this gland for the same purpose.

- The tarsal gland is large and significant, located on the inside of the whitetail's leg at the tarsal joint. It is marked by a raised tuft of long hairs. Like a large brush, this tuft becomes "painted" with the pheromones released from within, as well as with urine, which the deer deposits on this gland through a behavior called "rub urination" or "scent urination." In this technique deer of both sexes hunch up slightly and urinate on the inside of their rear legs. As the breeding season progresses, the tarsal gland of mature bucks becomes stained from the frequent rub urination, and the odor of it is detectable even by humans. The tarsal gland is generally considered by hunters to be the most important of the "communication" glands.

ANTLER GROWTH AND PURPOSE

Sure, antlers do serve the whitetail buck as weapons against predators and other whitetail rivals. But for the most part, these elaborate ornaments are there so bucks won't have to fight, at least among themselves. Social dominance in the male whitetail's world is largely governed by size of body and size of antlers. Since large bucks generally also produce large antlers, this headgear serves as a visual means of displaying one's status. Small bucks fear large bucks, limiting the rare actual combat to rivals of equal stature. Thus, in the grand evolutionary mastery of nature, these fascinating antlers, though they could be used for deadly means, prevent most fights simply through display.

Antlers are deciduous—grown and shed each year—and are actually made of bone and are living tissue. A cow's horns, on the other hand, are made of keratin, a dead tissue, and are not shed.

Bucks produce their first antlers in the spring just prior to their first birthday, although fawn bucks sometimes grow short buttons (not to be confused with the longer "spikes" of some yearling bucks).

Antler growth is triggered by the pineal

When fawns sometimes sprout small antler nubs, they are referred to as button bucks. Don't confuse a fawn's buttons with a yearling's longer spikes.

Big whitetails can have small antlers and small whitetails can have big antlers. Just as genetics, age, and nutrition determine body size, they also determine antler size and shape.

gland, which in turn triggers the release of testosterone, the hormone most responsible for antler growth. The pineal gland is sensitive to photoperiod; antler growth begins as the days lengthen in spring, between the spring equinox and summer solstice. Whitetails in the Far North have a more defined schedule to their antler growth than do those deer near the equator. For

example, Minnesota bucks are growing antlers by May, while those in Florida don't start until June.

Antler growth is incredibly rapid, and is, in fact, the fastest growing bone known to science. Although antler growth is started by the lengthening of days in spring, it is hastened by the shortening days of late summer. By the time the rut occurs, antlers will have been hardened bone for two full months. Growing antlers are covered in a modified skin and fur known as velvet. Rich with blood and nerve tissues, velvet nourishes the growing bone, and consists almost completely of a protein called collagen. Antlers are susceptible to damage when in velvet, and an injured antler bleeds profusely, but clots quickly. Misshapen antlers are often a result of accidental damage during this growth period.

Antler velvet dies in early autumn and either falls off the hardened bone, or is scraped away on brush and trees by the buck. The color of the antler, which can range from near white to mahogany brown, is determined by the amount of blood staining during the velvet stripping process. Antlers are high in mineral content, which the buck will steal from his own skeleton if his diet provides inadequate amounts, replacing them from his diet once the antlers are fully hardened.

White-tailed deer antlers sweep forward on the main beam, then grow upward on the tines. This basket shape seems to be designed to "catch" the antlers of an equal-size opponent, thus lowering the risk of injury to either combatant.

Antler size is determined by both nutrition and genetics. That is, some deer just have the genes for big antlers, but even then, their antlers won't be as big as they could be without good nutrition. With both good nutrition and the right genes, a yearling buck (his second fall) may have three or four points per side. Lacking one or the other of these elements, his first rack may only consist of two single spikes.

Recent research also indicates that the doe, as well as the buck, contributes genes that control antler growth. Bucks continue to grow antlers all their lives, with their peak rack occurring when they are 5½ years old. As they age beyond that, their antler size may diminish.

Antlers are cast in January through March, again as a reaction to photoperiod. At the point where the antler erupts from the skull is a joint known as the pedicle. Resulting from decreased testosterone after the rut, the bond between antler and pedicle weakens, and the two antlers fall off, often within hours of each other. In only a matter of a few short months, however, the buck will again start to grow antlers—the only regenerating living tissue in the animal world.

BREEDING BEHAVIOR

It's the rule for all species: The greatest amount of each individual's effort goes into the breeding cycle or to the rearing of young. Life is no different for white-tailed deer—the effort to pass on its genes is the central mission in a deer's life. Everything a deer does—escaping predators, surviving winter, scent-marking trees, even just feeding—are simply steps toward successfully reproducing itself. Exactly how a deer goes about it, however, depends upon its sex.

MATURITY AND SUCCESS RATE

Even though some male whitetails reach puberty as fawns, and all are sexually mature as yearlings, they rarely breed. Breeding rights among bucks are determined by size, so they spend most of their early lives just trying to grow large and old enough to get a chance to breed. To this end, body size is more important than antler size. Forced to make a choice (physiologically, not consciously), a buck will divert scant nutritional resources to putting on size and weight, rather than antler growth, which consumes tremendous energy.

Once bucks mature at 3 to 5 years of age, they then exert enormous effort into ranging widely beyond their home range in an effort to find receptive mates. Since bucks spend years denied the chance to reproduce, once mature enough to outclass rivals, they reproduce with as many does as possible. This helps ensure some of their offspring will themselves live long enough to perpetuate their genetic contribution. This then could be called a buck's reproductive strategy: Grow big and range widely. A buck is the wind that scatters seed.

A doe's strategy is different. Her genetic contribution is carried, born, and defended by her. She does not directly compete with other does for a mate. Although she grows restless during the breeding season and advertises her presence in her home range, she rarely needs to leave it to seek a mate, since he will invariably find her.

Even large whitetails such as this can have relatively small antlers.

Many hunters are motivated by the appearance of a late-season monster, like this buck. As bucks age, they become more nocturnal, but also more clever.

How Trophy Bucks Survive

Bucks, especially big bucks, are very secretive animals. Older bucks commonly live near people, yet they are almost never seen. We know bucks become more nocturnal as they age, so it's not too surprising that trophy bucks are so elusive. Some suggest that such big bucks leave an area when disturbance increases, but that seems unlikely—one study found that a density of 1 hunter per 10 acres did not force bucks to abandon their normal haunts.

A 1995 Texas study considered the way whitetail bucks react to human disturbance. The study showed that bucks were less flighty as they got older. Middle-aged bucks from 3½ to 4½ years old traveled farthest when spooked; bucks over 7½ years of age traveled the shortest distance. This research confirms what most experienced whitetail hunters already know—a big buck is secure in his home range. He's learned that slow, deliberate movements away from potential danger work better than a long, panicstricken run.

Bucks that survive to old age are cagey about the bedding areas they select, too. In skimpy cover like the farm country of the Midwest, bucks may travel several miles from choice nighttime feeding areas to the dense cover where they bed down during the day. In the South's extensive timber plantations, good cover and browse are nearly always close together, so bucks don't have to travel as far between forage and secure bedding areas.

A pregnant doe eats for herself and her unborn fawn in the spring, so she often generally beds close to prime feeding areas and maximizes her chow time. For this reason, it's not unusual to see does in strips of cover near farming operations. Trophy bucks aren't as desperate for food and often prefer to bed as far away as possible from human disturbance. This may leave them far from the best feed. Some biologists suggest that this habit may have evolutionary value. The mature buck may leave the best feed to his does so that his offspring are born healthy and vigorous, preserving his genes in the next generation. As the summer progresses, a buck's antlers and body begin to demand more energy and he may move into prime feeding areas nearer the does.

Trophy bucks spend much of their time in impenetrable cover. These areas provide bucks with such dependable sanctuary that they often use them as bedding sites for months, even years. Often as small as 1 to 2 acres, these refuges provide the buck with the cover he needs to hide during the day and ready access to nearby feeding areas at night.

In the South, these hideouts are often in swamps. In the Northwest, they may be impenetrable willow thickets next to a major river, positioned so that prevailing winds allow safe ingress and egress. In the North, they may be thick conifer stands; hawthorn thickets; abandoned fields with dense tangles of sumac, prickly ash or aspen, or a combination thereof. During the rut the trails to and from these bedding sites will be marked with many rubs. The bedding area itself will have some major rubs, perhaps a scrape and lots of deer pellets in a small area.

Trophy bucks may claim a reliable bedding site for an entire hunting season or even multiple years.

Antlers are biological wonders—
the only regenerating living
tissue in the animal world!

Thus, the doe's well-established home range may have a reproductive role—by staying in a small area, it is much easier for a mate to find you when you're ready to breed. If both sexes wandered widely during the breeding season, sexual encounters would be much more happenstance. Does, therefore, ensure their reproductive success by skillfully choosing habitat that provides the vast energy stores needed for a successful full-term pregnancy, offers a secure birthing area, is dense enough to hide fawns, and contains enough and appropriate food.

Among large mammals, white-tailed deer are considered a prolific species. They reach puberty at an early age (as fawns in some populations, as yearlings in all others). Exactly when they reach puberty has much to do with the quality of the range in which the deer is found, since the onset of puberty is determined by body weight. With good habitat and a population density within the carrying capacity of the habitat, fawns can reach the weight needed—70 pounds for southern deer, and 80 pounds for those in the North—by their first autumn.

During the rut, hardened antlers begin to turn to "velvet." Rich with blood and nerve tissues, velvet nourishes the bone and is composed almost entirely of protein.

Bucks shedding their antlers can be a jarring sight, but it is a natural and welcome process. Shed from January to March, antlers often drop within hours of each other, and soon start growing again.

In general, though, it is best for a population if fawns don't breed. Fawn does that do breed usually bear only one fawn, lack the birthing and rearing skills of older does, tend to breed later in the season (which results in later birthing dates that leave their fawns little time to grow before winter), and have a higher rate of stillbirths and fawn abandonment.

Fawn bucks (and yearlings) that breed in the absence of mature bucks have not been tested by the rigors of life. It is possible that these animals might never have attained the age or dominance status to breed, and so by mating early in life, possibly introduce inferior genetics to the population. Usually, nature ensures that this doesn't happen, but in populations where too many mature bucks have been removed, young bucks do get a chance to reproduce.

Most bucks don't reach their physical peak until they are 5 years old. In some heavily hunted areas, "old" bucks may merely be 3½ years old; in more pristine settings, some bucks retain dominance status past 10 years of age.

Does are sexually active by the time they are yearlings. A doe's breeding success improves with age until she is about 8 years old. Once mature, she'll usually bear twins and is a skillful mother. Given this scenario, a doe may have as many as eight or nine fawns before a same-age buck mates for the first time.

It's clear then that how quickly a deer population grows depends upon the number of does. Think of the sex ratio in mathematical terms: does "multiply" while bucks "add or subtract." Does, of course, "multiply" themselves. Remove a doe from a population and you remove not just one deer, but at least two or three (the doe, and the one or two fawns she would have born the next spring), and perhaps even more if you consider that she might have lived to reproduce for a number of years. Remove a buck from the population and you merely subtract one deer.

When bucks enter the rut, their genes and pheromones accelerate into hyper-activity as thousands of years of evolution tell them to breed. They become aggressive, but also vulnerable!

Because of the early age at which does breed, and the number of fawns they can carry, white-tailed deer in good habitat can double their population in just two years, and even whitetail populations in poor habitat have the potential to grow by a factor of 1.7 in four years.

THE RUT BEGINS

Biologists refer to the three main phases of the rut as the pre-rut, the primary rut, and the post-rut. Whitetails exhibit characteristic and behavioral changes during each

Does rarely need to leave their home range to find a mate, and often patrol the same area to let bucks know where they'll be.

Does are ready to breed before bucks are, thus accounting for recent overpopulations of does in states such as Minnesota and Wisconsin. The exponential growth of does is often deleterious to the health of the herd.

phase, and hunters who know what to expect will have a decided edge when it comes to getting within range of a good-sized buck.

In autumn, as the days shorten, strange and wonderful things occur to bucks and does, building slowly at first, but eventually cresting in a wave of activity that is unmatched at any other time of the year. With the first cool September nights (in the North), whitetails' thoughts turn to reproduction. Both sexes begin to alter their behavior by changing their daily patterns and adding new, reproduction-centered behaviors. The rut

is short and intense—so much so for the male of the species that he can destroy his own vitality, expending great energy in wandering and feeding so little that the effort can leave him vulnerable to the rigors of winter.

But the rut doesn't begin overnight. Gradually, as the days shorten, the old magic of photoperiod affects the pineal gland located deep in the brain, releasing the hormone melatonin. Now you may not care much about this chemical substance, but this hormone's influence starts the irreversible events that prepare each deer for reproduction.

The rut drives bucks mad. Their pursuit of does is relentless, and often leaves the buck exhausted and weak once the rut is over.

The biggest fallacy about the rut is that it's short and occurs only during cold weather. Cold weather does play a role in the activity levels of deer. However, it is not the genesis of the rut, as many hunters believe. During the rut, cold weather motivates bucks to move throughout the day seeking does. In extremely cold conditions, movement keeps them warmer. During a warm rutting period, on the other hand, deer become lethargic and bed throughout the day. They breed mostly at night when the air is considerably cooler.

A warm rut means less sign, a cold rut means more sign, simply because there's much more movement during the colder weather. Warm fall or cold fall, however, all three phases of the rut will take place generally at the same time each year. Deer hunters can count on it.

For the does, the released melatonin is critical to the production of yet other hormones. New, elevated levels of the female hormone estrogen begin coursing through does causing physical changes, such as preparing her uterus to receive eggs. And while the picture of a swollen-necked, hormone-charged buck is familiar to us all, does also change behaviorally thanks to estrogen, gradually becoming more and more restless and increasing nighttime activity greatly as the rut peaks. Although she will usually stay within her home range, the doe's restless movements increase her odds of encountering a mate.

The same chemical melatonin that stirs the doe biologically and behaviorally triggers testosterone production in bucks. This primary male sex hormone first causes antlers to harden and velvet to shed, then drives him to battle with shrubs. Eventually, it forces him to sometimes battle other deer, to create buck scrapes and to wander widely. At the peak of the rut, bucks are sometimes so driven to distraction by this hormone, they often throw caution to the wind in their wandering. This inattention to their own welfare puts them at risk, making them more susceptible to both human and four-legged predators.

ANTLER RUBS AND DOMINANCE HIERARCHIES

One of the most evident forms of deer sign is the buck rub. In early September (in the North; later in the South), antlers harden and velvet is shed. As one would expect, these steps occur first in dominant bucks, since mature bucks produce more testosterone than their younger cohorts. As they are shedding their antler velvet, bucks

During warm rutting periods, bucks need to rest and often bed for the day in heavy brush. Many hunters pass them by, completely unaware that their trophy rested near.

Though this doe rests in the cold weather, you can be sure the bucks are on the move.

As a buck grows, he generally seeks out trees that offer some resistance to his size. It is folly, however, to think that small bucks only use small trees to rub and large bucks only use large trees.

begin to rub their antlers on brush and tree trunks. Although it was once thought that rubbing was done to remove velvet (which it may do to some small degree), it probably has other causes and purposes, since antler velvet sheds without this rubbing. The entire shedding process takes only about 24 hours, but depending on many seasonal factors, some bucks may not shed their velvet until March. Given the amount of rubbing bucks are doing at this time, it is unlikely that it is governed simply by a desire to remove the velvet.

Instead, antler rubs probably signify the beginning of the dominance hierarchy among bucks. This rubbing may also help bucks determine the size and shape of their antlers. Mature bucks, because of their higher levels of testosterone, rub trees more frequently than young bucks and begin to do so much earlier in the autumn than subordinate bucks. The presence of a large number of antler rubs seen early in the autumn indicates that there's an old, dominant male in the vicinity. Dominant bucks also continue to rub trees well into, and

A typical rub tree has smooth bark, few lower branches, and is about 1 inch in diameter. But rub trees can vary in size from ½ to 4 inches.

Does entering the rut often seek solitude from other does and even their own fawns.

sometimes even after, the rut. Yearling bucks make less than half as many antler rubs as dominant bucks, and begin to do so later in the fall (because they produce less testosterone).

The rub phenomenon is 10 times greater in frequency, size, and intensity within the buck's range from October to December. Rubs found during this time indicate where the buck is traveling to seek out does. Fresh rubs found from January on indicate the location of a buck's core area—an ideal place to plan an opening day archery ambush.

Buck rubs will also show you a predictable pattern regarding where a deer is traveling, what time of day he's using that particular route, and what food source he's heading toward most frequently. Most important, rubs can betray a buck's bedding area. For

instance, when a hunter locates a spot where a buck has rubbed as many as 18 or more trees within 50 yards, he has discovered the buck's core area—where a buck spends 90 percent of his time. Bucks will rise several times a day from their beds to change position. Often, as they stretch, they will walk a few feet, defecate, and rub brush or a sapling before lying down again. By paying attention to wind direction and locating the most heavily used trail into this area, a hunter can plan a successful ambush for this deer.

Although bucks will rub just about anything with their antlers, including fence posts, they seem to prefer soft-barked trees. In some regions they seem to prefer trees that produce pungent sap, such as balsam fir, spruce, cedar, or hemlock, perhaps because these trees enhance scent-marking. Remember that whitetails have a forehead gland, so that beyond just testing their antlers, bucks are leaving a chemical marker for their rivals and potential mates. Antler rubs, particularly those made during the actual rut, are often along buck "highways," routes used for many years.

The buck rubs most hunters come across can also be used to determine the travel pattern of a mature whitetail buck throughout his entire home range. When you discover a rub, lie or kneel down with the rub in front of you. Slowly look left and right. You should discover other rubs on trees, saplings or brush in front of you. Usually, each additional rub will be about 30 to 50 yards ahead of the other. Also, by knowing whether you are heading to or from feeding or bedding areas

and which direction the rub is facing, you can tell if he is using this route in the morning or evening.

There are some misconceptions about rubs, too. A seasoned hunter never allows himself to be fooled into believing that all large rubs are made by large-racked bucks. This just isn't so. Many small bucks, spikes, and forkhorns rub large saplings (6 to 10 inches around) totally bare of bark as high as 4 feet from the ground. It's easy to be duped into thinking some rubs are made by a buck with a larger rack. Generally, smaller-racked bucks rub larger trees than most hunters believe. Larger-racked bucks, however, seldom rub smaller trees because of the lack of resistance the tree offers them. Trophy-sized bucks spend much less time rubbing their antlers

Buck rubs on trees is the most evident deer sign, but shouldn't be viewed as proof of the buck's size.

Secondary scrapes are often characterized by a nibbled or broken overhead branch, which the buck rubs his forehead and orbitals glands upon.

on trees than they do thrashing and tearing up thick, resistant brush. When you find a large bush with roots that have been dislodged and branches broken and strewn about, you have found an area where a trophy buck has displayed his aggressiveness to all subordinate deer to see and smell.

Rubs made on branched trees 16 to 20 inches wide showing bark stripped on both trunks have most likely been made by bucks with wide racks. Rubs with many deep gouges are usually made from burrs and kickers on the antlers of mature bucks. If the tree or sapling is dripping sap, the rub was made within 48 hours. The most exciting aspect of finding a rub is that you will know it was made by a buck in your hunting area. If there are fresh shavings hanging from the tree and on the ground, look around—he may be only 100 yards ahead of you, establishing another rub marker.

Few hunters get to witness an equally matched pair of bucks duking it out to win a doe. Bucks are not generally territorial, and smaller bucks almost always yield to larger ones in the presence of females.

It is commonly believed by hunters, although not confirmed by science, that big bucks rub larger trees. Since it is well known that some large trees are used year after year for this ritual, and that large dominant bucks do most of the antler rubbing, the "big tree—big buck" hypothesis is probably at least partially true.

During the pre-rut stage, bucks are doing things other than thrashing trees. They are finalizing the "pecking order" that they had been working on all summer in their bachelor groups. As the levels of testosterone rise, bucks begin to test each other in sparring matches. These aren't the all-out battles that sometimes occur in the rut. Bucks test each other more gently, locking antlers carefully so that they don't injure each other. These brief tests, most often initiated by the younger bucks, are tolerated by the dominant animal. These sparring matches allow deer to "size each other up," crystallizing the dominance hierarchy. Later, during the rut when the bucks will be stressed enough just by their extensive travels, this pecking order will eliminate many fights, saving needed energy, leaving the true battles for bucks that encounter an equal-size rival.

DOE BEHAVIOR

While much attention in research and literature is generally afforded bucks during this period, does are no less affected. As the rut intensifies she goes through some conflicting urges. She becomes less protective of this year's fawns, and so will allow her yearlings of the previous year to rejoin her, forming larger, family units. However, does will not allow the return of their yearling buck offspring, who probably just got kicked out of the bachelor group as testosterone levels made everyone a bit testy. If he returns to his mother, she will drive him mercilessly away, to avoid his breeding with her or any other of his near relatives. Even a mother's tolerance of yearling and fawn daughters isn't unconditional. Once she enters her estrous cycle and impatiently awaits her mate, she seeks solitude. Her daughters will only be allowed to rejoin her after she's mated.

As she succumbs to the inevitable urges of hormones, a doe becomes increasingly restless, often at night. Within her home range is a section that she considers her "core" area. Like the buck that wanders and advertises his presence through rubs and scrapes, the intense use of this core area causes her scent to permeate the vicinity, helping to attract bucks to her home.

A doe's urine provides the most important clues to wandering bucks about her condition to breed. About 20 days before she enters "heat" or estrus, rising levels of progesterone are revealed in her urine. This serves as a chemical odor clue detectable by any passing buck. Does sometimes pause to urinate when they know a buck is following them. If she isn't ready to mate, she saves herself the trouble of avoiding his sexual overtures, which also saves the buck the energy he might otherwise expend in the chase.

Actual estrus lasts between 24 and 48 hours. Mature does in good physical condition enter estrus before young does, or does that are in poor shape. Fawn does that do experience estrus do so late in the breeding season, sometimes into December and January, even in the North. If a doe isn't bred during her first estrous cycle, she'll enter a second estrous cycle in about a month.

BUCK BEHAVIOR

In the full grip of hormonal overload, bucks seek mates by extending their travels. Home ranges increase in size up to 3 square miles, and truly superb dominant bucks, called "dominant floaters" by biologists, roam over a large territory. These bucks fear few rivals, and enter the home range of other, but smaller, dominant bucks, usurping the breeding rights as they pass through. Sometimes called "hermit" bucks by hunters, these superb specimens are usually at least 5½ years old.

White-tailed bucks aren't truly territorial. They will tolerate the presence of other breeding-age bucks as long as these other bucks exhibit subordinate behavior. There is some evidence that does seek to breed with the most genetically superior buck available. When unable to drive a young suitor away, does have been known to lead him to a big buck that will finish the job of driving him off. In such cases, the subordinate buck literally high-tails it out of the vicinity without risking a confrontation. True dominance battles generally only take place between equal rivals.

Dominance fights rarely lead to death, but that outcome does occur. Sometimes the combatants' antlers

Gregarious scrapes are evidence of a group of bucks frequenting the same area—
if you encounter gregarious scrapes, post nearby and call in the bucks!

become locked, leading to the death of one or both. Bucks have been seen with the entire head and rack of a rival still locked in theirs, apparently able to paw themselves free of the rival's dead body with their sharp hooves. Injuries, such as puncture wounds or eye loss, also occur. Yet both death and injury are fairly rare. The whitetail's rack, with its basket shape, is designed to "catch" an opponent, not spear him, lowering the risk of serious injury or death. In addition, most dominance fights are short lived—less than a minute. It is better for the "loser" to break off the fight and flee so that he might breed elsewhere than to risk death or injury battling a superior rival.

SCRAPES

The most pertinent information about scrapes is that they are sexual calling cards of both bucks and does. Although there are some half-dozen types of scrapes, you'll need to pay attention to only a few: primary, secondary, and gregarious scrapes. As testosterone levels continue to increase in northern bucks into October, peaking near the middle of the month, they begin to make ground scrapes, coinciding with when the most mature does of the herd come into a brief estrous cycle, usually lasting less than 36 hours. Bucks who discover this early estrous scent respond by making numerous small scrapes throughout their territory. These scrapes, which are usually not refreshed, are the least likely scrapes to produce buck sightings—for the most part,

hunters shouldn't pay much attention to them (the same philosophy applies to scrapes made by does, which often do not produce well for hunters). Just use these scrapes to confirm that there are deer in the area. Bucks in the Southeast start making scrapes in November, while those in the Southwest take on this task in December.

Buck scrapes are an important form of whitetail communication. They let other bucks know who's boss of the neighborhood, and they also serve to let does know that a breeding-age buck will again be passing this way. Scrapes are a message, a note made of odors, and the dominant buck's way of asserting himself even when he can't physically be present.

Although bucks are still making antler rubs at this time, these sign posts begin to play a subordinate role as

The most aggressive message bucks leave for does is accomplished by urinating down the hind legs and rubbing them together. Fertile does will often respond in kind, urinating nearby.

Scraping and Rubbing Activity by Age Class of Bucks

Research conducted in Michigan's upper peninsula found that 3- to 8-year-old bucks begin scraping and rubbing earlier than 1 ½-year-old bucks. For both groups, scraping reached its maximum level during November 3 to 9, about 14 days before the peak week of breeding—November 17 to 23.

When a buck pursues a doe in heat, he'll often emit short, low noises called "tending grunts." She may lead him around for days, however, before she is truly ready.

the rut intensifies. Scrapes become the most important message-bearing device, and unlike antler rubs, which are often made in dense cover, scrapes frequently are made where the understory is more open. Bucks choose these sites to maximize their "advertising" potential—they are usually on or along well-worn trails, and are frequently found on high ground (which may help make their scent carry farther). They are also often clustered near each other.

One well-worn buck route where I hunt has scrapes every 40 to 50 yards for a length of 1/4 mile, after which they become much less frequent. It may be just coincidence, but this cluster is also in an area heavily used for bedding sites by a group of does. The message seems to be "I'm around, and I'll be back."

Secondary scrapes are the most prevalent of all scrapes and are usually 2 to 3 feet round. Bucks will make between 20 and 30 such scrapes throughout their home range during the rutting season. Usually these scrapes are 3 or 4 feet across, although they can be much larger. Almost invariably there will be an overhead branch, some 3 to 5 feet above the scrape site, frequently with a bare, broken tip. The buck licks this branch tip, and rubs his forehead and orbital (eye socket) gland on it. It is also possible that he deposits scent from his nasal glands. Licking of the limb tip may transfer other scent-producing materials, such as residue from the tarsal gland, which he sometimes pauses to lick. After completing this task, he scrapes the earth bare of leaves and grass with his front hooves. While

Pay Attention to Acorns!

It happens occasionally: The deer that feed in those alfalfa fields, showing up like clockwork every evening, just stop showing up. Or maybe the well-defined trails leading to that big patch of soybeans begin to show signs of disuse.

But the deer didn't just disappear. They've probably switched food sources—to an acorn-dropping oak back in the woods.

Whitetails eat a variety of foods, and agricultural crops are among their favorites. But when acorns are available, all bets are off. Available throughout whitetail range, acorns sustain deer (as well as grouse, bears, turkeys, and squirrels) when succulent vegetation disappears each fall. In some areas, acorns comprise over half the whitetail's diet for a six-month period. They're a convenient source of the fat and protein that deer need for winter survival. Acorns are tasty (to deer) too—biologists note that once deer find an acorn-producing oak, they'll revisit it until most of the nuts are consumed. If that fruitful tree has some neighbors, it could be awhile before whitetails get serious about finding other food sources.

Individual oak species are typically divided into two families: white oak and red oak. You can identify a tree's family by its leaves. Red oak leaves end in sharp, spiny points, while white oaks show soft, rounded lobes. White oak acorns usually mature in one season; you can count on modest-but-consistent crops annually. Red oak acorns require two years to develop and are much more cyclical, varying from bumper crops (every three to five years) to near-zeros.

What causes such fluctuation in acorn numbers? Foresters muse over that one as some biologists ponder grouse cycles. Undoubtedly a number of variables determine nut production for an oak tree: site, soil, sunlight, rainfall, drought (a drought-stressed tree may produce a final bumper crop before succumbing), with no one factor consistently predominating. To nail down specifics about acorn production in your hunting area, it's a good idea to talk to a local forester (or go out and look for yourself).

If you hunt woodland that hosts both oak families—most of us do—you'll undoubtedly wonder which one deer prefer. The answer is dependent on many factors, not the least being the mood of the individual deer at the time. Biologists and foresters I've spoken with agree that white oak acorns contain less tannin than do red oak acorns. Therefore, whites are less bitter (or "more palatable," as one

game manager put it). Also, since white oaks produce a crop virtually every year, deer may rely more on those acorns. Here all speculation ends. The party line is that deer love them all. Again, if you want to know what kind they're eating, scouting is the only sure way to find out.

Obviously you'll be a big step ahead if you can evaluate the acorn crop before hunting seasons begin. A mild, wet spring without a killing frost will get acorns off to a good start. Adequate summer rainfall helps, too. As fall approaches, visit mature oak stands (where trees are 30 feet tall and over) and scan the branches for acorns, using binoculars to search the loftiest crowns. If you spot an abundant acorn supply, note the location, either mentally or on a map. It's a solid bet that deer will be visiting these spots as acorns fall. The more areas like this you can locate, the greater your options will be once deer switch over to mast feeding.

With hunting seasons near, keep watching for signs that acorns are falling. An abundance of squirrels might tip you off to an acorn-laden autumn, but it could also mean that last fall's crop was the dandy. Gaggles of grays and flocks of fox squirrels could also mean that other nut crops—hickories, butternuts, etc.—are doing well. Determining each year's acorn crop, assuming you haven't been able to scout it, boils down to a quick visit to your favorite oak stands.

When acorns start dropping, you'll have plenty of evidence that deer have found them: Whitetails will churn up or scrape away leaf litter as they forage for the nuts. It'll be tempting to place a stand right in the thick of the sign, but it's better to set up on the trails deer use to enter the area. Deer probably won't be as alert while approaching, and they won't associate the feeding area with danger should you spook them. If you're lucky enough to find several acorn areas, spread out your hunting efforts—avoiding repeat vigils in one spot will keep it "fresh."

Hunting acorn-bearing oak stands may also be your best bet for taking a large buck. A trophy bowhunter from my region focuses almost exclusively on oak stands when hunting mature whitetails. Mike finds that bucks feed through these acorn-laden areas well into the morning as they head for bedding cover, and evening hunts have produced big bucks too shy to enter fields before dark. Even if you're just after venison, a good acorn crop is a true gold mine—one October evening last fall I watched 14 does gather under a single red oak. Now that's a true deer magnet.

The fat and protein hidden in acorns proves a valuable resource to deer fattening up for the winter.

When the air turns crisp and traditional food sources wither, deer turn to acorns to meet their nutritional needs.

pawing, he probably deposits some scent from the interdigital glands, which are found between his toes. Because of the sheer numbers of secondary scrapes, you can rest assured they are within a few hundred yards of a buck's core area. A hunter positioned over secondary scrapes is almost certain to see bucks because most of these scrapes are made where bucks spend a majority of their time.

When the rutting season reaches its peak, the secondary scrapes diminish in number and the remaining ones are used more frequently. These remaining scrapes become wet, churned up, and are transformed into primary scrapes. These primary scrapes, which are usually twice the size of a secondary scrape because of increased pawing, will undergo the peak of activity this time of year. Don't spend a lot of time around secondary scrapes in the early season. But keep track of the scrape activity; when the secondary scrapes become primary scrapes, hunt them until the rutting period is over.

A gregarious scrape can be either a primary or a secondary scrape that is used by several bucks of the same age group. Usually they are found in the same areas as secondary scrapes. These gregarious scrapes are nothing more than overused secondary scrapes. Because

Buck Food: Clear-cuts, Acorns, and Apples

Without a doubt, woodland bucks are attracted to 2- to 7-year-old clear-cuts like their farmland cousins are to alfalfa. Clear-cuts, especially those irregularly shaped with a lot of edge, may offer everything a buck requires. Here is where he finds food, in the form of succulent new growth early in the year and browse once late fall and winter arrives, plus cover, in the form of ½-inch to 3-inch saplings and replanted softwoods. If there is water and an ample resident doe population, a buck really has little need to venture out of the clear-cut.

Stands of oaks are a food source that attracts bucks with wild abandon. Indeed, when available, acorns are a whitetail's first food choice, with about a dozen preferred varieties distributed throughout their range. Beechnuts and hickory nuts are also an important mast crop to pay close attention to.

Apples are the third concentrated food source deer can't seem to get enough of. Fortunately, old orchards are as easy as clear-cuts to locate. Simply examine your topographical map for those rows of irregular green circles indicating an orchard, or you can hike through abandoned farmland. It seems every old farm had a crab apple tree or two in the backyard.

Many hunters overlook clear-cut areas for bedded bucks. Can you imagine glassing a buck in this area? It'd be nearly impossible, which is exactly why they seek out new-cut areas.

Deer do not mate for life. They may stick together for a day after mating, but the buck will continue hunting for does until the rut is over.

they are used by submissive bucks rather than the most aggressive bucks, they receive a lot of attention. They can be identified by their irregular shapes and beat-up look. Hunters watching such scrapes will usually score more quickly than if they watch any other type of scrape.

All scrapes are made in a relatively straight line over several hundred yards. Scrapes, like rubs, show up in the same places year after year. By identifying the most active scrapes in an area, hunters can count on bucks making scrapes in the same spot the following year. Even when a buck is shot near a certain scrape, do not forsake that exact area next year. Bucks are like big trout. If you catch one out of a certain hole, within a few days another fish will have claimed the territory.

The real scent-marking, however, occurs when the buck rub-urinates into the middle of the scrape. Hunching slightly, the buck urinates down the inside of his rear legs while rubbing his tarsal glands together.

This scent-marking routine continues through the rut, peaking about two weeks before the majority of does enter estrus.

About half of the scrape sites will be reworked by their maker, often intensely over a short period. He may just as mysteriously ignore them for days or weeks, then begin using them again. Once the rut is in full swing, dominant bucks usually cease to freshen their scrapes, probably because they've got more work than they can handle by mating with willing does. At this point, a buck no longer needs to advertise his presence to them.

Does, on the other hand, sometimes leave scent messages of their own by urinating near these scrapes. The scent messages they receive from buck scrapes may even be important to stimulating their own estrous cycle, and the scents they leave probably help the scrape-maker determine where does are located, and their readiness to breed.

THE MATING GAME

While all this scent-marking and signposting is going on, deer are evaluating each other as mates or rivals. By the time the rut is fully engaged, and the does start coming into estrus, bucks have nearly worn themselves out traveling over a large area, in some cases, thousands of acres. By early November in the North, and a month or two later in the South, the prime-age, prime-condition does will be in estrus and cease running away from bucks. Up until the estrous cycle came into full swing, dominant bucks traveled largely at night, so a sure sign that the rut is peaking is the sight of mature bucks during the daylight hours. Before it's all over, dominant bucks may lose 20 percent or more of their body weight in their around-the-clock, never-ending pursuit.

When a buck pursues her, a doe in estrus often pauses to urinate. When bucks encounter the urine, they stop to lick it and then perform what is called the lip-curling flehmen. Not only does this act tell him if the doe is ready to mate, it may be important to prepare himself for copulation. If he is convinced she is ready, he follows her rather politely in short, choppy steps, holding his head low and neck outstretched. When doing this, or trailing her, a buck might emit short, low noises called a "tending grunt." But just because she allows him to tend her, it doesn't mean she's fully ready to mate. Until she is ready to allow actual physical contact, she may lead the buck in circles for as much as a day, during which he "courts" her patiently.

After they mate, the pair may separate, or may stay together for up to another full day. If they do remain together, some pairs mate a second time. Once they separate, the doe returns to her normal routine while the buck continues to pursue his amorous ways. Because does expend less energy than bucks during the rut, they enter winter in much better physical condition. Although we tend to think of big bucks as the very finest physical specimens, they expend so much energy during the rut that they are second only to fawns in winter mortality.

Eventually, the rut ceases. But like its beginning, it doesn't happen abruptly. Decreasing daylight again causes photoreceptive responses in both bucks and does, slowing the mating urge. Those does not bred during the first cycle will come into estrus about a month later.

Bucks with enough testosterone still coursing through their veins will find and mate with them. But gradually, and surely, the rush to reproduce ends. Deer travel to winter habitats to pass the winter. Does concentrate on preserving their strength so that it might go to nourish the embryos they carry. Bucks seek a rest to regain their lost vigor and, by January or February, will drop the impressive racks that they had grown at such an expense.

HABITATS AND HOME RANGES

For most of its life, the average white-tailed deer lives in an area of about 1 square mile, often called its "home range," where it finds its basic needs—security cover, food, and water. In the North where special winter cover is necessary for survival, whitetails may have a second, separate "winter range," or deer yard. This may be located adjacent to, or even in, its regular home range, or it may be many miles away.

Most home ranges are oval. Fidelity to home ranges is strong. Deer have starved to death in their home range, even though better browse existed within just a few miles. That bond may be so strong because it is generally learned while a deer follows its mother through her daily and seasonal routine. Because does pass on this knowledge to their own offspring, which will then pass it on to their own young, generations of related deer often utilize the same home range.

Bucks seem to have a larger home range than do does, and they are particularly prone to wandering during the breeding season. Don't think of a home range as a place that encompasses all the deer in that vicinity. Home ranges are unique to the individual, and while a doe and her fawns may have exactly the same range until the fawns mature (and even afterward, if they are females), bucks and other doe groups in that area will probably have a different range. These ranges do overlap, however, putting the deer in contact with each other.

Bucks select a slightly different range than does based on their antler-growth nutritional demands. Does select a home range that favors the rearing of young. The ranges of the two sexes overlap least during the fawning season and most during the winter.

In heavily variegated habitats, buck ranges can be massive. Some Canadian bucks have been tracked patrolling over 3,000 acres, travelling circuits of 20 to 30 miles during the rut.

One reason bucks are so elusive during hunting season is that they adapt to the movements and habits of hunters. Shifters often leave their home territories if they suspect they've been compromised.

Home Range Size by Acres

	Buck Fawns	Yearling Bucks	Adult Bucks	Doe Fawns	Yearling Does	Adult Does
Spring	310	450	410	390	210	190
Summer	160	410	350	160	105	145
Fall	140	675	1090	110	260	275
Winter	150	310	290	275	300	400

Home Range Size by Acres

Buck and doe home ranges vary in size throughout the year. Data from 20 years of radio-tracking in Texas show that adult bucks during fall have the largest home ranges. This is the result of mature bucks traveling through several doe home ranges searching for a doe in estrus.

Travel Routes and Bedding Areas

- Shorelines, creek beds, and steep ravines all block a buck's forward progress. Bucks walk parallel to these features until they find suitable openings, which make these crossings ideal ambush sites for hunters. The tips of bays, shallow riffles, and the tops of ravines can be especially productive in this regard.

- Terrain features that promote travel include gentle slopes, spurs, and saddles where bucks can save energy going up and down a hill or crossing over from one valley to the next. Ridges adjacent to steep country or sheer cliffs are another travel route bucks choose to save calories.

- Thick tangles of various types of vegetation are a magnet for bucks seeking refuge—and the thicker and more impenetrable, the better. In the Northeast, for example, mountain laurel thickets, patches of dogwood, as well as cattails and swamp grasses, offer ideal cover. Not only do they hide a buck's form, but they make it nearly impossible for a hunter to walk through without getting tripped up. In the South, kudzu and honeysuckle can be just as impenetrable, as can alder swamps and thorn apple thickets in the Midwest and elsewhere east of the Mississippi. Planted pine plantations and unharvested cornfields also offer superb cover.

- When storms approach, look for whitetails to move to bed down in alder thickets and thick stands of evergreens around swamps, or patches of dogwood and tamarack on the lee or protected side of a hill.

- One of the most overlooked bedding areas is created during the timber harvesting process. Slashings, a byproduct of the axe and chain saw, consist of tree tops, rotten logs, and other debris that big bucks bed around. Tree trunks lying askew and dead branches piled atop one another are more often than not impossible to climb through quietly. Blackberry briars, alders, and replanted softwoods soon take over, offering even more cover.

- Unlike the summer when bucks seek deep shade as protection from the sun, in the winter you often find them herded up and bedded down on open and south-facing hillsides. All they need here are a few briars and some brush to break up their outline. Be sure to scrutinize these areas well!

- In big woods settings, whitetails seek protection from the bitter cold by wintering under the canopy in stands of native evergreens, such as hemlock, white pine, and mixed spruce/fir. Adequate thermal cover is often crucial to the survival of a wintering northern deer herd. Avoid hunting those areas where loggers have removed the thermal cover, especially after a long hard winter. You may see fewer deer in the vicinity due to high deer mortality.

In the winter, whitetails seek out southern-facing bedding areas to maximize their exposure to the sun.

Bucks become more clever as they age, but they also become more aggressive. Yearlings are easier to find during hunting season not because they're dumb, but because they've been driven from familiar territory.

HOW WHITETAILS MOVE

You've probably heard a thousand explanations for the disappearance of bucks at the beginning of hunting season: They got killed, they've become nocturnal, they've patterned the hunters. But in some cases, the disappearance—or better yet, the reappearance—of deer relates more to home range usage and natural movements than to any particular brainpower on the deer's part. You don't always have to outsmart them—you simply have to be in the right place at the right time.

Travelers

In fragmented habitat and areas with low deer numbers, whitetails, particularly bucks, roam much larger home ranges. In the hardwood forests of Mississippi, Dr. Harry

Bucks often change their territories once winter arrives. Few sights are as thrilling to hunters as watching or stalking a buck as he silently moves through the snow.

Jacobson calculated the average annual ranges of does at 1,820 acres and bucks at 3,733 acres, with the largest at nearly 5,500 acres. Whitetail researcher Dr. James Kroll said that bucks in Alberta may occupy core areas of 3,000 acres or more and travel circuits of 20 to 25 miles during the rut, and that in the boreal forests of eastern Canada, bucks commonly travel 15 to 20 miles every five to seven days, searching for does. In the Dakotas and other prairie states with scattered cover, bucks may travel a dozen or more miles from one cover pocket to another. So they're here today, gone tomorrow.

These long-distance travels explain why bucks in some areas disappear and suddenly reappear, especially during the rut. Under these conditions, a hunter's concern isn't so much being patterned by the deer, but getting in the path of a buck when he decides to show up. For far-ranging bucks, it often makes sense to analyze the country for the best travel routes, and then to stick with one good spot for several days until one of those roving bucks comes by.

Roaming families of does can often be seen in the winter, foraging for food.

Normal Buck Bedding Areas

During the early season and pre-rut, unmolested bucks generally bed within ¼ mile of a preferred food source, but bucks will travel 1 mile or more to feed in an alfalfa lot or a recently harvested cornfield. In farm country, you can find bucks hiding in brush lots, overgrown fields, old vineyards, cornfields, heads of ravines, cattail swamps, hardwood ridges, and thorn apple thickets. In wilderness areas, add high peaks, plateaus above clear-cuts, logging slashings, river banks, beaver flows, and humps inside large swamps to the list.

When the rut reaches its peak, bucks abandon these bedding sites and follow estrous does around, bedding and feeding where the does bed and feed. They rarely return to their summer and early-fall bedding areas.

In the late season, you can count on bucks bedding near food sources in the thickest cover available. Winter storms, however, push them to bed under the boughs of pine, hemlock, and spruce trees, as well as brush-choked ravines and the lee sides of hills. Hillsides with a southern exposure are another good bet when winter temperatures turn bitter.

Do bucks bed in the same location day after day? Sometimes, but not always. Approaching storms, early-morning air temperatures, a change in wind direction, emerging food sources, barking dogs, trespassers, bird hunters, and children playing can all force a buck to bed elsewhere.

Late in the season, bucks will go where they feel safe, which almost always means thick cover near a food source. You can bet this buck doesn't have to wander far to find acorns, abundant plant growth, and even a water source.

Shifters

During a three-year study conducted in the early 90s on DeSoto National Wildlife Refuge in Nebraska, Kurt VerCauteren verified what most hunters know—whitetails respond to hunting pressure. Near the DeSoto National Wildlife Refuge, where the Missouri River separates Iowa and Nebraska, VerCauteren witnessed that when the season opened in Nebraska, some deer swam to Iowa. When it opened in Iowa, they swam to Nebraska. (Even this proved hazardous, as one was hit and killed by a boat.)

Those that stayed at home also made distinct shifts. During the muzzleloader season on the DeSoto Refuge, eight collared deer moved into a strip of posted land 60x100 yards and remained there until the season closed. Once the pressure let up, the deer quickly returned to their home ranges. In only two cases did deer stay in new ranges; most returned within two weeks.

The lesson? If bucks vanish in the face of heavy pressure, look for places where they might seek temporary refuge. Keep in mind that once the pressure eases, they'll probably return to their original home ranges. Plan to meet them there.

Migrators

In some regions, whitetails migrate between summer and winter ranges. Even in prairie and farm states, some whitetails migrate, but migrations are far more dramatic in the West, where deer travel from high summer ranges to low-elevation winter ranges.

Snow-Tracking Mature Bucks

Tracking a buck in the snow and then shooting him is one tough job. It's certainly more difficult than ambushing driven deer or bushwhacking an unsuspecting buck from an elevated tree stand. Snow-tracking trophy bucks successfully, however, is seen by many as the epitome of woodsmanship.

- One of the best times to follow a buck's trail is during the rut at the tail end of a snowstorm, when new snow is no more than 6 inches deep. Family groups of does and fawns are still bedded, but the bucks are up and about looking for a doe near estrous as soon as they sense the storm is waning. You'll be able to age their tracks very easily if the snow is still falling, as any deer tracks you come across will cover up quickly with the last vestiges of the storm.

- It takes a few days for deer to get used to having snow on the ground. They think you can't see them even though their dark coats silhouette them against the white. Thus, the season's first snowfall is also one of the best times to track down a buck. Be in the woods just as the storm wanes.

- Look for pointed and elongated tracks with the dew claws set deep. These are almost always made by a buck, although a big doe can fool you now and then. Doe tracks are generally smaller and quite dainty.

- A rutting buck stops to sniff-test each deer track he crosses, and if he has a trophy rack he leaves antler impressions in the snow during the process. Now you know how wide his rack is and maybe how many points it has, too.

- Bucks also dribble urine and sprinkle deer pellets as they walk, whereas does generally stop to urinate and defecate.

- While on the trail, never cross an opening without first glassing the far side for deer or evidence of deer activity in the snow. Remember, you can see farther in the woods with snow on the ground, but so can the deer.

Snowfall can be a hunter's best friend; the bucks are easier to track and certainly easier to see. The tail end of a snowstorm is a great time to get out in the woods—the bucks won't waste any time continuing their pursuit of does in estrous.

In 1990 and 1991, Thomas Baumeister, as part of a continuing study, radio-collared 69 whitetails (26 adult bucks) in Idaho's Clearwater River drainage. He found that these deer occupied small summer home ranges of about 190 acres in the drainage's upper reaches. Then, in October and November, the deer migrated an average of 24 miles to winter ranges, some stopping at transition points along the way, others migrating straight through in four days. Many hunters believe deep snow triggers this migration, but so many deer migrated before any snow accumulation that weather can't be the only factor.

Hiders

In his Nebraska study, VerCauteren radio-collared several dozen deer and through telemetry relocated those deer a total of 17,000 times, plotting each one's home range. These ranges averaged 400 acres, although they varied greatly in size.

Holding and social areas are reliable spots to spot a large buck. They are often found in areas of dense coverage and close to a water source.

Southern deer often enjoy abundant acorn crops.

VerCauteren found that the most transient deer tended to be yearlings forced by their mothers from established home ranges to make room for new fawns. On average, transients dispersed 12 to 15 miles, although some subadults did travel 40 to 50 miles.

Many did not survive. "As soon as these deer leave familiar ground to fill vacant habitat off the refuge, they're vulnerable," VerCauteren said. "Of all the transients we monitored, 16 percent were killed by vehicles and 36 percent by hunters." One year VerCauteren radio-collared five yearling bucks, and four left the refuge in August and September. The radio batteries went dead on two, so their fate is unknown, but the other three were killed by bowhunters that fall.

Another buck summered securely in a small area, but then, in late October, swam the Missouri River and three days later was shot by a bowhunter.

In contrast, most adult deer became sedentary and virtually refused to venture from familiar home ranges; they had little reason to because food, water, security (and does during the rut) lay close at hand. One doe, for example, despite all intrusions, would not vacate a 40-acre parcel. And an old buck apparently had a similar lifestyle. On January 27, 1991, VerCauteren trapped and ear-tagged the buck and one month later caught him again in the same trap. Then VerCauteren never saw that deer again until a hunter brought him through a check station two years later. The hunter had shot the deer 200 yards from the original trapping location. VerCauteren surmises the buck had been living right there the whole time.

Hunters assume yearlings are easy prey because they're young and dumb, which is partly true, but the fact that they are forced into unfamiliar, marginal habitat is often what dooms them. Conversely, old deer become almost invisible—not because they're particularly smart, but because they claim prime ranges where a sedentary life ensures a certain invincibility.

Obviously, transient yearlings can be easy pickings. But older, sedentary bucks are tough because they're on intimate ground and instantly recognize intrusion. To prevent detection, a hunter must stay out of their core areas; move constantly, hunting different locations each day to keep the deer guessing; and hunt only those spots where conditions, particularly wind, are perfect at that moment.

Winter Changes

Whitetails in the North shift from their home range to their winter range in response to sharp drops in temperature. This is important to hunters, because this shift can occur during hunting season. If you've scouted your chosen hunting grounds in early fall, and your hunt occurs after the first snowfall or prolonged cold snap, you may find that the deer are no longer using the same trails, bedding areas, or feeding grounds that you discovered in September. It pays, then, to learn just what winter habitat looks like, so that you'll be able to adjust.

Winter deer yards are most often located in areas of dense conifers. A conifer's dense foliage and conical shape help to deflect snow away from the ground beneath, leaving areas of less snow where deer can move more freely.

In addition, whitetails create networks of trails through the yards to further enhance movement. Because conifers are dark in color, they also serve as solar collectors, creating a warmer micro-climate beneath them. By bedding beneath such thick overhead cover, which reduces heat loss to the sky, a deer's body heat loss is further minimized. Winter cover is crucial to whitetail survival in the North. Those deer with access to such deer yards frequently survive conditions that kill other deer whose range lacks adequate stands of conifers.

Even winter cover can be segregated into two types: bedding and browsing. The best bedding areas are about 80 percent conifer, while the browsing areas will be comprised of about 60 percent conifer—enough conifers to keep the snow depth down, but with adequate space in the canopy through which sunlight can pass so that woody browse can grow. Upland cedar probably provides the best winter cover since not only does it deflect snow and retain thermal energy, it is also a very nutritious browse. Hemlock is also a good choice, followed by lowland cedar groves. Balsam fir and spruce groves are a bit further down the list—they provide good winter cover but are poor dietary fare. Still further down the list are the pines: jack, white, and Norway. Because they have more open crowns than other conifers, pines aren't as efficient at intercepting snow, and none have much food value.

Southern whitetails generally travel less than northern deer because they don't face such severe winter challenges. That doesn't mean they don't migrate. Some movement occurs to take advantage of seasonal food sources or to avoid flooding. Generally, though, the greater the extremes in weather, the farther a deer will move in both the span of a year and over its lifetime. It is believed that in those populations of whitetails that must migrate long distances to winter habitat, fawns learn the complex route from their mothers. Some researchers believe that the deer in a particular winter yard are all closely related and come from the same, or adjacent, summer ranges. Thus, if a massive die-off in that deer yard occurs, the summer range that would have been utilized by those deer will largely remain vacant.

Holding Areas

Holding areas can also supply useful information. Deer tend to mill about in these areas before continuing to their destination. I refer to these spots as "social areas." They are often located where there is low brush, foxtails, and cattails, and are usually found between bedding and feeding areas. Deer that congregate here leave behind discernible sign. These areas always contain numerous droppings of all sizes and matted high grass where deer have temporarily lain down. There is an excess of heavy trails coming in and out of these spots. And almost every social area I have ever encountered is within 100 yards of both bedding and feeding areas.

Social areas are good places to ambush deer, especially in the evening. The best way to avoid confusing a holding or social area with a bedding area is to look for available food. Social areas do not provide much in the way of food. Most offer only browse. A few will have overgrown grasses, such as timothy. It is simply a semiprotected area for deer to hole up in prior to feeding in the evening or bedding in the morning.

GEOGRAPHICAL VARIATIONS

Whitetails are amazingly adaptable animals. They are found in nearly every state and province, from sub-tropical Florida to the Northern Great Plains. This means that the types of habitat they can inhabit varies greatly by region.

A hunter in the Great Lakes states, for instance, will likely seek out mixed deciduous forests. In the more northerly part of this range, young aspen forests will provide both good whitetail habitat and hunting opportunities. In the southern part of this range, and throughout the mid-latitude states, forest with adjacent acorn crops can support very large populations of whitetails.

On the Central and Northern Plains, whitetails most often are found along river bottoms and in the occasional woodlot, from which they can venture out to feed on farm crops. Wetland areas, with dense stands of cattails, are particularly good hiding cover for whitetails and can be a real challenge to hunt. Similarly, standing corn can hide an entire herd of whitetails and, provided you have the landowner's permission, is a great place to practice your stalking skills.

In drier regions of the Plains and Mountain states, water becomes a critical factor both for whitetails and those who pursue them. Typically, foothills of the dry mountains will have the most consistent watering areas, whether they take the form of ponds or creeks. Stock ponds, created by farmers and ranchers, serve a similar purpose. Hunting near natural or artificial watering areas is a sound strategy in these parts of the country.

No matter where you hunt, keep your eyes peeled for three types of habitat: bedding/hiding areas, which are typically dense, and often elevated so that the deer can see; travel corridors, through which deer move from resting places to feeding grounds; and feeding areas. Travel corridors are most often located in low areas, where deer can pass without being seen. Creek bottoms and draws are good places to look.

Feeding areas are often either the easiest or most difficult to find. In places with truly defined food sources, such as crop fields or stands of oak trees, it is quickly obvious where deer are feeding. But in many places, whitetails feed on a variety of plants, and so can essentially make a living just about anywhere. In these places, patterning deer is much more difficult, and hunters would be wise to instead focus on hunting near naturally defined corridors.

During most of the year, and throughout much of their geographic range, white-tailed deer can choose from a variety of succulent plants. Their diet changes with the seasons and with their physiological requirements, and those needs are different for deer of different ages or sex.

For instance, does are severely stressed just before they wean their nursing fawns in early autumn, but bucks are at their nutritional peak, having spent the summer building reserves for what is their biggest challenge—the rut. Mature bucks weigh 30 percent more than same-age females, but have a lower metabolic rate. This seems to allow them to subsist on poorer fare than can does; the does' dependency on more nutritious foods is likely related to the energy requirements of pregnancy and nursing.

Whitetails in the Southwest frequently consume prickly pear cactus during the summer, while their cousins in the Southeast are eating grapes, and midwestern whitetails are eating late varieties of berries. Fruits (often referred to as soft mast) are, by the way, a much favored food of whitetails wherever they live.

The variety they eat is only limited by the location and season—apples, blueberries, persimmons, blackberries, and huckleberries are among the most desirable. Obviously, whitetails in more southerly latitudes enjoy an advantage in this regard, since warmer weather and longer growing seasons provide more of a bounty.

But it is the succulent parts of woody plants that are the most important component of the whitetail's diet. Leafy portions of trees and shrubs, such as red-osier dogwood, aspen, oak, and an array of vines, find their way frequently to the whitetail's menu.

Deer in the Midwest seek out fertile deciduous forests for their habitat and nutritional needs.

Deer in the mountains are often found next to man-made lakes and reservoirs.

FOOD SOURCES

In some areas, agricultural plants are an important source of nutrition, and deer eat not only the ripened plant, but the seeds and fresh shoots as well. Woodland-bound whitetails without access to farm crops do fine by substituting leaf-bearing annuals and perennials from the forest floor, such as aster and clover. Even plants we consider toxic, like poison ivy and inedible mushrooms, are digestible for the adaptable whitetail.

Mast, such as acorns, is an important food in season, particularly autumn. Whitetails also eat both red and white cedar. The white cedar is considered the only woody browse capable of sustaining whitetails through the winter and is a critical food source in the North. Unlike whitetails in the South, those in the most northerly range are often forced in winter to subsist on less-desirable forage, such as woody browse, the least digestible.

The home range of a deer isn't large. But the deer knows it as well as you know the inside of your home. There are no shortcuts to becoming a master of whitetail hunting. You must learn at least the basics of whitetail feeding, mating, and travel strategies before you'll truly stand a chance of catching one off guard.

DISEASES

Whitetails are robust animals, and generally aren't susceptible to a lot of health problems. However, in recent decades, some "new" diseases have sprung up that not only impact some white-tailed deer, but may also be transmitted to humans. Hunters, because of their contact with deer during field dressing and butchering, are at a higher risk than the general public.

Lyme Disease

Lyme disease was named in 1977 when arthritis was observed in a cluster of children in and around Lyme, Connecticut. The disease is still largely a problem in the Northeast and Great Lakes region. Not truly a disease of the whitetail, since they serve primarily as a host of the tick that transmits the disease, it is included here because these ticks are common on deer, and may transfer to a hunter.

Woodland animals carry woodland parasites, and deer are no different. The most well-known parasite for deer is the deer tick, which is responsible for most cases of Lyme disease in the United States.

The deer tick (*Ixodes dammini*) is responsible for most of the cases of Lyme disease in the United States. The tick has three life stages: larva, nymph, and adult. Each stage takes a single blood meal. The bite is painless so most victims do not know they have been bitten. The nymphal stage appears to be responsible for most Lyme disease cases. The adult ticks (about the size of a sesame seed) prefer to feed on white-tailed deer. The entire life cycle requires three separate hosts and takes about two years to complete.

About half of the humans who've contracted Lyme disease develop a characteristic rash a few days to a few weeks after the bite from an infected tick. The rash generally looks like an expanding red ring. At about the same time that the rash develops, flu-like symptoms may appear with headache, sore throat, stiff neck, fever, muscle aches, fatigue, and general malaise. Some people develop the flu-like illness without getting a rash. Hunters should check themselves thoroughly after handling a deer to ensure they've not become a host to a deer tick.

Bovine Tuberculosis

Bovine tuberculosis (TB) is a contagious respiratory disease caused by the bacterium Mycobacterium bovis, and can infect most warm-blooded animals, including humans. The federal government has done nationwide testing of cattle herds to control bovine TB, but it still occurs in cattle and penned exotic livestock, such as elk and wild deer. TB has been diagnosed in captive elk herds in several states. Michigan has found TB in its free-ranging white-tailed deer since 1994.

Although it rarely occurs, bovine TB can be transmitted to people. TB is generally transmitted through the air by coughing and sneezing, and it is highly unlikely a person would contract the disease from field dressing or eating the meat of an infected deer. However, it is always a good idea to wear gloves when field dressing any animal. There is no specific test that can be easily done to check for TB in deer meat. Michigan recommends any deer meat collected from a TB infected area not be smoked or made into sausage or jerky, but be thoroughly cooked until it is no longer pink, and juice from the meat runs clear.

Chronic Wasting Disease

Chronic wasting disease (CWD) occurs in North American deer and elk. It belongs to a group of infectious diseases known as "transmissible spongiform encephalopathies" (TSEs), the most famous of which is the well-known mad cow disease. It is caused by an abnormal protein called a

Deer leave little to waste. Their teeth are perfectly adapted to chew and digest an entire plant—leaves, stem, seeds, and shoots.

Chronic Wasting Disease (CWD) can devastate local deer populations. Its more famous cousin is mad cow disease, but CWD is always fatal. Scrawny does like this one can sometimes indicate an outbreak of CWD.

and at the time of this writing, has been discovered in wild or captive deer or elk in South Dakota, Nebraska, Kansas, Oklahoma, New Mexico, Montana, Minnesota, Wisconsin, Illinois, Saskatchewan, and Alberta. Several wildlife agencies have decided to reduce the density of animals in the infected area to slow the transmission of the disease. In Colorado, Nebraska, and Wisconsin, large numbers of animals are being killed to accomplish this.

To date, there is no known case of CWD infecting a human, although the risk remains. The closely related mad cow disease has been known to jump the species barrier to people, which has resulted in a number of human deaths.

Hunters can minimize their exposure and risk by following several precautions. Don't eat meat from animals that look sick or ill, and don't touch or eat the brain, spinal cord, eyes, spleen, tonsils, or lymph nodes. In fact, it is important that you not cut into or through these body parts while field dressing or butchering. Prions can be spread, and they cannot be killed by cooking. In fact, they are virtually indestructible. The best defense is to not spread them from the above body parts, where they are known to be found.

Although the origin of CWD remains clouded, it has become clear that the movement of the disease from state to state is the result of the transfer of infected game-farm elk and deer. Inevitably, some of these animals either escape or come in contact with wild deer, and the dangerous release of this disease into a new region is complete.

Just about every state wildlife agency has increased its efforts to watch for CWD. To slow the spread of this disease, many states have now banned the importation of deer and elk. These game-farm animals are known to be a primary cause of CWD moving so rapidly around the U.S. and Canada. Some states have also banned supplemental feeding programs and the baiting of deer, because close contact between deer facilitates the spread of the disease. Hunters who travel should study regulations carefully because several states have implemented regulations that allow only boned meat, quarters (without spinal column or head), or processed meat from deer or elk to be transported out of certain areas with CWD. Other states have limited the importation of hunter-killed deer and elk to only boned or processed meat.

prion, which affects the animal's brain and is invariably fatal. Usually, months to years pass from the time an animal is infected to when it shows signs of the disease.

Whitetails that have contracted the disease sometimes display visible signs, such as drooping head or ears, poor body condition, tremors, stumbling, increased salivation, difficulty swallowing, or excessive thirst or urination. The disease was first discovered in Colorado and Wyoming,

CHAPTER TWO

EQUIPMENT FOR WHITETAIL HUNTING

Depending on where and when you hunt for whitetails, you may choose different equipment for different occasions.

The right rifle, for instance, makes your hunt more enjoyable and boosts your odds for success. Shotguns are widely used for deer hunting in agricultural or densely populated areas where rifle hunting is not allowed. Some southern states also permit the use of shotguns with buckshot.

Blaze orange and camouflage
is the most common equipment
for whitetail hunters, but
a wide bevy of tools and
techniques are available for the
savvy huntsman.

With a muzzleloader, you'd better make your first shot count because it'll likely be your only shot. Many states have muzzleloader-only seasons, allowing you to extend your time afield and escape the hunting pressure of regular firearms seasons. Using handguns also increases the challenge of hunting whitetails. They do, additionally, allow some disabled hunters to enjoy the sport.

Bowhunting for whitetails was once enjoyed by only a few highly skilled archers. But new designs have made the bow easier to shoot accurately and opened the door to many more hunters.

Clothes for deer hunting should keep you quiet, safe, and comfortable. A good tip when choosing accessories is to travel light with a pack containing only what you need—don't overload yourself with gadgets.

RIFLES AND AMMUNITION

A wide range of rifles and calibers are suitable for deer hunting. Selecting the right rifle for your needs is a personal decision that should be based on thoughtful consideration of action, caliber, fit, and sights.

Actions

A rifle action is the mechanical means used to deliver a cartridge from the magazine to the chamber. The simplest action is the single shot, where the shooter places the cartridge in the chamber. The single shot is preferred by some marksmen who enjoy shooting these

The rifle is as beautiful a weapon as it is useful, a perfect blend of form and function. Lever-action and bolt-action rifles are seen here.

Knowing the parts of your rifle will help you learn how it works, making you a better shot. Ballistics tables can help you determine the best caliber and cartridge for your style and type of hunting.

Ballistics Table for Common Calibers

The first number is energy in foot-pounds and the second is trajectory in inches above (+) or below (-) line of aim.

Type of Cartridge	100 Yards	200 Yards	300 Yards
6mm Remington (100-grain)	1775 / +1.4	1470 / 0.0	1205 / -6.7
.243 Winchester (100-grain)	1615 / +1.6	1330 / 0.0	1090 / -7.5
.257 Roberts (117-grain)	1710 / +1.9	1445 / 0.0	1210 / -8.2
.25-06 Remington (117-grain)	1985 / +1.6	1645 / 0.0	1350 / -7.2
.270 Winchester (130-grain)	2225 / +1.8	1818 / 0.0	1472 / -7.4
.280 Remington (150-grain)	2370 / +1.7	2015 / 0.0	1695 / -7.5
7mm Remington (150-grain)	2667 / +1.7	2196 / 0.0	1792 / -7.0
.30-30 Winchester (170-grain)	1355 / +2.0	989 / -4.8	720 / -25.1
.30-06 Springfield (150-grain)	2281 / +2.1	1827 / 0.0	1445 / -8.5
.308 Winchester (150-grain)	1957 / 0.0	1610 / -3.9	1314 / -14.0
.300 Winchester (180-grain)	3011 / +1.9	2578 / 0.0	2196 / -7.3
.35 Remington (200-grain)	1280 / +5.4	840 / 0.0	575 / -23.3

lightweight, accurate, and reliable rifles.

Consistent accuracy and reliability make bolt actions the most popular rifles. Bolt-action rifles are available from most manufacturers in a wide selection of calibers. Scopes are easily mounted on them.

The lever-action rifle, recognizable from countless western movies, is a traditional deer-hunting favorite. Although they've been eclipsed in popularity by bolt actions, levers are still chosen by hunters who prefer a quick, lightweight gun.

Pump actions are worked by moving the forearm, a physical action that comes naturally to many shooters, especially those who use pump-action shotguns for bird hunting. Pumps can be fired rapidly, but may jam in hunting situations.

Semi-automatic actions are worked by the expanding gases of a fired round. Although they can be shot as quickly as you can pull the trigger, semi-autos are prone to failure if they become dirty in cold or wet weather.

Calibers

Advances in cartridges and bullet performance give today's deer hunter an unprecedented selection of loads to choose from. The caliber you select should be appropriate for you and your hunting situation.

Whitetails have relatively thin skin and light bone structure. With proper shot placement, they can be killed by bullets delivering at least 900 foot-pounds of energy at the point of impact. This rules out the small-caliber cartridges, such as .22s. Most states and provinces have minimum caliber standards.

Although they have fallen out of favor with some modern hunters, low-velocity, medium-caliber cartridges, such as the 30.30 Winchester, .300 Savage and .35 Remington, were long the standard rounds

for deer hunters, especially east of the Mississippi. The famous Model 94 Winchester lever action, typically chambered for .30-30, is by far the all-time best-selling American hunting rifle. The limitation of low-velocity cartridges is that they are restricted to ranges of 150 yards or less, which usually isn't a problem in the whitetail woods. The advantage is these calibers are often found in light, easy-to-carry guns. Bullet weights of 150 to 170 grains are recommended. For lever actions with tubular magazines, be sure to use round-nose bullets, because a pointed bullet could fire a round in the magazine from recoil.

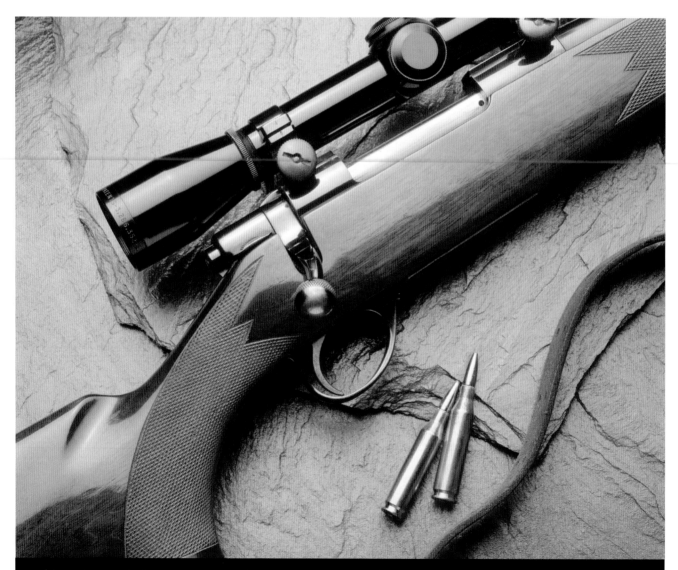

Careful consideration of caliber and cartridge will help make your hunting experience much more enjoyable—depending on your strength and body size, you may opt for a lighter rifle set with a low recoil, or a heavier rifle set for stronger hunters.

Not flinching while discharging a firearm isn't always easy. The best way to overcome it is to practice with your favorite rifle and cartridge to grow accustomed to the recoil and blast.

High-velocity, smaller calibers, such as the 6mm Remington, .243 Winchester, 25.06 Remington, .257 Roberts, .260 Remington, and 7mm-08, are effective to 250 yards or more and capable of tack-driving accuracy. The disadvantage is the calibers have smaller bullets. Most hunters who use these calibers prefer bullets weighing at least 100 grains. Mild recoil and lightweight guns are advantages to these calibers, especially for children or women.

High-velocity, medium calibers offer the most versatility in loads and typically have adequate down-range energy to 300 yards or more. Popular calibers include the .270 Winchester, .280 Remington, 7mm Remington, 30.06 Springfield, and .308 Winchester. Bullet weights may range from 130 to 220 grains, with 150 to 180 grains being the most common. These calibers are also suitable for larger game, such as elk and caribou.

A seven-pound 30-06 shooting the popular 150-grain factory load kicks twice as hard as a 257 Roberts shooting a 117-grain bullet. Not surprisingly, most shooters are capable of better marksmanship with the softer-kicking rounds. When you opt for a light-recoiling cartridge, you get less punch at both ends. In the deer woods, this often translates into marginal killing performance at extended range. For instance, a 165-grain bullet fired from a 30-06 strikes with 2,350 foot-pounds of energy at 100 yards, and still has 1,220 foot-pounds remaining at the 400-yard mark. In contrast, a 100-grain bullet from a 243 Winchester factory load delivers 1,516 foot-pounds at 100 yards and just 882 foot-pounds at 400 yards.

To be effective on whitetails and mulies, a rifle bullet needs to strike with at least 1,000 foot-pounds of energy. That makes the 30-06 a solid performer out to

Sighting In

Every season, hunters miss their chance at a trophy because their rifles were not sighted in. Many people think that bore-sighting is sufficient. It is not. A bore-sighted rifle may shoot 20 inches or more from point of aim. Before hunting, take several practice sessions with your hunting ammunition.

You can sight in most easily at a shooting range. Most ranges have bench rests and sandbags to provide a steady rest and minimize human error. If sighting in your rifle in the field, make sure you shoot into a solid backstop, like a tree or large stump.

To shoot accurately, take a deep breath, exhale halfway, then hold your breath as you squeeze the trigger. Do not jerk the trigger as you shoot.

Sights on a new rifle may be so far out of adjustment that you miss the target completely. To solve this problem, bore-sight your rifle. Look directly through the bore of the bolt or falling block action. You cannot look directly through the bore of most other actions, so you must use a bore-sighting tool.

You can also rough-sight your rifle by simply aiming at a close target through the sights, firing, then making any adjustments needed to hit the bull's-eye.

Once you have rough-sighted at 25 yards, back off to 100 yards. Continue to fine-tune the sights until you can center the shot group on the bull's-eye. If you plan to shoot at longer ranges, sight in a few inches higher at 100 yards. Then try a few long-range shots and make any necessary adjustments.

Always hunt with the same type of ammunition you used to sight in. Changing brands or bullet weights often makes it necessary to realign your sights.

Always wear eye and ear protection when on the range.

Rest the forearm and butt stock on sandbags when sighting in. Do not support the barrel; the result will be inaccurate shooting. Hold the stock firmly against your shoulder.

Recoil Comparison Chart

Cartridge	Bullet Weight (grains)	Muzzle Velocity (feet per second)	Rifle Weight (pounds)	Recoil (foot-pounds)
7.62x39mm	123	2,300	7.0	6.2
			8.5	5.1
			10.0	4.3
250 Sav	100	2,820	7.0	9.4
			8.5	8.5
			10.0	6.6
30-30 Winchester	170	200	7.0	10.4
44 Magnum	240	1,760	7.0	10.6
257 Roberts	117	2,650	7.0	10.7
			8.5	8.8
			10.0	7.5
243 Winchester	100	2,960	7.0	11.9
			8.5	9.8
			10.0	8.4
6mm Remington	100	3,100	7.0	14.2
			8.5	11.7
			10.0	9.9
7x57mm	140	2,650	7.0	15.3
			8.5	12.6
			10.0	10.7
7mm-08 Remington	140	2,860	7.0	18.3
			8.5	15.1
			10.0	12.8
308 Winchester	150	2,820	7.0	19.2
			8.5	15.8
			10.0	13.4
30-06	150	2,910	7.0	21.6
			8.5	17.8
			10.0	15.1
270 Winchester	130	3,060	7.0	22.7
			8.5	18.7
			10.0	15.9
7mm Remington Magnum	140	3,175	7.0	28.2
			8.5	23.2
			10.0	19.7
300 Winchester Magnum	150	3,290	7.0	36.4
			8.5	30.0
			10.0	25.5

Some hunters prefer to customize the barrels of their rifles with a muzzle brake, which diverts expanding gases and diminishing recoil forces.

the 400-yard mark, while the 243 pretty much poops out past the 300-yard mark. But since most deer are shot at ranges well shy of 200 yards—with many of those less that 100 yards away—recoil-sensitive hunters find this trade-off well worthwhile.

Relatively new additions to deer-hunting calibers are the short magnums, which achieve magnum performance with shorter cases and have noticeably less recoil. Short magnums come in .243, .270, 7mm, and .300 calibers. They are well suited to long-range shooting, having flat trajectory and retaining energy at distances exceeding 300 yards.

Magnum calibers are better suited to larger game such as elk and moose, but are also used by some deer hunters. Calibers such as the .300 Winchester Magnum and .338 Winchester Magnum are best suited to long-range shooting or hunting especially large, northern white-tailed bucks. These are not calibers for beginners and they have substantial recoil many shooters find uncomfortable. The recoil can be tamed with a muzzle brake system, but at the expense of a much louder report that can damage your hearing.

When shooting short magnum or magnum loads for deer, bullet selection is especially important. Be sure to choose a bullet designed to kill deer at the ranges you are likely to shoot. At short ranges, be especially careful with shot placement to minimize damage to meat.

Recoil

Every shooter is affected by recoil. Some learn to manage it and shoot powerful hunting rifles accurately; others do not. Practice helps, but doesn't always provide a cure for flinching. Even experienced sportsmen flub shots on occasion, and recoil is often a contributing factor. Magnums aren't the only offenders, either. The jarring thump of a 270 or 30-06 is enough to make many riflemen miss their mark. In fact, we'd all shoot better if our rifles didn't kick so hard.

Your deer rifle doesn't have to thump you, though. You can reduce recoil by selecting the right cartridge, using a heavier rifle, or adding a muzzle brake. The action you choose can even make a difference. An eight-pound rifle shoots softer than a six-pound ultralight model. An autoloader delivers less apparent recoil than a bolt-action, single-shot or lever-action rifle.

Weight

If you hunt deer in mountain or desert country, or simply aren't willing to pass up those occasional long shots, there are ways to ease the bite of even a hard-kicking magnum. One proven way to reduce the punishment any cartridge doles out is to use a heavier rifle. Pass up those featherweight models in favor of something heftier. A Ruger Model 77 Ultra Light model in 270 Winchester weighs only six pounds, while Ruger's M77 Express rifle is a full pound-and-a-half heavier. Weatherby's Vanguard rifle scales eight pounds, while Browning's Model 1885 single shot runs just four ounces shy of the nine-pound mark. The right scope, mount, and sling can add another pound or so.

The extra weight reduces recoil. A 270 firing a 130-grain factory load recoils with 22.7 foot-pounds of force in a seven-pound rifle. The same load generates 18.7 foot-pounds in an 8-pound rifle, and just 15.9 foot-pounds in a 10-pound firearm. The 10-pound 270 kicks only 1.7 foot-pounds harder than a 7-pound 6mm

Open sights have a front post, which must be centered in the notched rear sight. They are the most difficult type to align because the target becomes covered.

Peep sights require you to center the target in a hole in the rear sight, then place the front bead on the animal. Large peepholes are easiest to use.

Scopes feature easy-to-use crosshairs and are by far the most popular and simple to use. You can aim precisely without obscuring the animal.

Remington rifle—and few consider the 6mm punishing to shoot.

If you're supersensitive to recoil, you can tame kick even further with a bull-barreled varmint rifle. Remington, Ruger, and Savage all offer 9- or 10-pound varmint rifles, while Winchester's "Heavy Varmint" Model 70 scales a hefty 11 pounds. These rifles sport 24- or 26-inch barrels and are more tiring to tote than is an ultralight carbine, but they sure soften recoil. Scoping a Model 70 varmint rifle can bring the weight to an even 12 pounds; in 243 Winchester chambering, recoil will be held to a powder-puff 7 foot-pounds.

Most deer-hunting rifles weigh between 6 and 9 pounds. Increasingly, hunters are choosing bolt-action rifles weighing less than 7 pounds without a scope, although recoil may be excessive in larger calibers. When buying a rifle, go to a gun shop and try several makes and styles. The gun should come easily to your shoulder when wearing hunting clothing. Work the action and the safety to determine the style you prefer.

Rifles come with wooden stocks and blued actions and barrels, or with all-weather synthetic stocks and stainless-steel barrels. The type you select is a matter of personal preference. Most rifles sold today have a recoil pad suitable for the caliber. On older, used guns, you may need to have a recoil pad installed by a gunsmith. Trigger pull, which should be adjusted by a gunsmith, is typically set at about 3.5 pounds.

The Automatic Advantage

Yet another way to tame the punishment hunting cartridges dole out is to carry an autoloader. The cycling of the self-loading action uses up a small amount of recoil energy, but the real benefit comes in how the remaining energy is meted out to your shoulder. A bolt-action, or any other fixed-breech rifle, delivers a short, sharp blow. Autoloaders spread that recoil out over several milliseconds—more like a firm push than a rabbit punch. The energy transmitted to your shoulder may be the same, but the autoloader is a lot more pleasant to shoot. Recoil pads work in much the same way—they spread recoil out over a longer time span, as well as over a larger surface area.

Remington's Model 7400 autoloader and Browning's BAR both weigh around 7 pounds in most deer calibers. The Browning is also offered in four magnum chamberings; the magnums scale 8 pounds 6 ounces before you add a scope.

DIY Featherweight

The single most effective way to reduce your rifle's recoil requires a little gunsmithing. It'll cost you somewhere in the neighborhood of $200 to have a muzzle brake installed, but these devices work surprisingly well. Good muzzle brakes can actually reduce recoil 50 to 70 percent. They're most efficient with high-velocity rounds: The faster the bullet, the better the brake works.

A muzzle brake consists of a screw-on tube, or muzzle extension, with a number of holes drilled in it. The holes can be drilled into existing barrel muzzles on some rifles as well. These holes divert expanding gases sideways and to the rear. This goes a long way toward off-setting recoil forces. There are trade-offs, however. In addition to being relatively costly, muzzle brakes can be extremely hard on your ears. Actual noise level rises only 10 to 15 decibels (an increase of less than 20 percent), but the report is much sharper and more piercing.

Hearing protection is definitely recommended.

There are several excellent muzzle brakes on the market, including the KDF Recoil Arrestor, Barnes Straightline Quiet Brake, Gentry Quiet Brake, and the New Answer System brake. The Mag-Na-Port system also tames recoil, but is better known for reducing muzzle jump. Ask your local gunsmith for details or write directly to the manufacturer.

What's your best bet for a low-recoiling deer rifle? If you're willing to limit your shots to 125 yards or so, Ruger's Mini Thirty autoloader is the least punishing deer rifle on the market. With iron sights, the rifle produces just 6.2 foot-pounds of recoil. Add a scope, and it kicks with less than 5H foot-pounds of force. Because it's an autoloader, felt recoil is even less. In an 8H-pound rifle, the 257 Roberts cartridge develops 8.8 foot-pounds of recoil. The 243 Winchester packs a 9.8 foot-pound kick. Both are effective out to 300 yards.

If you find that much recoil a bit bothersome, adding a good muzzle brake will more than halve that punch. Cartridges like the 6mm Remington and 7x57mm Mauser are also noted for their civilized shooting manners and are great choices for hunting deer.

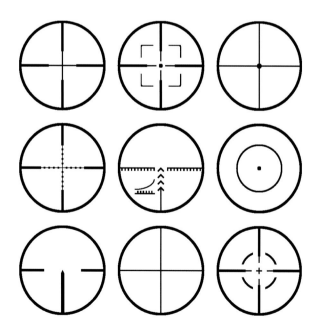

Scopes feature a wide variety of reticles—find the one that suits you best.

Scopes have multiple adjustments in which to customize the zoom, position, and space between the scope and your eye. Be sure to position the scope far enough away to not strike your head once the gun has been discharged.

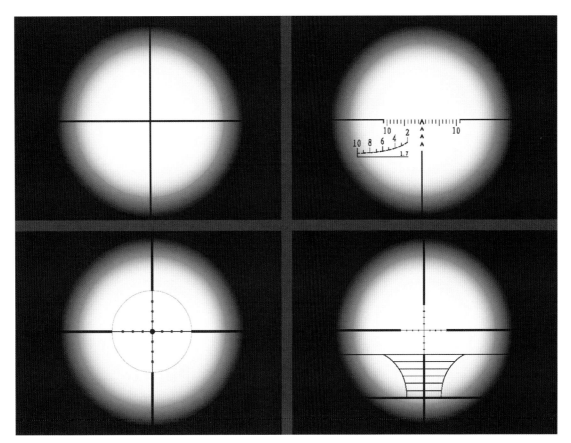

Your choice of reticle may also influence how bright you wish the scope to be—you don't want to obscure the built-in sights with under- or over-exposed brightness settings.

The absolute ultimate in a light-kicking 300-yard deer rifle? Probably a 243 Browning or Remington autoloader fitted with a muzzle brake and a one-pound scope. This kind of rig should practically pull you forward when you shoot.

Sights

With the exception of many lever-action and single-shot guns, open and peep sights have been largely replaced by variable and fixed-power scopes. Shooters who are proficient with open or peep sights are by no means at a disadvantage in the deer woods. However, scopes offer the advantage of magnification and improved light-gathering capabilities in low-light situations, and the modern hunting scope is fogproof, durable, and compact.

Fixed-power scopes are typically 4X, which makes the target easier to see, but doesn't magnify it so much that it is difficult to find and aim at a moving deer. Variable scopes range from 1.5X up to 9X, which is suitable for virtually all deer-hunting situations. When mounting a scope, be sure to adjust the eye relief—the distance between the scope and your eye—so that you have a full field of vision. The scope should be far enough from your eye so it doesn't strike you from recoil.

Pros and Cons of Magnification

For a long time, the 4X has been touted as the best all-around scope power for big-game hunters. Truly, if you were stuck with a 3X or 6X for the rest of your life, you'd find it adequate. But a 4X has the best mix of field, brightness, and magnification.

Hunters who like variables reject fixed-power scopes as they might a television with no channel selector. But while variables give you flexibility (useful for people

Firearms Safety

Most people would be surprised to learn that hunting is not among the most dangerous sports. A National Safety Council study showed the fatality rate for hunting to be less than half that of boating or swimming.

Improved hunter education and increased use of blaze orange clothing account for the low accident rate. Every state and province sponsors some type of firearms safety or hunter education program. Many states require beginning hunters to pass such courses before they can purchase a license.

Nevertheless, the potential for a serious accident always exists. To avoid an accident, follow these safety rules:

- Treat every firearm as if it were loaded. Never assume a gun is unloaded because someone said so.

- Make sure your safety is on at all times, unless you intend to shoot.

- Positively identify your target before shooting. Never fire at a silhouette, a vague form, or an area where you saw or heard something move. Blaze orange clothing greatly improves your own visibility.

- Control the direction of your muzzle at all times. If you start to fall, point the barrel away from yourself and other hunters. After a fall, check the barrel for obstructions like dirt or snow. A plugged barrel could rupture when you shoot, possibly causing serious injury.

- Never lean a gun against a tree, fence post, vehicle, or any place where it could fall over and accidentally discharge.

- Never shoot at hard surfaces or water with bullets or slugs. They could ricochet and strike another hunter or building.

- Never drink alcoholic beverages before or during a hunt. Alcohol does not keep you warm; in fact, it speeds the loss of body heat.

- Use only the ammunition recommended for your firearm. Do not carry two different types of ammunition in your pocket at the same time.

- When not hunting, keep the gun unloaded and the action open.

- Keep all firearms and ammunition out of the reach of children.

- Refuse to hunt with anyone who does not observe the basic rules of firearm safety.

- Open your action before crossing a creek, climbing over a fence, or in any other situation where you are unsure of your footing.

- Avoid shooting over the tops of hills and ridges.

Hunting safety is part and parcel to an enjoyable hunting experience. Practice responsible carries, as this hunter is doing, with the barrel down and away from surrounding households and people.

- Carry your firearm so the muzzle points away from others. Safe positions include: shoulder carry (resting the barrel over your shoulder with the muzzle pointing backward); cradle carry (resting the gun in front of you, barrel down, between two cradled arms); and trail carry (holding the gun by the stock outside the trigger and the barrel, with the muzzle pointed toward the ground).

It is your responsibility to always follow safe gun-handling rules. You can avoid accidents when you're in the field by keeping these tips in mind:

- Always be aware of where your barrel is pointing. Around other hunters, keep the barrel pointed up. When you load a firearm, stand away from other hunters with the barrel pointed toward the ground.

- Don't use your gun scope to look at distant hunters.

- Some lever-action rifles commonly used for deer hunting, as well as some other firearms, have exposed hammers that are cocked and must be uncocked if the gun isn't fired. Step away from other hunters and point the gun toward the ground when you uncock it. Use firm thumb pressure on the hammer and ease it forward as you squeeze the trigger.

- Most lever-action guns have a safe, half-cock position. In the fully uncocked position, the hammer rests against the firing pin mechanism and, if jarred, the gun may go off.

- Always leave your safety on until you are ready to shoot. Get in the habit of checking frequently to make sure your safety is on as you hunt. If you shoot at a deer, make sure to put the safety back on before you move.

- Unload your gun before climbing into a tree stand, crossing a fence or jumping a creek. Also unload it when you take a lunch break with other hunters or quit hunting for the day. Keep the action open, so everyone (including you) knows the gun is unloaded.

- Carry only the ammunition that you will use in your firearm so you won't mistakenly load it with different ammo.

- Be certain of your target and what is behind it before taking a shot. Take your time and aim carefully. A rushed shot is a poor shot.

Veteran hunters know that discipline saves lives and minimizes risk. When this hunter's trail becomes difficult over the ridge, he unloads his rifle and leaves the action open.

Common sense rules the day for years of safe and enjoyable hunting. Wear blaze orange, never point the rifle unless you intend to shoot, and keep the muzzle pointed away from yourself, your hunting partners, and structures like fences and buildings.

A scope is a valuable tool while deer hunting, but it must be calibrated perfectly so you actually hit what you're aiming at.

with only one rifle, but who want to hunt varmints and big game), they cost and weigh more and give you less latitude in ring spacing. You might find you settle on one power setting and rarely turn the dial.

Some hunters buy variables so they can crank them up to high power to glass a shaded draw or evaluate antlers. Bad logic. Most variables for big-game guns have a top end of 6 to 10 power, about the magnification you get in binoculars. Binoculars are easier to use and more effective. Besides, using a scope to search for game is dangerous. You could find a hunter behind that crosswire!

Field of view, or the size of an area visible through a scope, is the obvious sacrifice when you boost power, because the bigger the target image, the smaller the field. A typical 4X scope might offer a field of view of 38 feet at 100 yards. An 8X scope gives you only half that

field. Finding a buck walking through brush 100 yards away, in a field of view of 19 feet, isn't always a simple task. The only way to increase field of view would be to increase the size of the ocular lens—but then your bolt handle wouldn't clear it.

High magnification brings other woes. Eye relief (the range of distance between your eye and the ocular lens that gives you a full target picture) is most generous on low-power scopes. High-power scopes have "critical" eye relief: The sight picture blacks out if your eye is just a bit too far forward or back. For urgent shooting, critical eye relief is as useful as a fork in soup.

How Bright?

The objective lens doesn't have anything to do with field of view or eye relief. It does affect light transmission.

Objective lens diameter (mm) divided by magnification yields "exit pupil," a measure of light transmission. Our eyes have pupils that dilate in the dark to about 7.1mm and constrict in daylight to 2.5. Maximum dilation during normal hunting hours is around 6, even on a cloudy evening. A scope with an exit pupil of 6 gives you all the light your eyes can use (assuming top-quality multicoated lenses). A 4X scope with 32mm objective has a large exit pupil of 8. A 6x32 scope's exit pupil is 5.3, on the small side for woods hunting. My 6x42 Leupold has an exit pupil of 7, with an objective bell that still lets me use low rings. I'm not sold on variable scopes with 50mm objectives. They're bulky and require high rings. You just about need a sledge and a jack to get them into and out of scabbards. And the big glass helps you only at magnifications of 8X or higher in bad light.

Use a coin or screwdriver to carefully adjust the vertical position of your scope atop the rifle. The same scope can be used for different rifles, but take notes as to the proper setting for each.

An extra-large exit pupil can make shooting easier in bright light because it allows you to see a full field if your eye is a bit high, low or off to the side. That's why front bells make sense on 4X scopes. A straight tube with 22mm objective yields an exit pupil of 5.5—adequate, if not ideal. A 32mm lens is much more forgiving when you must shoot quickly and your eye isn't centered.

Other scope terms include "relative brightness" (the exit pupil measurement squared) and "twilight factor" (the square root of the product of objective lens diameter and magnification). But exit pupil is all you really need to know when comparing similar scopes.

A 4X scope (or standard 6X, or a 2-7X or 2.5-8X variable) is light and trim enough to mount low. It shouldn't affect a rifle's balance. Popular 3-9X and 3.5-10X variables can make lightweight guns top-heavy. Straight-tube variables and fixed-power scopes, and the new compact models, are most appropriate for short, wispy guns. Last season I met a hunter carrying a six-pound rifle mated to a high-power variable scope. It fit like a cowbell on a cat.

Some scopes are larger than others. Don't mount a giant scope on a small rifle—it will only get in the way.

On the other extreme, riflemen looking for top performance at any cost are buying European scopes with 30mm tubes. They're heavy and expensive: A 2.5-10X Zeiss weighs 24 ounces and lists for over $1,400! In contrast, Bausch & Lomb's 2.5-10X scales 16 ounces and costs $653. It has an adjustable objective to correct for parallax (reticle displacement caused by off-center eye position).

Optical brilliance conceded, a big scope can be a poor choice, even when properly matched to a rifle. Not long ago a hunter came to elk camp lugging a rifle with a barrel the diameter of a truck axle, matched by a 12X scope. He expected to kill an elk far away. By hunt's end, he was wishing that gun had wheels. Puffing up a mountain, he muffed a shot at a handsome bull at 250 yards—easy range for a practiced hunter with a hardware-store 30-06 and 4X scope.

Customize Your Scope

For years hunters have been told that long shots require huge scopes and rocket-like cartridges, that short shooting means iron sights and fat bullets. Sounds sensible, but it isn't. Your hunting style, not hunting conditions, should guide your choice of gear.

How you use a scope is more important than its specifications. Proper mounting is the first step: the lower the better for quick aim and good gun balance. Many hunters mount their scopes too far back, pulling the tube to within 3 inches of their eye while standing as if at attention. In the woods, you may have to shoot

quickly, thrusting your eye at the scope as you jam the rifle into your shoulder. A scope mounted well forward will bring the full field smoothly into view; one that protrudes too far to the rear will cost you time as you jockey your eye back and forth. If you crawl with your stock, or if you must shoot prone or uphill, a protruding ocular housing will bang your brow on recoil.

Make sure the reticle is properly centered. After you've snugged one ring to hold the scope where you want it, put the rifle in sandbags and loosen the ring so you can rotate the scope and true up the reticle. Bring your head back behind the gun. You'll lose most of the field but see enough reticle to plumb the vertical wire with the buttplate. Throwing the rifle to your shoulder for a peek can give you a false sense of vertical.

Next, adjust the ocular lens so your reticle looks sharp. Do this by loosening the lock ring in front of the ocular housing and spinning it forward. Now thread the housing rearward. Pointing your rifle at the northern sky, look through the scope. The reticle should be fuzzy. Next, screw the ocular housing in one turn at a time

In many states, deer season overlaps goose or duck season. Some hunters carry an extra shotgun in case the deer are scarce.

The ideal shotgun for whitetail hunting has a rifled barrel and scope. Proper ammunition is also very important. Rifling in the barrel imparts spin to the slug, stabilizing it and increasing accuracy.

until you see a sharp reticle. Don't stare! Your eye will automatically try to focus the reticle. When you get a sharp image instantly, tighten the lock ring.

"Sighting in" or zeroing is adjusting the scope so your line of sight coincides with the bullet's course at a given range. These paths cross twice; the second crossing is your zero range. I zero my big-game rifles at 200 yards regardless of cartridge or intended use. That way my bullets strike 2 to 3 inches high at 100 and drop six to 10 inches at 300, depending on the load.

Some hunters zero at 300 yards. They must then hold low between 150 and 200, where lots of game is shot. Some prefer to hold over at long range, and they take fewer shots and usually have more time to figure out where to aim.

Finding a well-built scope is easy. Matching it to your rifle and hunting style, then mounting and adjusting it so it brings your line of sight and bullet together at the target, is time well spent. Practicing so you can use it effectively is downright essential.

SHOTGUNS AND AMMUNITION

In farm country or more densely populated areas, hunters are usually prohibited from using rifles because of the long distance a bullet may travel, posing a safety risk.

In these areas, shotguns are the preferred alternative. A properly configured shotgun can be a very effective short-range (100 yards) whitetail firearm. A 12-gauge shotgun is the best choice, and a 20-gauge is the absolute minimum a hunter should consider.

Chokes

The constriction at the muzzle end of a shotgun barrel—the choke—is there to increase muzzle velocity and tighten the shot string by compressing both the shotgun pellets and the gas propelling it. However, a choke that does a good job on bird loads may be too

Quick Tips for Shotguns

Frontiersmen referred to the shotgun as a scattergun because it sprayed a swarm of lead pellets. Whitetail hunters don't use scattershot, but lead slugs can be just as effective as rifles and bows.

Bore Size Shotguns bores are measured in gauge or in inches. As the gauge number increases, the size of the bore decreases. The most common gauges are 12 and 20, but gauges range from as small as 28 to as large as 10. The smallest bore is the .410, the only bore measured in inches.

Choke The amount of constriction, or choke, at the end of the barrel affects the diameter and density of your slug. Common chokes from widest (most open) to narrowest (most closed) include: cylinder, skeet, improved-cylinder, modified, improved-modified, and full. Open chokes are best for close shooting, while narrow chokes are best for long-range. Many modern shotguns have interchangeable screw-in choke tubes that enable you to quickly change chokes to suit the type of hunting. They can even be installed on older shotguns by a gunsmith.

Action Most single-shot and double-barreled shotguns have a hinge action. The simple hinge design is more reliable than repeating actions, like the pump and semi-automatic. Pump shotguns are more dependable than semi-automatics, which can malfunction in cold weather. A pump ejects the spent shell and chambers another one each time you slide the fore-end back and forth. Most pump shotguns hold five shells, although it's doubtful you'll get five shots at a single whitetail!

Chamber Length Many shotguns are chambered for standard 2¾ shells. The proper shell length is usually engraved on the barrel—never shoot a shell that exceeds that length.

Weight A light shotgun works best for quick shots in heavy cover. When you have more time to shoot, a heavier gun works better. You can hold the barrel steadier and swing on a target more smoothly.

A hinge action shotgun opens when you push a lever or button at the rear of the receiver, allowing you to manually insert the shells. After firing, you break the action again. If your gun has ejectors, the spent shells pop out automatically; otherwise, you must remove them yourself.

Most shotgun barrels for whitetail hunting are 20–26 inches in length, and feature a rifle scope as well.

tight for slugs, causing erratic accuracy by deforming the projectile. Although almost any shotgun with an open choke can be used to hunt whitetails, the best shotgun for deer hunting will have a rifled barrel and some type of additional sights. In some cases, you can buy an extra barrel for your favorite pump or semi-automatic bird gun, allowing it to perform double-duty. If a rifled barrel is not available for your gun, consider buying a barrel that has an open choke—improved cylinder or skeet.

Barrels and Scopes

A rifled barrel will allow a shotgun to shoot slugs accurately out to 100 yards. Although it will never be as pinpoint accurate as a rifle, a slug barrel matched with proper loads makes it deadly. Most of these barrels run about 20–26 inches in length, and generally have rifle-type sights built in. The simple bead sight of a bird gun is a poor choice for deer hunting.

If your shotgun will accept one, consider buying a fixed low-power scope (2X) or a low-power variable (1–5X). There are many mount options for fixing scopes to shotguns. A good gunsmith can make suggestions for your particular gun.

Buckshot

Although a few states allow the use of buckshot for deer hunting, it is effective only at close range. If you use buckshot, try sizes 00 or 000. Take no shot beyond 30 yards. The larger the gauge, the better odds you'll have in making a clean kill, because the shell will carry more shot that will travel at a higher velocity. It is important to

pattern your shotgun, just as you would for bird hunting, when using buckshot. Try several brands to see which one works best with your gun and choke combination.

Slugs

Shotgun slugs can be grouped into three categories: sabot, trailing wad, and full-bore. All three are capable of 125-yard accuracy when matched with the proper slug gun.

Sabot (pronounced "say-bo") slugs revolutionized slug shooting during the 1980s. The slugs themselves are smaller than the bore diameter, which allows for a more ballistically efficient shape. The two-piece sabot encasing the slug is large enough to engage the rifling of a modern slug barrel, thus imparting a stabilizing spin to the slug. After the slug leaves the barrel, the sabot separates and drops away. Sabot slugs are generally best suited to rifled barrels—especially those with a relatively fast twist rate of 1 in 27 to 34 inches—yet shoot accurately through some smoothbore barrels. Rifled choke tubes produce surprisingly good accuracy.

A full-bore slug has a concave base, which expands when fired so it will fit the bore diameter of the barrel through which it is traveling. Since shotgun barrels vary considerably in diameter, no specific slug diameter would fit all barrels tightly. Full-bore slugs are comparatively wide and short, and are more accurate in rifled barrels with slow twist rates of 1 in 34 to 36 inches.

Most full-bore slugs are termed "rifled" slugs because the slugs themselves have lands and grooves on their outer surfaces. This rifled appearance lends the assumption that the slug spins when fired through

Buckshot is only effective at close range—generally 30 yards or less. Many hunters take to shotgun hunting for a challenge after years of proficiency with a rifle.

If you choose to hunt with buckshot, use a small shot size—00 or 000. The larger the gauge, the smaller the bead, and the more beads the shell will carry.

a smoothbore barrel, but such is not the case. Yet this "rifling" does promote the slug's expansion to bore size in both rifled and smoothbore barrels.

The traditional American full-bore slug, the Foster style, was designed long ago for use in smoothbore barrels. Although their style has not changed much, they still perform surprisingly well in modern slug barrels. I have gotten acceptable accuracy—three shots inside 6 inches at 125 yards—with all major brands.

On a trailing wad slug, the wad is attached to the slug itself to improve stabilization in flight. Trailing wad slugs can also be of the sabot, and full-bore categories and are suitable for rifled barrels, smoothbores or rifled choke tubes. Most of these slugs perform better in barrels with a slower rifling twist.

Results from the Range

Shotgun slugs have a short range and a low likelihood of ricochet. These two unchanging ballistic factors are precisely why more and more areas of high human population density are coming under "slug only" big-game hunting regulations.

What has changed significantly about slugs is their maximum effective range. A slug is still ballistically inferior to a rifle bullet, however, and two critical factors—trajectory and the effect of wind—rule out most slug-shooting at game beyond 125 yards.

A typical slug, fired from a gun parallel to the ground at shoulder height, will travel only about 240 yards. Tests of a variety of 12-gauge sabot slugs show an average drop of 6 inches between 125 and 150 yards (with sights zeroed at 100 yards). So a shooter's estimation of the distance to a faraway target must be close to exact. Misjudging the range by as few as 15 yards could lead to a miss or, worse, a wounded animal.

Many slug hunters mistakenly assume that wind does not have a large effect on slug accuracy. However, a mild breeze destroys accuracy beyond 125 yards; a stiff wind makes shooting beyond 75 yards difficult. Shooting straight into the wind is just as unpredictable.

Test Fires

That said, it is possible your particular shotgun may prefer a Foster to a sabot. The only way to know for sure is to buy some of each (and perhaps a couple of brands of each) and test-fire them. Fortunately, most slug ammunition is available in boxes of 5 or 10 rounds, so it doesn't require a large outlay of cash to do the proper testing.

Just as you would when testing a rifle, shoot three-slug groups with the two types of slugs, and several brands, to see which one performs the best. Ideally, you should set the target at the maximum distance at which you would be comfortable taking a shot at a deer. Most slug ammunition will shoot relatively flat out to 50 yards, but begin to drop at 75. At 100 yards, most will have dropped by ½ to 1 inch—a drop not serious enough to ruin the chance of a clean kill. But beyond that distance, slugs lose their effectiveness. At about 125 yards, a

Foster-type slug will no longer even have adequate energy for a clean kill on deer.

Shotguns are an extremely effective firearm for whitetails. You must, however, respect their limitations. In doing so, you'll be respecting your quarry as well.

Muzzleloaders

Imagine a time when a firearm was not just something used recreationally for a week or two per year, but as a tool to put food on the table year-round. Such a firearm would need to be relatively foolproof and accurate.

That firearm was the muzzleloading rifle, perfected in the United States through trial and error. Early muzzleloading long guns were smooth bores—their

Shotguns are popular (and challenging) choices for hunters near expansive areas with tall grasses or weeds; they can more easily approach unsuspecting bucks.

Handguns for whitetail hunting include bolt-action repeaters (top), break-action single shots (center), and revolvers (bottom).

barrels essentially no different inside than that of a shotgun. But with the advent of rifling, a leap in accuracy occurred.

This improvement meant hunters could take game at longer distances, but these guns had shortcomings. They were prone to misfire because of damp powder and hunters were relegated to a single shot.

Still, there is a romance to these guns and the skill it takes to handle them, which has led to great growth in modern muzzleloading, or "black powder" hunting. Many states and provinces now offer a primitive-weapons-only season and increased hunting tags issued—some states offer as much as 30 extra days of hunting.

Since there are fewer blackpowder hunters than modern-firearm hunters, there's less pressure on the animals during muzzleloader seasons. You'll see more animals moving in a natural manner, allowing you to pattern their feeding and bedding habits with less chance of other hunters interfering with your strategy or spoiling your solitude.

Today, the term "muzzleloader" is used to describe everything from the traditional Hawkins-style rifle of our ancestors, to the modern in-line rifles.

Ignitions

Muzzleloaders come in three basic ignitions—flintlock, percussion (caplocks) and the modern "in-line" ignition, which is akin to the caplock. The flintlock rifle does, indeed, use a piece of flint affixed to the hammer to create sparks in the frizzen to ignite the primer powder, which then ignites the main powder charge. Traditional caplock rifles look and work much the same as a flintlock, except that the hammer no longer contains flint, and the frizzen is replaced by a nipple over which a percussion cap is placed. When the hammer strikes the cap, it sends a flash through the nipple to ignite the charge. Caplocks are generally considered more reliable than flintlocks, and are faster in the sense that the main powder charge ignites more quickly than that of a flintlock.

Very popular are the newest black powder rifles, which have in-line ignitions. Looking much like a modern bolt-action rifle, these rifles use one of three types of caps to ignite the charge—the standard #11 cap, a "musket" cap (which produces more spark), or the 209 shotshell primer, the same primer used in many shotgun shells.

The Versatile Contender

One handgun, the single-shot, break-action Thompson/Center Contender, has brought thousands into the ranks of handgun hunters. By switching between the wide assortment of interchangeable barrels, a hunter can shoot any number of pistol and rifle cartridges in a single Contender frame. The action is simple, strong and accurate, and it makes scope mounting easy. Barrels are available for cartridges from 22 rimfire to the 30-30 Winchester, 35 Remington, and 45-70.

When even the Contender isn't enough, take a look at SSK Industries, the "handcannon" firm created by noted handgun hunter J. D. Jones. SSK starts with a Contender frame, then mounts a custom barrel chambered for a powerful factory or wildcat cartridge capable of taking the largest game or shooting at distances of hundreds of yards.

The first popular bolt-action handgun was the exotic-looking Remington XP-100, which was initially chambered for the 221 Fireball. Now the XP comes in several flavors, in composite and wood stocks, in varmint calibers, as well as big-game rounds like the 7mm-08 and even the 350 Remington Magnum, and in single-shot and repeater versions.

Other companies that make bolt-action or break-open handguns suitable for hunting include McMillan, Anschütz, Wichita Arms, Magnum Research, Ultra Light Arms, and Pachmayr. If you want magnum power in a modern revolver, consider the Freedom Arms 454 Casull. It's a big, stainless-steel, single-shot revolver chambered for the potent 454 Casull cartridge, which delivers more energy at 100 yards than the 44 magnum does at the muzzle.

What calibers are best for deer hunting? The 41 magnum and the venerable 44 magnum are good ones. In the long-range calibers, some of the better choices include the 7mm BR Rem, any of the JDJ wildcat cartridges, 7-30 Waters, 7mm-08 Rem, 30 Herrett, 30-30 Win, and anything bigger that you can shoot accurately.

The strategy for hunting deer with a handgun is the same as with a rifle, shotgun, or bow. Scout the area well and set up to give yourself the closest shot possible. Forget jump-shooting or any kind of deer drives that are likely to result in running shots. With a handgun, you want a stationary target, and you should use a rest for your gun whenever possible.

Before heading afield with your handgun, check the state and local laws, not just hunting regulations. You may be required to carry that gun locked in the trunk. Also, if you hunt with the gun in a holster, don't forget to take it off when you get back to your vehicle.

Powder and Projectiles

All of these rifles still load via the barrel end, thus, are still muzzleloaders. Most hunters who use the two more traditional designs still opt to measure powder (which allows for both error and custom loads). Many who choose the modern design employ an equally modern powder charge—pellets of powder that come in pre-measured sizes, usually of 50 grains each. Be sure to read the instructions for your rifle as some are rated up to 100 grains, while "magnum" black powder rifles can handle up to 150 grains.

True black powder is coded by coarseness of the grains—FFFg is the finest and used for priming flintlocks. Fg is the coarsest, and used for shotguns. Most rifles will perform best with either FFg (large caliber) or FFFg (small caliber).

Because black powder leaves a lot of corrosive residue, guns need a thorough cleaning after each use. To partially reduce the time needed for that chore, some hunters choose a black powder alternative called Pyrodex. Although Pyrodex is less expensive than black powder, and less corrosive, it is not as volatile—that is, it doesn't ignite quite as easily or burn as hot, leading some hunters to prefer the reliability of black powder, despite the need for cleaning. Two new black powder substitutes—Clean Shot and Triple Seven—are touted to be more volatile than Pyrodex, yet less corrosive.

Muzzleloading rifles come with varying amounts of rifling twist in their barrels, and the amount of twist often determines which type of projectile will work best with that rifle.

The most traditional rifles usually have a 1-in-60 twist (one full twist in 60 inches) and are best suited for round-ball projectiles. Some traditional guns in recent years have adopted a 1-in-48 twist, which still performs well with round balls, but will also allow the use of conical and sabot-type bullets. Most in-line rifles have a fast twist of about 1-in-32, which is great for conicals or sabots, but too fast for round balls, which become unstable.

Round balls are a short-range projectile, best suited for shots less than 50 yards, as they lose velocity more rapidly than the other two types of bullets. Sabot and conicals retain enough energy to kill a whitetail out to and sometimes beyond 100 yards.

Most deer hunters prefer a .50 or .54 caliber muzzleloader, but other options are available. Check your state's regulations to find out which calibers are legal. Also be advised that in many states, the addition of a telescopic sight is prohibited on muzzleloaders during muzzleloader-only seasons.

Finally, a few new black powder rifles now load through the breech with a bolt-like plunger, or break open like a double-barrel shotgun, and are loaded at that end. It is under debate whether these rifles truly qualify for use during primitive-weapon hunting seasons. Always check to learn what the area in which you plan to hunt allows.

Handguns for Whitetail Hunting

In the last 20 years or so, there has been a great increase in the use of handguns for hunting whitetails. While these hunters are only a small percentage of the total deer-hunting population, their interest in this method has prompted the development of new handguns and loads.

Handgun hunting presents a challenge similar to bowhunting. Shots must be close, so the hunter needs skill in getting near deer, and must also practice long hours to become proficient. In addition, handguns allow many hunters with disabilities to participate in the firearms deer season—hunters who could not otherwise handle a rifle.

Types

Handguns that allow a two-handed hold—one on the pistol grip, the other on the gun's short forearm—can be shot more accurately than those that offer only a one-handed grip (or two hands, but near to each other). It isn't that these guns are inherently more accurate than the latter, but the wider hand "stance" tends to steady the shooter more. These longer barreled handguns also propel bullets with more energy than a shorter barreled gun of the same caliber, for the simple reason that the expanding gas stays with the bullet for a longer time as it travels down the barrel.

These types of handguns are usually single-shot pistols that either break open like a break-action shotgun, or actually have a bolt, like a rifle. Some of the bolt-action pistols hold more than one round. Many of these are chambered for short rifle cartridges, such as the .30-30 or the .35 Remington.

Revolvers are another popular choice, as they offer quick-repeat shots. However, they are limited to handgun calibers only, and even the most powerful possess less than half the energy of common rifle calibers. Popular choices for revolvers are the .454 Casull, .44 Remington Magnum and .41 Remington Magnum. Some may be tempted to use the .357 Remington Magnum, and, in fact, in some states it is legal to do so, but it really is an ineffective deer load.

SCOPES AND ACCURACY

In order to improve your accuracy and to facilitate shots in low-light conditions, the addition of a pistol scope can be a great aid. Not only do these low-power scopes help the hunter to concentrate and hold on one spot, scopes gather light more effectively than the human eye and can make all the difference during that dawn or dusk hunt.

High-power scopes and long-range cartridges require a steady rest, and it's not unusual to see a handgun wearing a bipod. A handgun chambered for a cartridge such as the 7mm-08, with a good scope and a bipod, makes 250-yard shots at deer practical for a good shooter. To determine your maximum hunting range, shoot 10 shots at a round paper plate. The distance where you can consistently put nine out of 10 shots on the paper, from a hunting-style rest, is your maximum.

As with any deer-hunting weapon, make sure you check the laws for the state in which you hunt. Some states do not allow scopes, and all states have restrictions on which caliber handguns you can use. Because these large-caliber handguns do produce significant recoil, practice can be a painful affair. Many handgun hunters practice general accuracy by using a lighter caliber, but similar weight and configuration, handgun, then switch to their heavy hunting handgun a few weeks to a month before deer season. Practicing with the smaller caliber sharpens the eye and hones technique, but it is still necessary to shoot your hunting handgun—with the full loads you'll use for the hunt—to ensure that the skills you

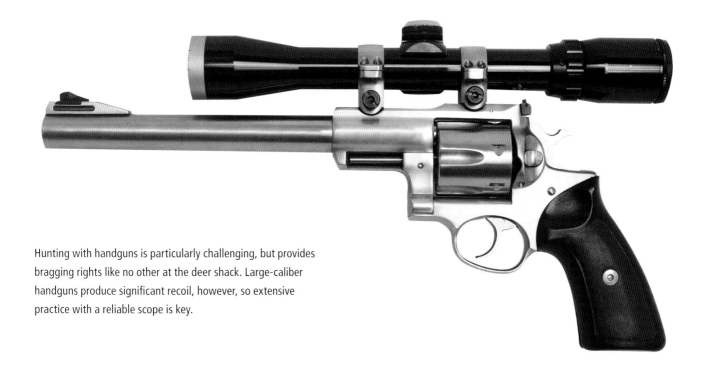

Hunting with handguns is particularly challenging, but provides bragging rights like no other at the deer shack. Large-caliber handguns produce significant recoil, however, so extensive practice with a reliable scope is key.

mastered with the other pistol transfer to your use of your hunting weapon.

Becoming proficient with a handgun is a very time-consuming task. Many hours of practice are required to achieve the consistent accuracy you need to make clean, ethical kills. If you are not willing to put in the time, then do not select a handgun as a hunting weapon.

ARCHERY EQUIPMENT

Longer seasons, less competition for hunting areas, and the challenge of killing a deer at close range attract hunters to bowhunting. Archery equipment continues to be improved and refined, causing some hunters to bemoan technological intrusions to a primitive hunting method. Nevertheless, the modern bowhunter still relies on a stick and string, and must have the hunting skills necessary to get close enough to a deer for a shot.

When choosing a bow, it is best to seek advice at an archery specialty shop, because it is hard for a beginner to sort through the array of choices available. A hunter need not buy the most expensive equipment, but it does make sense to invest in high-quality gear.

Bow styles fall in three broad categories. Compound bows, which use cams and pulleys to transfer the energy to the limbs and reduce the effort needed to pull back the string, are used by the vast majority of deer hunters. Recurves and longbows are used by some hunters who enjoy the challenge of shooting with more traditional gear.

The amount of effort required to bend the limbs of a bow at full draw is called the draw weight. About 40 pounds is generally considered the minimum necessary to kill deer, but every state and province sets a minimum draw weight for hunting big game.

The draw length of an arrow varies with individuals. It is important to determine your nocking point, the place where you will hold an arrow at full draw. Some archers draw to touch their cheek, others touch their chin. What is most important is that your nocking point is consistent. The draw length is measured from the bottom of the nock groove to the far side of the bow.

Compound Bows

The mechanical advantage that reduces the effort needed to draw a compound bow is called let-off. The advantage of a compound's low holding weight is that archers can shoot a bow with a heavier draw weight and hold it at full draw while waiting for a shot. Although the Pope and Young record book for bowhunting trophies sets a maximum of 65 percent let-off for eligibility, many compounds have a let-off of 75 percent or more.

Compound cam configurations include the popular single cam, as well as cam-and-a-half or two-cam systems. The cam and wheels function like block and

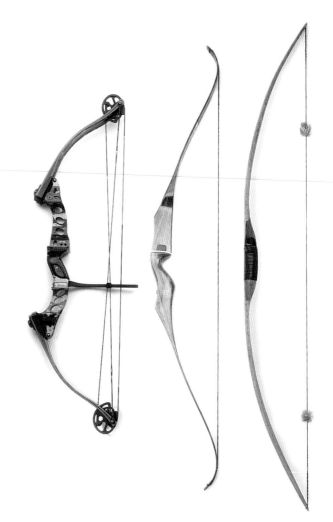

Bow types include compound bows (left), recurve bows (middle), and longbows (right). Compounds deliver the most energy for a given draw weight; longbows the least. A compound's limbs are manufactured from man-made materials, while recurves and longbows are usually made of fiberglass-wood laminates, though some longbows are solid wood.

tackle to transfer energy to the limbs. The limbs of a compound bow are attached to the riser, which is where the grip, arrow rest, and sight are located. An adjusting bolt where the limb attaches to the riser allows you to change the draw weight.

Recurves and Longbows

Hunters who savor tradition shoot recurves or longbows. With both, the archer must hold the entire draw weight at full draw, so it requires hours of practice to develop muscle tone and become a proficient shot. Typical draw weights are 40 to 60 pounds.

The longbow has straight limbs and is the most traditional design, because it dates to the early days of archery hunting. The recurve, with its curved limbs, delivers more energy to the target.

Be aware that traditional bows (often called "stick" bows) are more difficult to use. They cannot be tuned and sighted with the same precision as compound bows.

Crossbows

Although they are not legal for deer hunting in very many places and often scorned by archers, crossbows are effective for killing deer. Designed with a short bow fixed horizontally on a stock, crossbows are fired with a trigger and may have a scope sight. In some places, they are allowed for hunters who have physical disabilities that prevent them from using standard archery gear.

Unlike a rifle and its bullets, arrows are not always consistent—everything from wind speed to microscopic tremors in the hand can affect the flight of an arrow. Choosing an arrow shaft and fletching material that fits your style is key to enjoying the bow hunt. Popular shaft materials include aluminum, carbon, and wood.

Hunters wishing to extend the brief rifle season should buy a bow. The season is more than doubled in length, there's less competition, and the bucks are less wary.

Sights

Most archers use a sight. Typically, a peep embedded in the string is lined up with a pin on the riser that corresponds with the distance to the target. A wide variety of sights are available. Many incorporate fiber-optic material for better brightness in poor light conditions. Holographic and red-dot sights, incorporating technology developed for handguns, are also available.

Archers who do not use sights are called instinctive shooters, and usually are recurve or longbow shooters. Developing instinctive shooting skills requires significantly more practice than learning to shoot with a sight.

A sight system that is hard to see in low-light situations—early morning hours or in the shadows of a dense forest—is of little use. For this reason, bow-sight manufacturers are constantly developing and testing ways to improve visibility on sights.

Sights are especially valuable for beginners, because they make it easier to analyze mistakes. When shooting instinctively, it's hard to know if a miss is caused by bad form or a faulty aim, but with a sighting system, you'll know your aim is on target.

Whether you rely on simple pin sights or choose the latest in fiber-optic and laser-targeting technology, your selection is largely a matter of personal preference.

Releases

A mechanical release aid is used today by at least 75 percent of bowhunters to achieve a smooth, consistent release. The release is attached to a U-shaped loop on the bowstring and is released with a trigger device held in the archer's drawing hand.

Hunters who do not use a release draw the string with two or three fingers. They use a leather tab or shooting glove to protect their fingers.

With practice, either method of arrow release can be successful, but the outcome of many hunts often comes down to one shot, and using a release aid can help make that shot count.

Arrows

Any bow must be matched with quality arrows to achieve the best performance. Arrow selection is based on draw weight, draw length, cam design, and the weight of the broadhead. All of your hunting arrows should be identical.

Small variations in length, diameter, head weight, and fletching style can make it impossible to achieve consistent arrow flight.

Carbon is the most common shaft material, although some shooters use aluminum. Fiberglass or cedar arrows can be used with recurves and longbows. Many archers find wood arrows do not perform as consistently as aluminum or carbon.

The stiffness or "spine" of the shaft must be matched to the bow, or the arrow will fly erratically. Shaft diameter and weight, which affect penetration, are also important considerations when choosing hunting arrows.

Arrows are commonly fletched with three or four feathers or plastic vanes to give the arrow stability

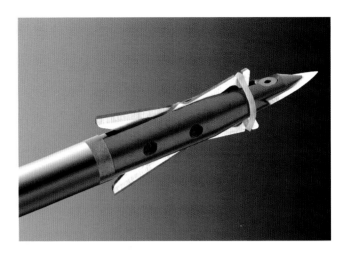

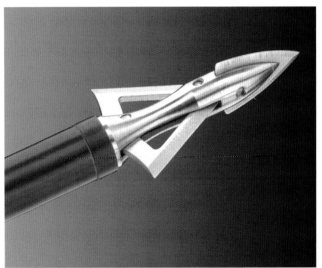

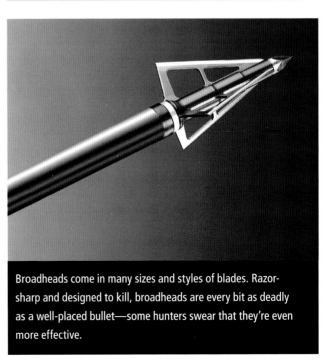

Broadheads come in many sizes and styles of blades. Razor-sharp and designed to kill, broadheads are every bit as deadly as a well-placed bullet—some hunters swear that they're even more effective.

in flight. There are three common styles of attaching fletching to the arrow shaft: in a straight configuration, offset, or in a helical pattern. You'll find feathers are wrapped left if they are left-wing feathers, or right if they are right-wing feathers.

An archery shop can help you select shafts that will perform well with your bow and suit your hunting needs.

Broadheads

Broadheads come in many styles, but all have one thing in common—they are razor sharp. Replaceable, fixed blades are popular. Fast-shooting bows are often matched with expandable broadheads, which have retracted blades that expand on impact, because the arrows are traveling so fast that fixed blades affect flight. Old-style, fixed blades that are hand-sharpened are used by some traditional archers.

Regardless of broadhead style or size, precision is key for best flight. A broadhead acts as a wing on the front of an arrow, and if that wing is crooked, the arrow will fly erratically. Before using a broadhead on game, you can test its durability by shooting it into a foam 3-D target. If it doesn't perform well, try another style or brand until you feel comfortable that the penetration will be acceptable for a successful hunt.

Practice points should be the same weight as your hunting broadheads. They come in various diameters to match different-size shafts.

If you practice with broadheads, be sure to replace or sharpen the blades before you hunt. Regulations regarding legal broadheads vary, so make sure the ones you intend to use are legal where you hunt.

Clothing and Accessories

The clothing you wear for whitetail hunting should be suitable for the area of the country you live in, the temperature and weather patterns in your region, and whether you'll be hunting with a firearm or bow. But all clothing for deer hunting has a few things in common: It must be quiet, comfortable, and durable. The most important thing to consider when purchasing accessories is to choose only those items necessary for safety and success.

Outerwear

Outerwear must be quiet. Deer have incredible hearing, and stiff fabrics that rustle when you move not only may spook deer, but make it difficult for you to hear them. Fabrics that are quiet include wool, fleece (and similar synthetics), and cotton. However, except for warm weather hunting, cotton is a poor choice because it too easily absorbs moisture, ruining its insulating qualities. In fact, in regions prone to wet, cool weather, cotton clothing can be downright dangerous since becoming chilled in these settings could lead to hypothermia—a sometimes fatal condition.

For those who walk to deer stands and then sit quietly for long periods in cold weather, outerwear should be packable. Wearing a heavy parka on the walk in will cause you to sweat, and once you stop, you will chill quickly. Carry a parka and pants or bibs of a high-lofting insulation, such as down or polyester, in a daypack.

Layering is an important component of keeping comfortable. The first layer against your skin should be of a wicking material. For quickly drawing perspiration away from the body, you can choose from silk, wool, or synthetics like polypropelene and Thermax. Not only will this keep you more comfortable, it will help avoid hypothermia.

The next layer should also be of a material that allows perspiration to pass through. Fleece is again a good choice, as is wool. Each year it seems new fabrics with wicking capabilities are introduced, and many of these are available in pants and shirts. This layer also should be of a quiet material. Over this go your insulating coveralls or parka and pants.

In many locales, firearm hunters are required to wear blaze orange. Each state sets its own requirements, so become familiar with them. Some hunters who pursue whitetails in lightly hunted country may opt for natural-colored camouflage clothing over which they wear a blaze-orange vest. However, in places where hunting pressure is high, it is best to be safe and wear blaze orange from head to toe. Blaze-orange camouflage is also available and helps to break up your outline. While deer do not see color, they do seem to be able to more easily spot blaze orange because of its brightness, which camouflage helps to reduce. However, blaze camo is also less visible to other hunters. At least some part of your middle layer should also be blaze orange since you may want to strip down to that garment while walking to and from your stand, or while dragging out your deer.

In most places, bowhunters are not required to wear blaze orange unless hunting with a bow during the gun season. Most archers prefer camouflage. The pattern you use largely depends upon the habitat in which you hunt or the time of year.

Pursuing deer in a hardwood forest early in the autumn when foliage is still present would demand a different pattern than deer hunting in a pine forest or during late season when there is snow on the ground. For this reason, many hunters buy lightweight shell garments, each of a different pattern. These are worn over other clothing, and are an inexpensive way of building a wardrobe of camouflage patterns that can match any situation. Generally, camouflage patterns made up of large blocks of contrasting colors are more effective in breaking up your outline than patterns that are small and tight.

A trend has been toward clothing that is designed to control or eliminate human scent. Most of these garments contain a layer of odor-trapping carbon. In all cases, it is best to keep your deer-hunting clothing clean and as odor free as possible. Washing it in a scent-free detergent that contains no UV brighteners, then keeping it in a plastic bag until the hunt, is a good start.

It used to be that if it rained during a deer hunt, you were stuck either getting soaked, or wearing noisy raingear. Those days have ended. Several companies now offer raingear that is nearly as quiet as wool or fleece. The outer layer is a soft polyester material, and is usually bonded to Gore-Tex or some other breathable and waterproof membrane. While deer tend to restrict movement in a downpour, they actually move more often during periods of light rain or drizzle. These rain garments also help protect hunters who go afield during wet snowfalls, and they provide excellent protection from wind, which means you'll stay warmer.

Footwear

One of your most important clothing choices is footwear—and what you wear will obviously depend upon terrain and climate. Hunters in the North frequently wear pac boots—boots with a rubber bottom and leather or nylon tops—insulated with removable

Nothing ruins a good hunt like being ill-prepared. The old maxim holds true here—failing to prepare is preparing to fail. Fortunately, there is a wide array of gear and accessories to maximize the hunting experience and ensure safety and enjoyment.

liners of wool felt, Thinsulate, or other materials. These are wonderful boots for sitting in a blind or stand, but they are often awkward for walking long distances, and their large profile makes it difficult to walk quietly.

Boot makers also produce lighter weight pac boots, and build much warmer leather hunting boots. In some cases, these boots, when filled with 800 or more grams of these super-insulations, rival the warmth of heavy pac boots, yet are much better suited to walking.

Thinner soled boots are well suited to stalking. They are reasonably lightweight and waterproof, and give a good feel of the ground beneath your feet. Hunters

Choosing Camouflage Patterns

So why wear camouflage hunting clothes if whitetails don't see colors the same as you do? The answer may lie in the deer's ability to distinguish brightness.

Studies have shown that deer can assess brightness, although not as well as humans. What this means to hunters is that a camouflage pattern that uses large areas of dark and light colors for maximum contrast will best break up the human outline. Camouflage clothes with too "fine" a pattern appear to be a solid color when viewed from a distance. As a result, they lack contrast in brightness and are more easily seen by deer.

Be sure to choose camo for the season you will be hunting. Of course, the most important factor to avoid being spotted by deer is to remain motionless. While it is impossible never to move, you can hide much of your movement by leaving as much natural cover around you as possible.

Deer pick up different visual signals than humans; blending into the background will give you a leg up in the hunt. These hunters will be all but invisible when they enter the nearby forest.

Blaze orange is not always required by law. Most archers prefer camouflage, and during bow season can wear it in full.

who frequent rough, rocky terrain will do better with a lug-soled boot. In snake country, knee-high snake-proof boots might be a good option. Bowhunters often wear knee-high rubber boots to reduce scent.

Because wet feet mean cold feet, consider buying waterproof boots or Gore-Tex socks. The latter go over your regular socks, but are worn inside of any boot, providing excellent protection from the elements. Avoid wearing cotton socks, which soak up too much perspiration, leading to cold feet or blisters. A thin liner sock of polypropylene, olefin, or similar fabric is a great blister-proofing tool. Over that should go a sock of wool or synthetic material to provide warmth and cushioning.

Head and Hand Gear

Hats and gloves are important, not just for added warmth, but because they complete your camouflage wardrobe. The flash of a hand as you scratch your nose can be seen a long way off. Even bowhunters afield in hot weather often wear lighweight camo mesh gloves for just this reason. Cold-weather hunters should consider wearing a very lightweight liner-glove under heavy gloves or mittens. If the deer suddenly stops, and makes you wait after you have removed the warmer outer gloves—which happens often—the light liner-glove provides some protection to your hands as you wait for the shot.

Many hunters swear by the use of face masks and headnets, which not only help hide you, but can protect you from biting insects, and, in cold weather, offer added warmth.

Hats need to match your conditions. In hot weather, the lighter the better, and cold-weather hunters obviously will want an insulated hat. A brim helps shield you from the sun, reducing eyestrain.

Camouflage

In addition to wearing camouflage clothing, hunters also disguise their guns, bows, and stands while hunting. Many hunting-related products now come in camo pattern finishes. Or, hunters may customize by adding camo tape or paint.

In warm weather, hunters often opt for face and hand paint over masks and gloves, and many arrow manufacturers offer arrow shafts with camo paint.

Packs

You could easily double your own body weight with all the gadgets now available for hunters, many of which are unneeded. The best advice is to pack only what is necessary for safety and success.

Packs should be of a quiet material. Hunters can choose from many pack designs made of fleece or other quiet fabric, and even in a wide range of camouflage patterns or blaze orange.

Into that pack should go some things that are considered absolute essentials. These include:

- means of starting a fire (waterproof matches, disposable lighter, or candle stub)
- map of the area
- emergency food, such as jerky, chocolate, or granola bars (in addition to your lunch)
- flashlight
- small first-aid kit
- compass (even if you also carry a GPS), which should always be carried on your person

Other items that should be in your pack are:
- a drag rope
- some hunks of parachute cord for hoisting your gun or bow up into your tree stand
- toilet paper
- water
- disposable field-dressing gloves
- a couple of stout plastic bags to store the heart and liver
- moist towelettes for cleaning up after gutting your deer

Optics

Binoculars are a great aid to deer hunters, even if you hunt in country where visibility is limited. Don't "check things out" through your rifle scope, since the thing you might be studying could be a person. Binoculars allow hunters not only to examine distant movement or terrain, but actually help see into the brush.

Don't buy cheap optics. It might be tempting to purchase those mini-binoculars; a mid-size pair is a better investment. They'll have a wider field of view, will gather light more efficiently, and are far easier to hold steady. The larger the objective end (the lens farthest from your eye), the better it will be for low-light situations. An 8x40 combination is a good place to start. Optics should be at least weather resistant, if not 100-percent waterproof.

If you wear eyeglasses, purchase a pair of binoculars with roll-down eyecups, and what is called "long eye relief." Together, these features will permit binocular use without having to remove your eyeglasses.

Compass

Always carry a good compass, and know how to use it. Some hunters even carry a spare in their pack. GPS (global positioning system) units are a very useful tool for finding your way around in the woods. They can also be used to plan your hunt or locate stands. Remember, however, that their batteries can run down. Compasses, when held level and away from your body and gun or equipment, are foolproof and dependable.

On the ground or in the stand, high-quality optics are essential. Most models come with a strap for easy transport around your neck, and small binoculars are generally favored over large ones—the distances you can reasonably shoot do not require extra powerful binoculars.

Binocular exteriors are manufactured to perfectly blend in with your camouflage pattern and surroundings.

The batteries of a GPS can fail—the needle of a compass will not. Map-reading skills and the ability to navigate using a compass is another valuable tool in the skillset of a hunter.

Knives

A knife for gutting a white-tailed deer need have a blade of only 3 to 6 inches long. Many fine sheath knives are available with blades of this length, as are many folding knives. Some have interchangeable (or multiblade) designs, incorporating a small saw blade, which is not only handy for splitting a deer's pelvis, but for trimming limbs that might be in the way near your deer stand.

A drop-point knife—a style with a slightly blunted tip—is a better choice than those with a swept-up tip, since it'll be far less likely to puncture the deer's intestines during field dressing.

Another option is the Wyoming knife. Hunters who have used one say it opens game like a zipper and handles with speed, safety, and efficiency.

Whatever type of knife you choose, remember to always keep it razor-sharp.

SELECTING AND SHARPENING HUNTING KNIVES

A good hunting knife is one of the best investments a hunter can make. Properly selected, used, and cared for, it may well outlive him. A cheap knife, on the other hand, may not last a hunting season.

When selecting a hunting knife, look closely at the materials, blade length and shape, and workmanship. The blade steel should be stainless, hard but not brittle. A blade with a Rockwell hardness rating of 57 to 60 is hard enough to hold an edge, but soft enough for easy resharpening at home when it becomes dull.

The handle should be made of hardwood, plastic-impregnated wood, or a tough synthetic. These materials last longer than brittle plastic, or than wood you can easily dent with your fingernail.

Select a knife that feels comfortable in your hand. Remember that your hands may be wet when you're using it, so look for a handle shape that's easy to hold firmly. A blade between 3.5 and 4.5 inches long is adequate for either small or trophy deer.

Clip-point and drop-point knives are good all-purpose types. The acutely pointed tip of a clip-point is good for delicate cutting, and penetrates the abdominal skin easily in field dressing. The tip of a drop-point is less apt to puncture the intestines when slitting the abdominal skin, or to punch a hole in the hide should you use it for skinning.

For convenience and safety in the field, many hunters prefer folding knives. They are shorter and easier to carry than a straight knife, and the folded blade is safely out of the way in the event of a fall. Choose folding knives carefully, checking for quality construction. When fully opened, the blade should lock in position with no trace of wiggle or sloppiness, and the back of the blade should line up exactly with the back edge of the handle.

Use your knife only for its intended purpose. If you use it to hack wood or pry the lid off a jar, you could destroy the edge. Be sure your knife is clean and dry before you store it at the end of the season. Over time, even modern stainless steel can be corroded by acids or salts.

A sharp blade is safer than a dull one. It gives you more control, and you need less pressure to get the job done. Dress the edge often with a sharpening steel. A steel does not remove metal from the blade, but simply realigns the edge. When the blade becomes so dull that the steel won't dress it, sharpen it with a whetstone.

Hunting knives include general-purpose types, such as folding drop-point (middle left) and folding clip-point (bottom left). The tip of a clip-point is more acute and curves up higher than that of a drop-point. Special-purpose types include: folding bird knife (upper left), with a hook for field-dressing birds; folding combination knife (upper right), with a blunt-tip blade for slitting abdomens without puncturing intestines, a clip-point blade, and a saw for cutting through the breastbones and pelvic bones of whitetails; and a big-game skinner (bottom right), whose blade has a blunt tip to avoid punching holes in the hide. The sides of the skinner blade are concave, curving down to a thin edge that's ideal for skinning but prone to chipping when used to cut against wood or bone. The other blades shown have sides that slant down straight, with thicker, sturdier edges.

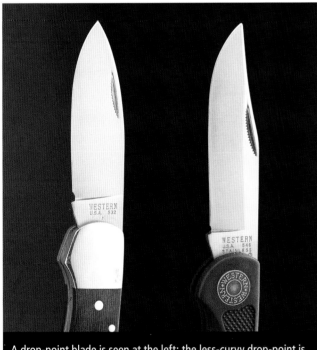

A drop-point blade is seen at the left; the less-curvy drop-point is seen on the right.

Hunting knives are multipurpose. Many have folding blades, and feature a pointed tip, razor edge, and even a serrated section for the sawing of deer limbs and tree branches. A good hunting knife can last a lifetime.

How to Sharpen a Knife

Select a medium whetstone at least as long as the blade (if the blade is extremely dull, use a coarse stone first, then the medium stone). Place the stone on a folded towel for stability, and apply a little honing oil.

Hold the base of the blade against the whetstone at the angle at which the blade was originally sharpened (usually between 12 and 17 degrees). Using moderate pressure, push the knife away from you in a smooth arc from base to tip, as if shaving thin pieces off the face of the stone. Keep the edge of the blade at the same angle, in constant contact with the whetstone. Repeat this motion two more times. Draw the knife toward you in an arc three times, maintaining the same angle. Continue sharpening alternate sides, adding oil if necessary, until the blade hangs up when drawn very gently over a fingernail.

Repeat the previous steps on a fine whetstone. If the stone clogs, wipe and re-oil it. The knife is sharp when it slices effortlessly through a piece of paper. Clean the whetstone with soapy water for storage.

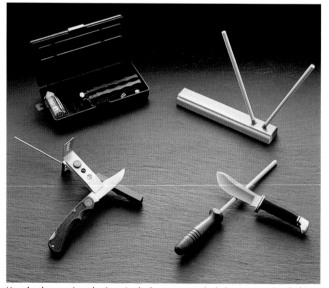

Handy sharpening devices include a pre-angled sharpening kit (left); ceramic sticks, which have a light sharpening action (upper right); and diamond-impregnated sticks (lower right), which remove as much metal as a medium stone.

MISCELLANEOUS

There really are very few other things a hunter needs in the woods, but there are some items that you might want to consider:

- Chemical hand warmers are a nice touch in cold weather, and can also be considered a possible survival tool if you are forced to spend the night in the cold deer woods.

- A space blanket is another good thing to have if you find yourself spending a night in the woods. Most models roll up into a very small package and it can be a life saver.

- A small camera for capturing memories of days afield.

- An extra pair of dry socks, though not a necessity, can really make the second half of a full day's hunt much more pleasant.

- Some kind of seat—whether a soft, quiet pad you place on the ground or on a five-gallon bucket, a folding stool or a seat that clamps to a tree—can add immeasurably to the length of time you can sit quiet and motionless.

Two-way radios are convenient, efficient, and can be used to get help if needed. Good for keeping in touch with hunting buddies.

Waterproof matches are a must in any emergency hunting kit. Many hunters carry multiple forms of fuel, including disposable lighters or even candle stubs. The value of light and heat cannot be overstated in an emergency situation.

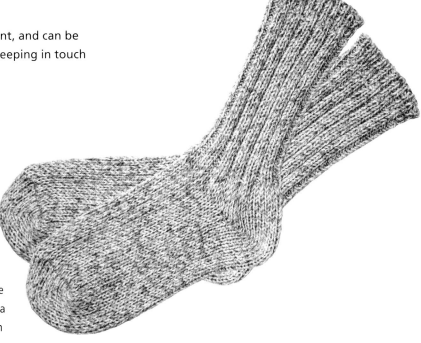

Never underestimate the power of effective footwear. A thick pair of wool socks is often the difference between a good day of hunting and a bad day of hunting. Some hunters even keep an extra pair to swap out for the afternoon.

CHAPTER THREE

PREPARING FOR THE HUNT

Many deer-hunting stories begin with that split second
it takes for a shot to hit home. But most successful
hunts begin much earlier, sometimes more than a year
in advance. Doing a little research will help to make
the best use of your time afield and improve your odds
of taking a deer.

Knowing your hunting area will go a long way toward informing when, where, and even how to hunt—is the ground tamped down, indicating a common deer path? Is there a bedding area nearby? Shed antlers can be valuable clues in discerning the habits of the buck.

GATHERING INFORMATION

A wealth of information is available to help you find good places to hunt. Start with a copy of state or provincial hunting regulations to learn about seasons, legal methods, and bag limits. Natural resource agencies also have web sites that show public hunting opportunities, deer population and harvest statistics, and other pertinent information. If you are traveling to hunt, a web search will help you find guides and outfitters. Whenever possible, try to talk with individuals who have hunted in the area previously, such as friends, co-workers, or members of your local sportsman's club.

As your search narrows for potential hunting areas, gather maps. Excellent maps are available on the Internet or as software. You can also get free or inexpensive maps of state and federal public lands. Statewide county atlases, sold at bookstores, are invaluable. The best maps show topographic detail, including land contours, wetlands, roads and trails, and vegetation types. Aerial photos, which are updated regularly, give you a bird's-eye view of actual terrain. A plat book, showing the individual properties and landowners for a local area, is published by each county.

Helpful sources of local information are wildlife managers, foresters, and conservation officers. You should be able to locate their telephone numbers on natural resource agency web sites or by calling the public information number listed in hunting regulations booklets. Don't expect wildlife professionals to tell you exactly where to hunt—most don't want to concentrate

Use every resource to your advantage, including local land owners and wildlife or conservation officers. Local professionals have intimate knowledge about the land and deer habitats, and can often provide free or inexpensive topographical maps or charts to aid your hunt.

Quick Tips for Finding Whitetails

Scouting ahead of the rut is a good strategy to gain the upper hand during deer season. Many hunters employ a spotting scope and hunker down for a few hours to see what kind of deer are passing through, where the trails are, and if they make a regular habit of it.

Young forests produce big bucks. Young forests have more open canopies than old, thick forests, which often obscure sunlight from reaching the forest floor. Sunlight prompts plant growth, providing easier access to abundant plant food for whitetails.

Though whitetails range all over North America, hardwood forests are their favorite. Hardwood forests provide ample food and cover. A young forest is best, because sunlight can reach the forest floor to grow shrubs and grasses.

- Farmland also offers considerable food supplies. Farmland can support large numbers of deer if they have cover like brushy draws or stream corridors.

- Lowlands like swamps, bogs, and river bottoms provide dense cover. Whitetails usually feed in surrounding fields or woodlands.

- Whitetails are creatures of habit, even though they prove wily during the rut. Don't make the mistake of thinking a single deer path is frequented both day and night by the same deer—different trails serve different purposes. Day trails wind through thick brush and trees, but seldom cross clearings to offer hunters easy shots. Wait in a ground blind or tree stand near a day trail early in the morning when deer are most active, because they won't be moving through a field by day.

- Night is a different matter—night trails often lead through meadows or open croplands. Do not choose a stand along this type of trail, however, because deer seldom use them in the day. Instead, post nearby in edge territory or thick brush, but be sure to get there early, otherwise you might miss them.

Locating Nocturnal Bucks

What makes a buck go nocturnal? In many cases it is human intrusion. Bowhunters, for example, may spook him during their preseason scouting forays by leaving their scent on his runways or near his feeding areas. They might even jump him from his bed, causing the buck to bed elsewhere for at least a while. Of course, hikers, bird watchers, and small game hunters can also push bucks into the twilight zone, as can those who spotlight open areas at night. These tips will help you find the bucks who enjoy burning the midnight oil.

- The first step for locating a buck that has pulled the disappearing act is to get a better feel for his home territory. Try glassing for him in open feeding areas after sunset and before sunrise around open feeding areas.

- If you're not seeing a particular buck anymore, that doesn't necessarily mean he has gone nocturnal, assuming of course he is still alive. A buck may have been visible all summer long, but as soon as he sheds his velvet, he prefers solitude and remains bedded down for as long as possible during daylight hours.

- A buck can also change his bedding area, and as a result you aren't likely to see him. As corn plants grow, for example, bucks move off the ridges and out of the swamps to take advantage of the cover offered by mature plants. Large unharvested corn lots are such good hiding places you may not see the bucks that live here until the corn is picked.

- If you fail to get a shot at a buck that has gone nocturnal, and either jump him or spook him with your scent, you may as well look for another deer to hunt, as this buck is definitely unkillable now during legal shooting hours.

- Some bucks go nocturnal as a function of age. Indeed, most bucks past three years of age are shy. Yet even yearling bucks can go nocturnal after their first encounter with a human, which is another reason to avoid contact with bucks during your preseason scouting sessions.

- Your best opportunity to ambush a nocturnal buck will be the very first time you set upon him. If he is a mature buck, light rattling or buck contact grunts might be all it takes to tweak his territorial instincts. He might just leave a bit early to see what all the commotion is about, and give you a legal shot.

- The real secret to getting a shot at any nocturnal buck is to set up as close as you dare to his bedding area, not his feeding grounds.

The nocturnal buck can be one of the hardest to hunt. Nocturnal bucks are often older animals, wisely keeping out of sight during the day. Often the best chance to bag a trophy nighttime mover is to try to find his bedding area, and hunker down nearby, then shoot him when you see him during legal hunting hours because you may not get another chance.

hunting pressure—but they will give you information about deer populations, hunter access, hunter success, and terrain. In some situations, they may direct you to private landowners who are experiencing problems with deer and are looking for responsible hunters to reduce their numbers.

To locate accommodations, campgrounds, and local services, contact the state or provincial tourism office for area listings. Use the Internet to find individual businesses and make inquiries or reservations. A call to the local chamber of commerce will help you find lodging and may lead to new sources of information.

If you are hunting in another state or province, begin researching a year or more in advance of the hunt so you can meet deadlines for nonresident license applications or apply for special hunts. Hunting outfitters are often fully booked for a year or more. You will also want to find out if nonresidents are required to have a hunter safety certificate from their home state.

When gathering information, ask about the weather during hunting season, hunting pressure, special clothing needs, and necessary gear. Make clothing and equipment purchases well in advance of the hunt so you have time to make sure that the clothes fit and your gear is in working order. If the hunting season lasts a week or more, ask how hunting conditions change as it progresses. When planning to hunt on private land, secure permission or pay access fees well in advance of your hunt.

If you seek a high-quality hunt, look for special seasons held before or after the general firearms season. Many places have lightly hunted, early archery or late muzzleloader seasons. Areas with exceptionally high deer numbers may hold special hunts intended to reduce deer numbers. Ask, too, about the timing of the rut and seasonal deer movements. Whitetails may change their patterns as they adapt to hunting pressure or the weather.

Trophy buck hunters must put extra effort into information gathering. Ask specific questions about local entries into record books, differences between trophy potential on public and private lands, and any recent trends in weather or hunting pressure that could affect overall numbers of mature bucks. When shopping for a guide or outfitter, ask for hunter success rates and always get references from previous clients.

Many hunters plan annual vacations or trips with friends and family to new hunting grounds. Careful study of the local area is absolutely necessary, to not only maximize the chance to land a buck, but also to minimize the chance to get lost or disoriented in unfamiliar territory.

SCOUTING

Have you ever wondered how some hunters take deer year after year, even in heavily pressured areas where deer seem to disappear after opening day?

These hunters aren't lucky. They're good. And the reason they're good is that they scout their hunting territory year-round. They know the deer in their area—to the point where they can recognize individual bucks and even does—and they know where those deer go to feed, bed, and escape from danger. While you're sitting at home, these hunters are out in the woods scouting.

Scouting is the primary tool used by successful deer hunters. The object of scouting is to locate a good buck (or bucks), then learn his feeding, travel, and bedding routines long before the season starts. If you can, learn his escape routes as well; knowing where he goes when he's on the run will be of great value come hunting season, and there is no substitute for time spent in the field. Avid hunters visit their hunting area throughout the year, so they become familiar with the land and the deer living there. They learn about seasonal deer movements, food sources, local population abundance, good stand locations, humane use of the land, and myriad details that become part of a successful hunting strategy.

The size of the area you scout is determined by things like the amount of property where you have permission to hunt, use by other hunters, and your personal hunting style. When scouting a new area, first learn the lay of the land. Use a topographic map and compass to locate property lines, roads, trails, water courses and prominent natural features. A handheld GPS (global positioning system) can be used to log-in specific locations for future reference. Bright-colored, plastic surveyor's tape can be tied to branches and saplings to mark forest paths and stand sites. On private land, be sure you have the landowner's permission to use the tape or other marking material. And on public land, be sure to remove the tape after your hunt.

Your first priority is to look for deer sign, the evidence that whitetails use the area. Hoofprints, droppings, trails, beds, rubs, scrapes, and browsed twigs are signs you may encounter while scouting. A good hunter becomes a student of deer sign and what it reveals about the local deer population. Generally, deer sign is easiest to find during fall and winter, and more difficult to see in dense, summer foliage. In summer, you may learn more about the deer in your hunting area by watching for them in fields where they feed at dawn and dusk.

Figuring out habit patterns isn't that difficult, as bucks tend to group together during summer. You can also determine which animals will have decent racks in the fall, because by July the main beams on most racks have started to turn forward. With binoculars, you can study a buck's growing rack and tell whether it's going to be large.

No matter where you hunt, you can count on the fact that a whitetail's movement patterns will be determined by five critical factors: food, water, cover, terrain, and hunting pressure.

Modern hunters use modern tools. The ability of handheld GPS units to flag various areas allows a hunter to scout, see, and, return to favorable spots to set up a drive, build a tree stand, or simply return to a lucky spot!

FOOD AND WATER

Being creatures of habit, deer generally stay on the same few hundred acres of land for their entire lives. Even when food sources change with the seasons, they usually won't move out of their home range in search of other things to eat.

If you hunt woodlots, locate oak trees yielding mast, wild apple trees, maples, and other preferred food sources during preseason scouting trips. Finding oak trees that produce more acorns than other oaks in the immediate area, for example, will give you a hot spot to hunt while other hunters are still searching for deer.

On terrain other than woodlots, such as agricultural areas, zero in on food sources that offer deer a high nutritional value, especially during periods of changing weather. When temperatures drop, for instance, deer

They may venture during the rut, but most bucks keep to the same area for the majority of their lives. Wooded water sources are reliable places to scout for signs of bucks.

are naturally attracted to corn because it raises body temperature. On the other hand, when the weather is warmer they prefer clover and alfalfa.

Although deer do not require watering holes in the true sense of the term, they will drink at specific spots along their normal travel routes. If you can find a watering area that's secluded and near heavy cover, you will increase your deer sightings immensely.

COVER

A deer's survival depends on cover that's secure from predators and hunting pressure. Locate cover areas that are hard to reach and generally inaccessible to all but the most persistent hunters. Look for the toughest, thickest, nastiest terrain. Generally, this means swamps, steep ledges, and overgrown thickets. This is where the buck will

be when the hunting pressure is on. Plan to set up along trails leading into and out of these areas.

TERRAIN

Use a topographic map to get a feel for the lay of the land and its natural and man-made obstructions. These barriers heavily influence how deer behave and travel. Deer are just like largemouth bass—you'll find them wherever there is natural structure to help conceal their movements.

Features to look for on topographic maps are saddles, natural funnels, flats, and edges. Once you've located them, inspect them in person and figure out how to hunt them in the fall.

Saddles A saddle is a depression in a ridge running between two mountaintops. Bucks feel safe in saddles

Getting Permission to Hunt on Private Land

For most hunters, the hardest part of taking any deer, including a trophy buck, is getting permission to hunt the land it calls home. Thousands of acres of private land in North America—small farms, huge ranches, broken suburban lots, and bordering crop fields—are closed to hunting. Hundreds of bucks live within such sanctuaries, safe from human predators.

How do you find such places? Just look for the signs: No Hunting. No Trespassing. Listen for rumors flying around town about the huge buck seen crossing a certain road. Ask at the local cafe and gas station. Who's been seeing big bucks? Who got the big bucks last year? Call these folks and get friendly with them. Join the local hunting club and exchange information. If you hear about a big buck on private land, make it your goal to gain access where no one else is allowed.

Your first strategy may be to take up the bow. Archers are often welcomed in places closed to gun hunters. Second, get to know the landowners. Don't be shy and don't let the "No" signs frighten you. Many farmers post their property just to keep from being pestered, or to cover themselves against frivolous lawsuits. If you know who owns a piece of hot property, make a phone call or drive out for a visit. If you don't know the owner, check county plat maps or ask around at the local co-op or farm-equipment retailer.

When you visit the landowner:
- Be open, honest, and friendly.

- Tell the landowner you're always looking for a beautiful, quiet place to hunt, where you can get away from the crowds and enjoy nature.

- Tell him you're after mature bucks only and have no interest in shooting fawns or females (unless the landowner wants you to remove a doe for management reasons).

- Mention that you hunt by yourself and want the challenge of hunting the smartest buck in the countryside.

- Offer to help the farmer with his evening chores as payment for the right to hunt on his property.

If he turns you down, respect his reasons, but try to counter them tactfully if you can. Many landowners post their land because they've had bad experiences with inconsiderate hunters. Here are some additional things you can discuss:

- Assure him you won't drop litter, start fires, or leave gates open.
- Offer to park in his yard while you hunt.
- Give him your hunting license number.
- Provide character references from other farmers and respected locals.

If the landowner still says no, thank him as you leave, but keep his name and address in your files. Several months later, send him a Christmas card or a brief note describing your latest hunting season. Try again the following year. Polite persistence sometimes wears down resistance.

Another strategy is to ask permission simply to take photographs or look for antlers on the property. If a friendship or mutual respect blossoms, you can later ask for permission to hunt.

In essence, you are "courting" the landowner or farmer. If you show a genuine interest in him as a person and can convey a sincere love of the outdoors and respect for his land, your chances are good for winning him over. In the end, you may find that making new friends only improves you as a hunter.

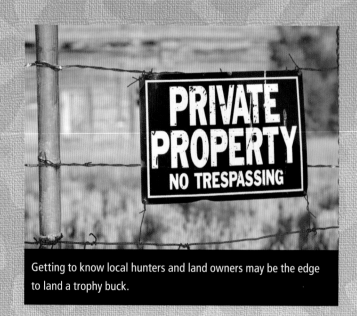

Getting to know local hunters and land owners may be the edge to land a trophy buck.

Being open, honest, and friendly about your hunting intentions is often all you need to get the permission to hunt private land, and it sure beats a fine or other legal consequences if you're caught trespassing.

Where's there's cover, there's bucks. A deer's survival depends on the ability to blend in with the surroundings, unseen by predators. Use topographic maps or old-fashioned scouting methods to seek out areas of heavy brush and difficult terrain. That's where they'll be come hunting season.

probably because the terrain breaks up their silhouettes. They also retreat to these areas during heavy winds.

Funnels These lanes of terrain offer deer an easy "flow" through the woods, letting them travel from one place to another unnoticed. They are usually long, narrow corridors that begin at a high point and flow to a lower area. Check your topo map and you'll be able to find them without too much difficulty.

Flats Deer often use these benches, shelves, or ledges (lying just below and parallel to ridgetops) as bedding areas. Bucks also make scrapelines across them.

Edges You'll find these on the fringes of swamps, where agricultural fields meet forests, or where stone walls border abandoned apple orchards. They can be anywhere one type of vegetation or terrain blends into another. Deer are attracted to them because they usually offer food sources with cover nearby.

PRESSURE

Try to figure out where other hunters will likely set up. Look for permanent tree stands, spent shells, ground blinds, marks on trees from climbing stands or screw-in steps—anything indicating the presence of other hunters. By knowing where other hunters will enter, hunt, and exit an area, you can better place your stand along known escape routes or other trails that deer are likely to use.

Finally, make sure you don't over-scout your area. Even light pressure can make deer alter their movement patterns. End your scouting missions by September. Don't invade promising areas again until the season opens.

PRESEASON

The most overlooked stage, and the one least capitalized on by hunters, is the pre-rut stage. Also called "the false rut," this typically occurs in early October. Archers who hunt during this time will attest to observing a yearly phenomenon regarding the rut where, all of a sudden, within a 24-hour period they begin to find a multitude of fresh scrapes throughout their hunting territory. What happens to cause this obviously intense breeding change in bucks? The onset of the pre-rut.

Because there is a lack of does in estrus in early September, bachelor herds of bucks continue with their normal behavior until early October, when a brief estrous cycle (18 to 36 hours) occurs. This brief cycle is brought on by the mature whitetail does (4- to 5-year-olds) that are coming into their first estrous period for the year. Once bucks discover the estrous pheromone permeating their range, their natural reaction is to start making scrapes and rubs. They'll continue to do this for up to 36 hours, all the while dashing throughout the woods in search of does.

Always try to start scouting at least a couple of weeks prior to your planned hunt. Look for trails the deer use when moving through the area. In farm country, you may find distinct feeding areas, such as crop fields and dense cover used as a bedding area. Trails leading between these two locations are excellent places to hunt. In large forested areas, deer movements may seem more random. Look for frequently used trails and edges between dense forest cover, such as conifers, and more open hardwoods.

In areas where deer habitat is limited by agricultural activity, residences and development, or land features, look for funnel spots that the deer must pass through when traveling from one cover to another. These are usually good stand locations. Be aware that you may find places with lots of deer sign, but little security or nearby escape cover. These locations are typically visited by whitetails at night and avoided during the day. Pay attention to prevailing winds, so that you can plan ways to enter your hunting area by walking upwind or crosswind. Make note of places that are sheltered from winds, because the deer will use them on windy or stormy days.

Preseason Tactics

If you learn to recognize the new scrape and deer activity signs as part of the "false" or pre-rut period, you will dramatically increase your chances of shooting a buck. By setting up around areas where bucks have

The Drop on Droppings

Another good indication that deer regularly use an area is the number of fresh piles of droppings you find. According to the Wisconsin Department of Natural Resources, deer defecate about 13 times during a 24-hour period. Therefore, if you are hunting an area with a high whitetail population, analyzing this sign becomes a little more difficult. Here are some hints to help you select the information you need. Adult buck droppings are clustered and are larger than adult doe droppings. A good rule of thumb to determine the approximate age of a buck is that a single pellet measuring about ¾ inch is from a buck about 2 to 3 years old. Larger pellets up to 1 inch long are usually from the truly trophy-sized animals. Mature buck droppings are thicker, longer, and generally clumped together in a shapeless mass rather than in single pellets. Finding a few dozen such droppings in an area perhaps 50 yards around is an indication you have found a buck's core (or preferred) bedding area. Consequently, you can eliminate the smaller loose pellets usually found in piles of 10 to 50 droppings; these belong to fawns, yearlings, and does.

All deer droppings will change in texture and consistency as the deer's food source changes. This information will help you determine whether deer are browsing or grazing, and where you should post accordingly. If a deer is feeding on grasses or fruit, the feces will usually be in a loose mass composed of soft pellets. If you find such sign, hunt along routes leading to alfalfa fields or apple orchards.

When a deer is browsing on drier vegetation, such as twigs, branch tips, and acorns, its droppings will be less moist because of a loss of mucus. Consequently, the pellets do not stick together when expelled from the deer. They will be hard to the touch, longer, and separated. If you find this type of sign, plan your ambush accordingly. Posting in an alfalfa field when most of the deer dung you are finding is loose, hard, and long will most likely prove to be futile, as the deer's droppings suggest they are not grazing but browsing.

When inspecting deer excrement, remember that weather affects its look and texture. If the pile you are examining is on top of a ridge, for instance, and is subject to wind and harsh sunlight and receives no moisture, it will dry much more quickly and appear to be stale, when in fact it may be fresher than you think. In places where deer pellets receive shade and moisture and are not exposed to wind, the opposite holds true.

You can eliminate the guesswork by picking up a few pellets and squeezing them between your thumb and index finger. Remember that pellets dry from the outside in. So one that looks fresh on the outside but is hard and dry and begins to break apart when squeezed is at least four days old. Shiny, fresh-looking pellets having the consistency of Play-Doh when squeezed and may be very fresh.

You will often discover the freshest sign in and around bedding areas. When you locate an area with eight to 10 beds grouped within a short distance of one another, you have found the bedding area of does and fawns. But it pays to investigate such an area. You can determine if a buck is within the group by measuring the size of the beds. Beds measuring about 2 to 3 feet long are those of does, yearlings, and fawns. However, beds measuring about 3 to 4 feet long are most likely those of a mature buck.

They're not pretty, but they are useful. The size of the pellets in a deer's droppings is a reliable indicator of general size. Pellets longer than 1 inch are from trophy bucks.

opened new scrapes, for example, you can simply wait out your quarry, figuring that sooner or later a buck will come to check out his scrapes in hopes of finding a mature doe in estrus. Or you might try attracting a passing buck with a deer call or by rattling antlers. Another good tactic during this period is to make a mock scrape and agitate a buck into responding. All of these tactics will work during the pre-rut as bucks are eager to respond to the first signals of the start of the breeding season.

It is important to keep in mind that the pre-rut does not last long. Generally, throughout the East, the pre-rut occurs about the 7th through the 10th of October, give or take a couple of days either way. Since only a few bucks actually get to mate during the pre-rut, the rest of the bucks become quite frustrated. This frustration is nature's way of laying the groundwork of behavior and activity that precedes the primary rut.

Every doe experiences an estrous cycle every 28 days until she is successfully bred. Therefore, a hunter can

During the pre-rut, bucks become frantic and begin making scrapes and rubs in multitude. They can often be seen on the move, pursuing does that have just entered their estrous periods.

Bucks often return to old scrapes during the pre-rut. They are looking for signs of does who have also broadcast their presence through the use of pheromones and scent-marking.

count 28 days forward from when he first discovers the above-mentioned activity during the pre-rut and he will place himself squarely within the primary rut.

THE RUT

Mating activity occurs from early autumn, when bucks begin polishing their antlers, into winter, when the does finish their estrous cycles. Initially, you'll see small saplings with shredded bark and broken branches made by bucks rubbing their antlers. As the mating season

nears, you'll begin to see small scrapes along deer trails. The early rutting evidence is often misleading, because the buck that made it may establish a territory elsewhere during the rut.

There are several obvious signs after pre-rut that indicate the start of the primary rut. Bucks are seldom seen traveling together now. They have an ever-increasing intolerance for one another and will often engage in immediate aggressive behavior upon simply encountering other bucks. In addition, because of the building tension and continuing decrease in daylight, they will take out their anxieties more often on saplings

Quick Tips for Scouting

While scouting, one of your primary goals is to identify those bedding areas preferred by bucks during the early season and pre-rut period. Start by assuming the greatest number of bucks bed high during the day, and then feed in the lowlands under the cover of darkness. That's because thermals help bucks keep tabs on what is below, and there are fewer contacts with predators at these elevations, including humans, for them to contend with.

Uneven terrain features are another draw to mature deer. Try to find ravines, creek beds, deep canyons, and slopes dotted with knobs and knolls on your topographical map. Bucks like them in part because swirling winds quickly warn them of impending danger. One sniff is all it takes for a buck to disappear from view.

Another terrain feature that attracts bucks is a small island in a swamp or on a large body of water. Locate such elevated hummocks by studying topographical maps or by backtracking deer in the snow after the water has frozen.

Bucks are also attracted to certain terrain features for food. Pinpointing these preferred feeding locations is not as difficult as it might seem. Begin your search by examining any blue ink on a topographical map;

creek beds, shorelines surrounding ponds and lakes, and the edges of swamps are all places where sunlight can reach the forest floor, producing plentiful new plant growth.

Another terrain feature worth a scouting trip is a plateau. These, and to some degree nearby ridges, are often choice feeding locations, especially if they're situated on south-facing slopes and have an oak, hickory, or beech grove present.

The food is not the only reason that deer gather here—plateaus are easy to navigate, requiring fewer calories. They also serve as transition zones, especially if there are no nearby openings, allowing deer to congregate until it's time to continue on to their primary food source. As such, it's not uncommon to find rubs and rub lines and scrapes and scape lines atop a plateau.

The most important terrain feature to examine for a feeding location, however, is undoubtedly a large opening. In the big woods, these include beaver flows plus burns, landslides, ice slides, and openings created by tornadoes, windstorms, and hurricanes. Man-made openings include clear-cuts, railroad beds, power lines, gas lines, and underground cable right-of-ways.

Mixed-terrain areas like this forest and pond are excellent sites for scouting for deer. The forest provides varying cover, while the plant growth and water offer plentiful sources of food.

During the height of the rut, bucks are rarely seen together...unless they're fighting. Aggressive behavior becomes more common as does reach the peak of their estrous cycles during the rut, and frustrated bucks often take out their anger by sparring.

or trees. Venting their frustrations also helps get them physically prepared for the inevitable battles that will come over the next few weeks.

This buildup also accounts for a sharp increase in buck activity, and buck sign is prominent for about three weeks in autumn at the height of the rut. You'll find large scrapes and sparring rubs. Fresh rut sign often means a buck is nearby. If you are hunting for bucks during the rut, scout within a few days of when you plan to hunt. Then, during the hunt, continue looking for fresh rutting activity. When you locate an area that is being used by a buck, plan a hunting strategy that will create minimal disturbances.

Unlike the pre-rut, when only a few mature does come into estrus, the primary rut has a majority of the does coming into their estrous cycle. This accounts for

a dramatic increase in doe activity, too. Hunters will see does checking out buck scrapes, making scrapes of their own, running erratically through the woods, and avoiding fawns. Like female dogs, as they come closer to actually accepting males, they will begin to flag their tails. For deer, this simply means they will be seen carrying their tails in a horizontal position, off to one side. Hunters who take advantage of all of the above signs will find themselves at the right place at the right time.

Rut Tactics

During the primary rut, try hunting off-hours from 10:00 a.m. to 2:00 p.m. This tactic works for a combination of reasons. First, you'll be hunting at a time of day when

Bucks aren't the only deer driven mad by the rut. Does can be seen making scrapes of their own, trotting through the woods in pursuit of bucks, and making much more of a ruckus in the woods than they do the rest of the year.

fewer hunters are in the woods. In addition, because deer are less pressured at this time, they move about more freely, giving you the chance to see more of them. Another tactic you might consider is to try using a variety of soft grunts (both buck and doe) throughout the day. Grunting works well throughout the entire primary rut period and should not be overlooked. Using certain agitating scents, such as buck urine and tarsal placed downwind from your stand, will also create opportunities that cannot be created in the pre- or post-rut periods, when deer are reacting to different stimuli.

THE LATE OR POST-RUT

Count 28 days from the primary rut date, and you will have the prime time of the "late rut." During the late rut, most of the immature (or latest born) does, and any other doe that has yet to be successfully bred, will come into estrus. Many hunters have had success rattling during the late rut: rattling can be effective into January and even February, as some does are still experiencing estrous cycles during these months.

The post-rut usually begins after a distinct low period in the primary rut. Throughout the East, the start of the post-rut usually begins around mid-December and runs for about 28 days. It is a period that is overlooked by many hunters who are sure that the rut is long over.

One sign to look for during this phase is a quick and dramatic increase in deer activity. Does that come into estrus during this period seem to have an intensity about finding bucks. They will often be seen trotting along depositing estrous urine. They will frequently make soft grunts, too. Any bucks scenting the estrous pheromone will quickly swarm to these estrous does. Often during the post-rut, hunters will see several bucks chasing one doe. It's almost as if the bucks have come to realize it's a "last chance" scenario.

Post-rut Tactics

One tactic that works amazingly well during the post-rut is the use of sexual scents to attract bucks. In fact, estrous scents seem to work better now than they did during the primary rut, especially when applied from a drip dispenser attached to your boot. By wearing a dispenser, you can walk around your hunting location and create mock estrous trails of does. Such trails can attract bucks that might not have come near otherwise. Another post-rut strategy is to imitate the blat of a doe in heat. This deer call often brings bucks in on the run.

By recognizing that the rut is three to four months long, you can prevent yourself from falling into the habit of believing that your only chance for a big buck is during cold weather in November. Understand that there are three peak periods of rutting behavior from October through January, and plan your hunting accordingly. You'll see the difference.

HUNT AND SCOUT

During the hunting season, scout for recent deer activity and new places to hunt. You can combine scouting with a still-hunt. Pay attention to details, such as the points from which other hunters enter your hunting area and where their stands are located. Then look for places where the deer go to avoid other hunters. Plan your hunting strategy accordingly. Even on heavily hunted public lands, you may find places infrequently visited by other hunters that are used as escape cover by deer. A physical barrier such as wet ground or dense foliage may make it difficult to enter these areas, but extra effort may pay off with a successful hunt.

Whitetail activity is affected by the availability of food. Learn to identify and locate the fall foods whitetails prefer in your hunting area. After killing frosts, deer in the forest shift from eating vegetative matter to woody browse. In agricultural areas, feeding patterns are associated with crop harvests. The abundance of natural foods, such as acorns, varies from year to year, and your hunting strategy may change accordingly.

POST-SEASON

Scouting after the season is over can be very helpful. Early-winter deer movements are usually similar to those used in the recently ended hunting season. The most

During the post-rut, catch a buck's attention with a well-timed rattle. Because of the increased activity of does late into estrous, bucks are susceptible to savvy hunting strategies.

significant difference is that the bucks are no longer in rut. Look for sign from the rut, such as scrapes and rubs, and mark where you find it. Very likely, rut activity will occur in the same place the next year.

Later in the winter and in spring, you can look for antlers shed by bucks. Many folks find shed-antler hunting an enjoyable way to scout and spend time in the woods. Focus your search on winter cover, such as conifer stands, south-facing slopes, and feeding areas. Walk slowly, scanning the ground around you for the telltale shape of an antler or an upright tine. If you find one antler, carefully search the surrounding area for a radius of 50 yards or more. You may find the other.

If you are lucky enough to find several antlers, you may learn something about antler sizes and the age-classes of bucks in your area. Finding a trophy-size antler can fuel your dreams, because the buck that dropped it may still be around next year.

PUTTING IT ALL TOGETHER

When you are out and looking for deer sign, remember to take a small tape measure with you. Doing so will eliminate guesswork, letting you accurately measure the size of droppings, the height and width of rubs, the size of beds and, later, the inside spread of your buck's rack! They're a useful tool for the hunter who reads sign.

The wise hunter doesn't stop reading sign after his buck is down. Now it's time to dissect and examine the digested and undigested contents of the four compartments of a deer's stomach. The information will let you know where and when the deer was feeding and what it was eating. The least-digested food is what the deer ate last. The food that's been further digested will be mushier, less identifiable, and will have to be investigated more closely — this is what the deer was feeding on first. By knowing the time of day your deer was killed, you will be able to backtrack through the stomach contents to discover the route the deer traveled. This information can be shared with hunting companions who haven't filled their tags. Or it can be used next season if the same general weather conditions and food patterns exist.

The end of the calendar hunting season doesn't stop the most dedicated hunters—clues for next year's hunt can be found in scrape and rub locations, and comparing those locations to areas where antlers are shed later in the year. Many hunters keep notebooks from year to year to compare notes like these.

Deer sign allows a hunter to eliminate a majority of the guesswork and to place himself at the right place at the right time. Luck now takes a backseat to knowledge and skill. So, by taking the advice of that old Adirondack guide and learning to correctly "read the water," you too can become a better deer hunter.

SIGHTING-IN AND SHOOTING FIREARMS

Deer hunters must be competent with the guns they use for hunting—whether rifle, shotgun, muzzleloader, or handgun. Being a good shot is not a birthright, nor is it a skill acquired through casual study. Shooting a few rounds prior to the hunt to make sure your gun is sighted-in is not sufficient practice to know that you can make the shot when a deer steps out. If you want to shoot well, you must practice until you are confident that you can hit what you're shooting at under field conditions.

Finding a place to shoot is a challenge for many hunters as urban sprawl and local ordinances lead to the closure of both shooting ranges and informal shooting places like gravel pits. Find a place to shoot long before hunting season begins so you have sufficient time for practice. To find nearby shooting ranges, you can simply check the Yellow Pages, or you can contact local law enforcement representatives, conservation department offices, or the National Shooting Sports Foundation (www.nssf.org). These sources will know of ranges operated by a sportsman's club, the state conservation department, or a private owner. Most ranges allow you to shoot for a small fee or the price of a membership. If you own or have access to rural property, you can set up your own shooting range.

At the range, shooting distances should be defined for 10, 25, 50, 100, and 200 yards so you can sight-in and practice with hunting guns. The range may provide bench rests, targets, and other amenities. A range officer oversees the area and is responsible for safety. Be sure you understand and follow the range rules.

Know Your Gun

Before you go to the shooting range, learn how your gun functions. With the gun unloaded, become familiar with the sights, the safety, the action, and the magazine.

There's no limit to the methods in which hunters can improve their chances at finding the kind of buck they can brag about for ages. Use the methods you find most effective, and you'll have more to look forward to before, during, and after hunting season.

Nobody is born with the innate ability to shoot straight and hit often. The ability to hit your target is borne from practice and repetition. Just as athletes use the weight room to enhance their on-field performance, hunters should consider the use of hunting ranges or private land to practice their marksmanship.

Perform a cleaning disassembly. If you want to try dry-firing—practicing pulling the trigger with an unloaded gun—get a snap cap, which allows the firing pin to make a strike without damaging the spring.

All guns work on the same principal. Igniting gunpowder causes an explosion that propels a projectile—called a bullet or a slug—down the barrel, launching it toward a target. Generally, bullets used for deer hunting travel at speeds ranging from 1,000 to over 3,000 feet per second, which means that they reach the target in an instant. In the course of flight, a bullet must counter the effects of gravity, which pulls it toward the ground. To compensate for gravitational pull, the bullet travels at a slight arc, which is called trajectory. The relationship between bullet speed and trajectory is called ballistics.

Study the ballistics information for the ammunition you intend to use while hunting. For factory-loaded ammunition, this information may be available on the cartridge box or in a manufacturer's brochure. Knowing the trajectory, measured in inches at specific distances, will help you select the proper ammunition and sight-in your gun. A selection of ammunition or loads is available for most calibers. If you are uncertain which load is best for your gun, seek advice from an experienced shooter or hunter. Gun stores have knowledgeable staff who can answer your questions.

Sighting-in Firearms

Sight-in your gun prior to every hunting season. If you travel a long distance, take a few shots before you hunt to make sure the gun is still sighted-in. If you accidentally jar the gun during a hunt (perhaps by falling down, or dropping the gun), or if you inexplicably miss a deer, shoot at a target to again check for accuracy.

Firearms should be kept clean, dry, and in a protective case when not in use. Begin the sighting-in process by

The advantage of shooting ranges is that they're ready made to provide you with all the information you need to improve your hunt. Pre-defined distances and endless targets allow you to get to know how your rifle will operate at various distances in the field.

Be sure to sight in your gun using every position you know you'll be using in the field—this hunter anticipates shooting from a prone position on the ground, so it only makes sense to practice that way. He uses a tripod to steady the barrel for a clean shot.

giving the gun a once-over to make sure that scope mounts are tight; look for any visible damage, and check the tightness of all screws and bolts. If the rifle has never been sighted-in, use a bore-sighting tool to make initial scope adjustments.

Use targets with a bull's-eye at least 3 inches in diameter. A 6-inch bull's-eye is easier to see. Begin the sighting-in process with the target placed at 25 yards. At that distance, all bullets are still on the rise of trajectory. When zeroed at 25 yards, most rifles will shoot about 2 inches high at 100 yards and return to zero at about 200 yards. Muzzleloaders, shotguns, and handguns, which have projectiles traveling at slower speeds, have a shorter range, but the trajectory principle is the same.

Always fire sighting-in rounds from a solid resting position. Ideally, you should use sandbags to steady your firearm on a bench rest, though you can also use cushions to rest the gun. With open sights or a scope, aim exactly where you want the bullet to strike the target. Keeping the same sight picture for each shot, fire

three rounds. Then check the target. Your shots should form a group and indicate where the gun is aiming. Make sight or scope adjustments if necessary and fire three more rounds.

When you are satisfied that the gun is sighted-in, move the target to a longer distance—50 yards for shotguns and handguns, 100 yards for muzzleloaders and rifles. Fire three-shot groups, which should strike 1 to 3 inches higher on the target due to rising trajectory. Make any necessary horizontal adjustments.

If your gun shoots inconsistent groups, try different ammunition. Many guns are more accurate with specific loads. If you remain unsatisfied with the accuracy, ask an experienced shooter to try the gun. If he or she gets the same result, the accuracy problem may be the gun or sights, and you should visit a gun shop or gunsmith for further advice.

Sight-in with the ammunition you intend to use for hunting. You can shoot less-expensive rounds for general target practice. Read shooting magazines and consult ballistics tables to select your hunting loads. For rifles, use bullets designed for deer-size animals. A common myth is that heavier bullets "bust brush" better than lighter ones. In reality, all bullets may deflect when they strike a twig or stem.

Once your gun is sighted-in, spend some time shooting it. Remember, sighting-in is done from a controlled setting such as a bench rest to make the gun accurate—a process that doesn't necessarily make you a better shot. Practice from the various shooting positions until you're confident that you can hit a dinner plate, which is about the size of a deer's vital areas, on every shot.

Distance Shooting

Every firearm has an acceptable range for making consistent, killing shots. Most handgun and shotgun hunters try to keep their shots within 50 yards, though some guns and loads—in the hands of an experienced shooter—are capable of greater distances. Black powder shooters limit their shots to about 100 yards, again with some exceptions.

Rifles are capable of greater distances, though just how far is dependent upon the caliber and the load. The venerable .30-30 is best at ranges of less than 150 yards. A .270 can reach out to 300 yards or more. In most of the whitetail's range, nearly all hunting shots are taken

In open areas of the country, hunters often lack the luxury of hunting from a stand. Prone is the steadiest position to shoot from, and often your only option in southern and central parts of North America.

Sitting is the most comfortable and natural shooting position, but it requires patience and discipline to accurately fire your rifle while doing so.

at distances of 200 yards or less. Many expert hunters strongly recommend that even if your rifle is capable of greater distances, hunting shots should be confined to 300 yards or less.

The longer the shot, the more variables come into play. First, you must accurately judge the distance. A range finder or range-finding scope is useful, especially if you are not experienced at making long shots in the field. With a flat-shooting rifle, you should be able to aim directly at the vitals out to 200 yards. But as distances increase, you must account for trajectory. If there is a breeze, you must also consider bullet drift.

Stories abound of whitetail hunters who make a Western hunting trip and are stymied by the long shots typical of open country. If you plan to hunt in the West, be sure you spend plenty of practice time at the shooting range before you go. Buy a range finder and learn not only how to use it, but also to become reasonably adept at judging distances. Preparation always pays off—no matter where you hunt.

Common Shooting Positions

Whenever possible, shoot from a resting position with the gun steadied by an inanimate object, such as the railing on a tree stand. In hunting situations, however, you don't always have the opportunity to shoot from a rest. It is essential to know how to fire from the basic shooting positions: prone, sitting, kneeling, and offhand. You can take shooting instructions or a gun safety class to learn more about these positions.

- **Prone** is the steadiest position. It is most useful in open country, where the deer is some distance away and you are able to lie down and shoot. Lie on your stomach with your body tilted at a 30-degree angle from the line of fire. The butt of the gun forms the apex of the angle. Spread your legs apart for support. Use your elbow to support the forearm of the gun. The elbow of your trigger hand should rest on the ground.

- The **sitting position** is nearly as steady as the prone position and more practical in some field situations. Sit with the lower half of your torso at a 30-degree angle from the line of fire. Spread your legs apart and rest your elbows on your knees. Some shooters prefer to sit with their ankles crossed.

- The **kneeling position** can be used when brush or high grass obscure the view from sitting or prone positions. Kneeling is less steady and many shooters find it a difficult position to assume. Kneel with the knee on the same side of your body as your trigger hand. Sit back on that foot and ankle. Slide your other foot forward and rest the elbow of the arm supporting the gun's forearm on the knee.

- **Offhand** is the least steady position, but is often used when you have just a few moments to make

the shot. It can also be described as a freestanding position. Stand with your feet apart and your body leaning slightly toward the line of fire. Tuck the elbow of the arm supporting the forearm beneath the gun. Raise the elbow of your trigger hand until it is horizontal. Practice shooting from this position until you are confident you can hit targets at typical deer-hunting distances.

Portable Rests

Shooting with a steady gun can mean the difference between a hit and a miss. Awkward positions can be greatly improved by using a steadying tool. Here are three suggestions.

- **The sling** is most often used to carry a gun and leave your hands free. Some shooters use a sling to become

Hunters making drives often only have a few moments to raise the rifle, sight, breathe, and fire. It's not the most accurate method of shooting, but sometimes there's no other choice. Practice walking, pausing, raising, and shooting at stationary targets or bulls' eyes to ready yourself for the real thing.

The most common method of safely walking with a gun is by using a sling. Almost every firearm is equipped to be fitted with a comfortable sling that can be adjusted to any body size.

more steady in all shooting positions. The sling goes around the outside of the arm used to steady the gun. Adjust the sling to fit you. When beginning a hunt, check the adjustment to make sure the sling fits with your bulkier hunting clothes.

- **Folding shooting sticks** are carried in a belt pouch and used to steady the gun, often from a sitting position. The sticks are crossed to form an X. The forearm rests in the apex.

- **Bipods** are attached to the forearm and folded up when not in use. Open-country hunters find them especially useful for prone and sitting shots. A telescoping monopod is lightweight and can be used for sitting and standing shots.

TUNING AND SHOOTING BOWS

Killing a deer with a bow and arrow is an achievement. You must first master the skills of archery and then learn to hunt well enough to get close to whitetails. Typically, bowhunters spend more time in the field, because it is difficult to get within arrow range of a deer. When you do, you get just one shot.

Becoming a competent archer requires lots of practice. Fortunately, it is easy to find places to shoot. Many hunters are able to set up a target with a safe backstop in their backyards. Archery ranges exist in many communities. Indoor ranges are available for year-round shooting.

Consistency

The motions of drawing and releasing an arrow come naturally for most of us. The challenge is acquiring the consistency to make the same motion time and again in a variety of conditions so you can reliably hit a plate-size target at typical hunting distances. Archers develop individual styles, but they practice until the steps of draw, anchor, sight, release, and follow-through become second nature. Consistency leads to accuracy.

When practicing, pay attention to shooting position. Find a comfortable upper-body stance and stick with it whether you are standing, kneeling, or sitting in a tree stand. To shoot at various angles, learn to bend at the waist. Hold the bow lightly, because a tight grip affects arrow flight.

The anchor point, which is where your string hand holds the arrow at full draw, must be the same on every shot. Varying the anchor point changes the course of the arrow. To hold a consistent anchor point, many archers touch their chin, cheek, or the corner of the mouth with their index finger or mechanical release on every shot. Find the anchor point that feels right for you and stick with it.

A smooth release leads to accuracy. Practice finger or mechanical releases to avoid moving or plucking the string. Focus on your aim, so that the release occurs when you are confident that you are on target. Then you won't hesitate when taking a shot at a whitetail. Remain steady after the release so the arrow flies true.

Sighting Methods

Today many archers use bowsights to improve their accuracy. If you are skilled at judging range, sights will help you achieve consistent accuracy. Instinctive shooters don't use sights, but instead rely on experience to place their shots.

Set sight pins for the distances you are most likely to shoot while hunting. To sight-in a bow, move the pin opposite of the direction you expect the arrow to go. For instance, if you are shooting low, move the pin lower. Practice until you can draw and then hold until you release.

Instinctive shooting requires more practice, but is really no different than learning how to throw a ball. Draw and release when the shot feels right. Focus on the target. Some shooters use the point of the arrow as a guide. Practice frequently to hone instinctive skills.

Whether using sights or a bare bow, begin practicing at 10 yards and move back in 5-yard increments as your shooting improves. The distance at which you can consistently hit a pie plate is your effective hunting range.

Practice Techniques

Use target points for practice at block targets or bales. If your practice area is in the backyard or close to home, remember that it is better to take a few shots often than to have an occasional long practice session. Remember, you'll only get one shot when hunting.

Large archery ranges may have a walk-through area where you can shoot at game-size targets in realistic field conditions. You can get similar practice by stump-shooting. Find a place where you are unlikely to meet other people and shoot at stumps or other objects at varied distances. Use judo points, which stop rapidly in grass or forest duff, so your arrows are easy to find. Don't shoot at hard objects such as rocks or tree trunks, which may damage your arrows or cause ricochets. Bowhunting for rabbits or other small game during the off-season is excellent practice for deer hunting.

It is a good idea to practice while wearing your hunting clothes so you know that they won't interfere with your shooting. Take shots from a tree stand and a ground blind. Shoot from varied positions, including crouched, kneeling, and sitting. If you hunt in open country, practice on windy days.

Prior to going hunting, take some shots with your broadheads, which fly differently than target points. Be sure you have a solid backstop, such as a pile of clean sand. Carefully examine arrows and sharpen the broadheads afterward, so they are ready for the hunt.

Tuning a Bow

Adjusting a bow to fit you and achieve good arrow flight is called tuning. You can learn how to make the proper adjustments from your bow's owner's manual or at an archery shop. Establish your draw length and the bow's draw weight. Use a bow square to set a nocking point. Place silencers on the string to minimize the chance a deer will "jump the string" when you release a hunting shot.

Test arrow flight by shooting through a taut sheet of paper placed 10 feet away. A straight-flying arrow will cut an even fletching pattern. An odd-shaped pattern means the arrow is wobbling in flight. Adjust first the nock point and then the arrow rest to improve performance. Step back to 30 feet and shoot the paper again. Make any necessary adjustments.

Using field points, test your hunting arrow shafts by shooting at a mid-range target. Try to keep the arrows in a tight group. Mark arrows that don't stay in the group and shoot again. Don't use inconsistent arrows for hunting. Never try to shoot groups with broadheads, because you may cut fletchings or damage shafts.

By tuning your bow and making performance tests, you'll gain confidence in your equipment and your ability as an archer. Now you are ready to go hunting!

SHOT PLACEMENT FOR BULLET, SLUG, AND ARROW

A good deer hunt ends with a humane, one-shot kill. If your shot strikes the vitals, the animal dies quickly, which makes it easier for you to recover the deer. Understanding whitetail anatomy is essential to shot placement, because you don't always get a perfect shooting opportunity. Whitetails may approach you from any direction, never stop moving, and be partially obscured by vegetation. Learn to identify the vital area from various angles. Practice shooting until you are able to shoot quickly and with confidence.

The primary vital area consists of the heart, lungs, and liver, located in the chest cavity behind the front shoulder. The neck contains major blood vessels and several vertebrae. A whitetail's brain is relatively small. Breaking the backbone will incapacitate the deer, but is unlikely to kill it.

A heart/lung shot is best, because the chest cavity is the largest target. The proximity of the liver and spine allows some margin of error. An open, broadside shot is preferred, but learn to identify the heart/lung area from various angles. The bone structure, including the shoulder, may cause your shot to deflect.

While neck and head shots may result in quick kills, both are risky targets. A near-miss may wound or maim the animal, but not be serious enough to prevent its escape. Every hunting situation is different and on occasion you may be compelled to shoot at the head or neck. Take the shot only if you are certain you will hit where you aim.

Ground-level shots tend to be the most successful—broadside exposes 100 percent of the deer's heart/lung area; quartering toward, 65 percent; quartering away, about 60 percent; and head-on, 35 percent. Steep-angle shots tend to be less successful, with quartering toward and quartering away exposing about 55 percent of the deer's vital organs. Walking away exposes less than half, about 45 percent.

Bowhunters often have a wider skill set than rifle hunters, as their practice requires them to not only master a more difficult weapon, but to get closer to a deer for a bow's shorter range. Many hunters, however, become proficient with both weapons and enjoy a long hunting season.

A deer bounding directly away from you generally doesn't offer a shooting opportunity unless it is wounded and you are trying to put it down. If you must make such a shot, aim beneath the white tail. Conversely, if a deer is walking directly toward you, it may be best to wait for the animal to turn and present a better, quartering shot. Do not shoot if a second deer is standing behind the deer you intend to kill, because bullet, slug, or arrow may pass through the deer and hit the other animal.

The traditional hunting theory that you should always aim behind the shoulder betrays many a short-sighted hunter. On paper, the concept seems infallible: Place your bullet or slug just back of the shoulder to hit the heart and lungs area. In reality, your chances of actually getting an unimpeded broadside shot at this area are small. You are more likely to see a buck walking toward or away from you, either directly or at an angle.

The key to dropping a buck with the first shot is to think in three dimensions. You aren't trying to hit the side of a deer; you're trying to put your bullet or slug into the heart or lungs. If you imagine these vital organs as sitting squarely between the shoulders, with the heart quite low, you can then picture the correct angle no matter how the buck is positioned.

Bullets and slugs kill with tissue damage and associated trauma. Use a bullet designed for hunting deer-size animals, which expands as it enters the body. Factory-made ammunition suitable for deer hunting is widely available.

Arrows kill by slicing and creating hemorrhage. Select broadheads designed to make cutting wounds. An arrow that penetrates the heart/lung area will kill as quickly and efficiently as a bullet.

Hay bales and block targets are an archer's best friend. It is better to shoot often in short bursts than to exhaust yourself in marathon sessions—short bursts are all you get in the field. Equip your arrows with blunted ends to ensure safety.

In archery, consistency is key. Practice a variety of positions and techniques that yield the best results. The ability to draw, anchor, sight, and release is something developed over time.

SAFETY

Years ago, hunting accident rates were much higher than they are today, even though there were significantly fewer hunters. The advent of mandatory hunter safety programs for young hunters and voluntary training for adults has made hunting one of the safest recreational activities. Nevertheless, preventable accidents still occur. You can take precautions to ensure the safety of yourself and other hunters.

Deer hunting is a strenuous physical activity. Be physically prepared to walk on uneven terrain, climb into tree stands, and drag out a deer. Wear foot gear with ankle support to prevent sprained ankles. Even if it is warm during the day, have sufficient clothing to remain warm if the temperature drops. Carry water and food.

Never go afield without basic gear that will allow you to meet situations you may encounter afield. Have a reliable means for starting a fire, such as waterproof matches. A small candle will help you start a fire even in wet conditions. Carry a flashlight, a length of rope, a knife, and gloves.

A GPS unit is a handy tool, but you should also carry a compass and know how to use it. Take out the compass at your starting point and determine what direction you will need to go to get out of the woods. For instance, if you walk west from a road running north and south, walking east will bring you back to the road.

It is hard to get lost in most whitetail hunting areas, but it may be difficult to find your way in unfamiliar country or after darkness falls. Be sure to tell someone where you are going and when you plan to return. Pay attention to natural features and landmarks. Above all, don't fear the forest or panic if you lose your way. If night falls and you don't know where you are, stop, gather firewood, build a fire, and wait for someone to come looking for you. If you are in good physical condition, at worst you'll spend an uncomfortable night in the woods.

Treat every gun as a loaded weapon. And when hunting with bow and arrow, remember that broadheads are razor-sharp and can easily inflict life-threatening cuts or puncture wounds.

Wearing some amount of blaze-orange clothing is required for most firearms deer hunts. Be sure you know the guidelines in the state or province where you hunt. Although some hunters believe whitetails can distinguish the brightness of the color, hundreds of thousands of whitetails are killed annually by orange-clad hunters. Wear as much blaze orange as you believe is necessary for other hunters to easily see you. Blaze-orange camouflage patterns, though somewhat less visible, can be worn to break up your outline.

Bowhunters usually are not required to wear blaze orange. Typically, they wear camouflage to blend in with the surroundings. If you are hunting in an area where small game or turkey seasons are open, consider wearing some blaze orange so these hunters can see you. You can carry an inexpensive blaze-orange vest to wear as you walk to and from your stand.

Avoid wearing white or brown clothing. In dim light or darkness, use a flashlight. Some hunters affix childrens' flashing safety lights to their hats so they can be seen. If you encounter another hunter who doesn't see you, say hello or make a noise to attract attention.

Keeping safety in the forefront of your thinking can go a long way to avoiding an accident afield.

These two hunters are exhibiting basic rules of hunting safety; they are easily visible in vibrant blaze orange vests, and are equipped for the colder weather. Their rifles are pointed away from each other and into the ground. Getting into the habit of safe hunting practices ensures a lifetime of worry-free hunting.

CHAPTER FOUR

HUNTING TECHNIQUES

Hunters use dozens of techniques to outwit whitetails. Stand hunting, still-hunting, and drives account for the vast majority of deer. But other methods—such as stalking, tracking, rattling, calling, using scents, using decoys—also have their devotees. Knowing how to hunt goes along with knowing where to hunt and when to hunt.

Still-hunting is as challenging as it is rewarding. The crisp snowfall may benefit this hunter in spotting a whitetail, but to do so, he must move in slow, quiet, deliberate steps, using wind direction to his advantage.

STAND HUNTING

There is no official tally, but it seems reasonable to assume that more whitetails are killed by hunters in stands than by all other hunting methods combined. Taking a stand, or waiting in a likely spot for a deer to approach, is a very effective way to hunt. Hunting from a stand is best at times when deer are moving, such as early and late in the day, during the rut, or when other hunters are on the move.

Stand hunting works anywhere whitetails are found. It is a safe method for heavily hunted or populated areas because you are in one place and usually elevated above the ground. Hunting from a stand is the most consistent way for novice hunters to see deer. Many hunters spend the majority of their hunting time on stand. If you can sit—alert, silent, and motionless—downwind from a deer trail or feeding area, sooner or later you'll see a deer.

TYPES OF STANDS

Permanent Stands

The term "deer stand" loosely defines places and objects used by hunters who are waiting for deer. A stand may be a stump on a northwoods ridge, a rusting farm implement beside a prairie wheat field, or an elevated shelter overlooking the brush country. Stands are divided into two categories: elevated stands and ground blinds. Either of them may be permanent or portable.

The most common elevated stand is the tree stand, a platform typically placed 6 to 25 feet above the ground. Years ago, hunters believed deer did not look up, and even today whitetails are less likely to detect a hunter perched in a tree. However, hunters have learned that deer may indeed look up, especially older, more wary

A deer stand is a loose term for just about anything that sits above the ground during hunting season. This stand not only helps keep the hunter warm during the chill winter months, but also obscures movement from within (a luxury most stand-hunters do not enjoy).

Portable stands become lighter and more reliable with each passing year. This one uses a hinged seat and a lever to create a right triangle with the tree, supporting the hunter from the ground up.

Tree Stand Exit Strategy

Get out of your tree stand quickly and quietly, avoiding all metal clanging. In case an unscrupulous hunter does find your stand, undo the lower set(s) of steps and hide them nearby. He may have found your secret stand site, but it is unlikely he will be able to hunt from it—at least on the day he finds it.

Next, choose an exit route that will help you avoid contact with any deer. Keep in mind that getting to your stand quietly is much easier in broad daylight than when it's dark. Can you sneak out without making a racket or disturbing nearby deer? After a morning hunt, for example,

you can cross most openings with impunity, but in the evening you would need to avoid meadows and other feeding areas, even if it means taking the long way around.

Don't walk out too quickly or in a forthright manner. As with your approach, you must "bob and weave," avoiding known trails and probably concentrations of deer. Sneak out! And when you get to your vehicle, don't talk, turn on the radio, or bang your gear around. Deer study your exit strategy as quickly as they study your approach.

Tree Stand Tips

Screw-in steps help you climb any tree. Folding models take up less room in your pack, but cost more than nonfolding models. If you plan to use the tree again, remove the steps and put matchsticks or twigs in the holes so you can easily find them next time.

Portable ladders are an alternative to screw-in steps. Most are made of aluminum and measure 12 to 14 feet in length. They break into 3- to 4-foot sections, strap securely to the tree, and come with carrying straps for easy backpacking.

Reflective tacks or reflective adhesive strips applied to trees beforehand make it easy to find your stand in the dark. Before moving to a new stand, be sure to remove the tacks so you don't clutter the woods and confuse other hunters.

Understanding what the deer see at ground level will help inform where to place your deer stand in the surrounding woods. You need a clear shooting lane through the folliage, but you must also account for enough natural cover to hide your aerial movements.

animals. Tree stand hunters generally use camouflage or screens to be inconspicuous.

Besides placing you above a deer's normal line of sight, an elevated stand offers other hunting advantages. Usually, you can see farther from an elevated position than from the ground, because you can look over and beyond any underbrush. From above the ground, human scent may disperse better and quicker, and not contaminate your hunting area. If a tree stand is comfortable and offers a good view of the surroundings, you can sit for longer periods of time—increasing your odds of seeing deer.

Permanent tree stands are built of lumber or natural materials in locations with consistent deer activity. A well-constructed permanent stand is safe and comfortable, and becomes part of the surroundings. Be sure you have landowner permission before building a permanent stand. Most public areas do not allow them.

On the subject of picking a tree, make certain that your tree is in good shape before you start building on it. The last thing you want to do is build a tree stand in a set of trees that may rot out in a few years.

When building a stand, do it in spring or summer. Deer know the forest, and anything out of the ordinary is going to be suspect to them. If you build your stand well before hunting season, they'll get used to seeing

it there, and won't view it as potentially dangerous. Building it during summer will also give the wood some time to weather, so it won't stand out once the leaves have fallen.

If you somehow find yourself in a situation where you must build a tree stand just before or during hunting season, it might make sense to use natural wood, as the deer may not notice it as readily. I generally prefer 2x4s from the lumberyard, however, as they last longer, and are easier to work with. Natural wood is wet, too, which means it's more apt to split.

When your stand is complete, sit in it for a while. Like the view? If not, it might pay to carry a limb pruner or handsaw into the woods and clear shooting lanes and any limbs that obscure your vision.

Finally, clean up the ground around your stand. Let

the woods revert to its natural state; the less human odor and evidence of human presence, the better. Never urinate near your stand, before or during deer season, as you'll simply be advertising your presence to the deer. For that matter, you should use scent on your boots, to further mask your presence.

Portable Stands

Portable tree stands offer mobility. Many makes are available, falling into the categories of hang-on models, tree-crotch models, self-climbers, and ladder stands. Freestanding tripod platforms are available, too. Choose a stand that is practical for where you hunt. Pay particular attention to platform size. A small platform may become uncomfortable if you intend to spend long hours in the tree. Weight and portability are other considerations, especially if you must walk a distance to reach your hunting location.

Climbing Stands

Where trees have straight trunks with few limbs, climbing stands seem natural. Some prefer the security of the platform under their feet (opposed to tree steps) while climbing. Many hunters, portable stand in hand, can be high above the ground and scanning for bucks within 15 minutes.

With all climbing stands, you strap your feet to the platform, cock it away from the tree, pull it up, and then tip the platform horizontally to bite back into the tree.

That's pretty standard. But methods for pulling yourself up vary. With some stands, you sit on a seat and then alternately stand and sit to climb the tree. These may be the easiest to use, but many sit-stand climbers are heavy and bulky, not ideal quick stands. With lighter models, a lightweight seat doubles as a hand climber; you lean on the seat as you pull up the platform, raise the seat, lean on it, and so forth. To further reduce weight, you can leave the seat home and simply hug the

Quick Tips for Stand Hunting

- Intersections of two or more heavily used trails make prime stand-hunting locations. Another good spot is an area with many fresh scrapes.

- Elevated stands place you above a deer's usual vision level. They also expand your field of view and keep your scent above the ground. But many hunters simply hide behind a tree or a pile of logs or brush.

- Raise and lower your unloaded gun or bow with a rope when hunting from an elevated stand. Make sure the barrel is pointed away from you.

- Tower blinds make it possible to hunt from a high elevation where there are no tall trees. Some tower blinds are permanent.

This western game farm in the distance employs tower stands to help hunters hide from whitetails. Though it may jar the deer at first, tower stands soon become permanent fixtures in whitetail habitat, and deer soon forget they're even there.

Deer Stand Locations

According to surveys, more deer are taken by hunters on stand than by all other methods combined. The primary reason is obvious: A moving predator makes noise and is easily seen, while a motionless one makes no noise and is virtually invisible to whitetails. The following tips show you where to stand hunt throughout the season, regardless of whether you use elevated stands or ground stands.

- Always stay downwind or crosswind of the location where you expect to see deer. This lessens the chance that deer will smell you. If the wind changes during the day, move to another stand.

- Pick a spot that has enough cover to hide your silhouette and reduce glare from your face, glasses, and hunting gear.

- Prune limbs and twigs from nearby trees and bushes to ensure a clear shot.

- Scrape away leaves from underfoot so you can move your feet silently when shifting position on the ground.

Forested ridges often have benches (sometimes called shelves, ledges, or flats) that lie just below a ridge top. Benches are an important area to stand hunt regardless of whether you're pursuing deer in hilly farmland or true wilderness. Because benches are relatively flat, they are easy spots for deer to bed, feed, and make scrapes. And, like saddles, benches are often used by deer in their daily travel routes.

Quality deer habitat contains a large amount of edge—the zone between two different types of habitat, such as a forest and a field. An edge typically provides deer with a variety of foods and access to cover. Whenever you scout for a good stand location, look first along an edge. For evening hunts, place stands on an edge and close to crop fields and other food sources; for midday and morning hunts, place stands on an edge near thick bedding cover.

As whitetails travel through a forest, they usually walk the easiest route while taking advantage of available cover. For example, whitetails typically avoid climbing over steep ridges and simply pass between ridge tops in the saddle. Like funnels, saddles are excellent places to sit during the firearms deer opener. As hunters mill about the woods, deer travel through saddles en route to escape cover. Place stands overlooking the saddle.

Travel corridors, or funnels, are narrow bottlenecks formed where open fields, lakes, rivers, or other obstacles force deer into a narrow area of cover. A funnel is one of the best places to be on a stand during the opening day of gun season. Hunting pressure typically keeps deer on the move throughout the day, and chances are excellent that many deer will be forced to travel through the funnel as they try to elude hunters. Place stands overlooking the funnel.

Many hunters give up the game long before they even know a deer is nearby. Understanding where the wind is coming from and where it's going is key to not being ousted by a buck and his sensitive nose. No matter where or how you hunt, always stay downwind of the animal.

The best deer habitat is a mixed bag of forest, fields, water sources, and cover. Areas with large amounts of edge, the zone between two different areas of habitat, are popular walking trails for whitetails.

tree to pull yourself up. Hug-climbing can be strenuous if you're not in shape, however. Climbing aids such as Loc-On's Rope-N-Stick, a bar with a rope that twists around the tree, enable you to pull yourself up to ease strain on the arms and chest.

Climbers can be dangerous on wet, smooth-barked trees. On wet trees, climbers may not be the best choice (the need for a safety belt goes without saying). Climbers can be a little noisy, especially as you bolt the climbing arm around a tree, and they're heavier, on average, than many fixed-position stands, although the total system may not weigh much, if any, more when you add steps to the fixed stand.

Many manufacturers produce a climber that consists of two small climbing stands, one strapped to each foot. In essence, you walk up the tree, and then bind the individual stands in place to form a foot platform and seat. No matter which stand you use, it must fit your body type and comfort level. The most obvious drawback is weight, but for many hunters, the benefits of being completely mobile and airborne are too hard to ignore.

Fixed-Position Stands

If wet bark, limbs, or other obstacles prevent use of a climbing stand, a fixed-position stand is the obvious alternative. In fact, many hunters prefer fixed stands

Tree Stand Tips: Fooling the Buck

Tree stands help nullify a buck's three primary senses: sight, sound, and smell. But there's more to it than simply sliding a tree stand up an old oak in the early-morning darkness, and then tagging a buck at first light. To be successful, you first have to fine-tune your set-up. Here are a few tips to do just that.

FOOLING A BUCK'S NOSE

- Your first consideration before erecting a stand is wind direction. Any tree stand you use should be set up downwind or crosswind to where you expect a buck to saunter past.

- If you hunt hilly terrain, then daily thermals must also be taken into account. Generally winds rise uphill with the rising sun, and rush downhill with the setting sun. Therefore you may have to erect your tree stand uphill of a preferred trail for an early-morning hunt, and downhill of a preferred trail for an evening hunt.

- You need more than one tree stand location to cover different times of the day and those days when the winds blow erratically. Be conscious of this need whenever you scout—you can never have too many tree stand sites!

- A buck can be alerted to your presence by simply sniffing the trail you took to your stand. He is so good at it, you may never know he was in the vicinity! Therefore, approach your stand location carefully. Rubber-bottomed boots and scent pad or drag-along rag dipped in fox or coon urine help keep your human ground scent to a minimum.

FOOLING A BUCK'S EYES

- Your first task is to avoid being silhouetted against the skyline. The best tree stands are set up in a copse of trees or against a large enough tree trunk to conceal your torso.

- The perfect stand allows you to make the perfect shot by raising your gun undetected. Sitting down is your first choice because it requires only a minimum of movement to complete the act. If you must stand to make the shot, then position your stand so you can use the trunk of the tree as a shield.

- When trimming, leave a branch with its green leaves hanging on the tree near the stand. Later, those fluttering brown leaves help hide not only your silhouette, but also those involuntary hand and head movements we all seem to make on the stand.

- It is also wise at times to wear gloves and a face mask, and/or paint all exposed skin, including face, neck, and ears with camo cream. Why? Exposed skin attracts a buck's attention like a moth to a bright campfire, especially when you move your head to see what that crunch, crunch, crunch is off to your left.

Bucks follow their noses—it is their most valuable asset throughout their lives. An ill-considered tree stand location upwind from bedding areas will end your hunt real fast.

FOOLING A BUCK'S EARS

- Be sure to dampen the base of your stand. Sometimes just dragging your boot across the base as you turn to shoot can alert a buck to your intentions. Most carpet stores sell indoor/outdoor samples or remnants that are ideal for this project. Make sure they are securely fastened to the stand and that they are not slippery when wet.

- If you stand is difficult to approach quietly, it's never a bad idea to clear a path and mark the trail with some form of fluorescent markers. Even then, you should plan on being on stand for an hour or so before shooting hours.
- Once your stand is secured on-site, test it for squeaks and groans by moving about the platform (and be sure to do so safely). Then remove any shards of bark that may come in contact with your body and any branches that might interfere with the swinging of your rifle or shotgun. Even a small dead twig can spoil a hunt if it rubs up against your gun's barrel.

The ability of bucks to swivel their ears in almost every direction lends them an excellent chance to pinpoint exactly where a sound is coming from. Being elevated helps, but it's often not enough if you're already making too much noise.

regardless of conditions, figuring they can put up such a stand almost as quickly, and more quietly, than they can a climber. Many manufacturers say they sell two to three times as many fixed-position stands as climbers. For a given platform size, fixed stands generally weigh less and pack easier because they have no climbing mechanism. Many fixed-position stands have a built-in seat, although some have a separate seat, and the lightest have no seat at all.

Attachment methods vary, but the most common are probably chain and polypropylene rope. Some hunters prefer the chain because it's easy to use and can be locked to a tree, and it never deteriorates. The rope is equally easy, it's quieter, and is actually stronger. Comparing rope and chain, you instantly have suspicions about the rope, but the tensile strength exceeds that of most chains used on stands. A friend of mine didn't believe that, so he tied together the chain and rope from two tree stands, attached one end to his tractor, the other end to a tree, and started pulling. The chain broke. Rope will fray and weather, however, so it should be inspected regularly and replaced at the first signs of wear.

Some stands attach to the tree with a strap and ratchet-tightening mechanism. And a fourth style hangs from a steel pin screwed into the tree with a backup strap around the tree for added safety. Pin-up stands are convenient, although the pin can be hard to screw into pines and other pitchy trees.

Ground Blinds

Ground blinds can be simple or elaborate. Use them where elevated stands are impractical, unnecessary, or unavailable. You can sit with your back against a tree trunk to disguise your outline or make a hiding place within a fallen tree. Use a few feet of camouflage material as a screen. Camouflaged tents with openings for shooting are commercially available. In open country, you can dig a shallow pit to use as a blind or hide behind hay bales.

When making a ground blind, be careful not to change natural features. Deer notice changes in their surroundings and are wary of them. A blind should be in place prior to your hunt so the deer become accustomed to it.

STAND PLACEMENT

Scout for trails, rutting activity, and feeding areas to help you choose stand sites. Select locations near feeding fields, fencelines, forest openings, escape cover, or anywhere you find abundant deer sign. Look for funnel locations where deer pass a certain place or trails leading to known bedding areas.

Pick a site that is inconspicuous, located in shadows, or screened with cover to break up your outline. Avoid having your human silhouette "sky-lighted" against an open background. Consider the prevailing wind direction and the angle of the sun when placing the stand. Always try to keep the wind in your face to control your scent and the sun at your back to avoid glare. If you put a stand on a ridge, morning air currents will carry your scent upward and away from the deer.

If possible, know the stand locations of other hunters who are in the vicinity, so you can avoid setting up your stand too close to another hunter. Generally, you should be at least twice the distance of your line of sight from other hunters. Don't place a stand along roads or trails regularly used by hunters or other people.

You can set up a stand anytime throughout the year, though most hunters do so during the weeks preceding the hunt. Select more than one stand site so you can move around to take advantage of changes in weather, hunting pressure, and deer movements. If you are using portable stands, try to set them up at least a day prior to your hunt. In some situations, especially on heavily used public land, this may be impossible. Set up the stand so you can wait comfortably and have a full range of motion. Test the stand to make sure you can turn and shoot at deer approaching from various angles.

JUDGING RANGE

Place your stand close enough to a trail so deer pass within shooting range, but not so close that they detect your presence. Stands for bowhunting should be within 30 yards of where deer are likely to appear. You can shoot to greater distances with guns, though in most situations whitetails will be within 100 yards of your stand. In open country, distances may be greater.

Use a range finder to accurately measure the distance to landmarks around your stand. Memorizing the distances will give you reference points when a deer appears.

SHOOTING LANES

Removing a few saplings, a windfall, or intervening branches makes it easier to see deer and get a clean shot. Clear twigs and brush that will interfere with your ability to move quietly or shoot. Use a pruning tool (where you have permission or the legal right) to cut shooting lanes radiating out from the stand. Unless you have the landowner's permission, do not cut down trees. Clear brush and fallen branches from your entrance/exit path to the stand, so you can approach quietly when you hunt there.

Take advantage of survey lines, logging skid trails, and other lanes already cut in the forest. Deer often follow these lanes because they offer easy walking. You can also watch for crossing whitetails. Don't shoot down a lane unless you are certain no one is in your line of fire.

SAFETY

Falls from trees account for a high percentage of hunting accidents. It's important to understand that all tree stand accidents are self-inflicted; a fall victim can blame no one but himself.

Equipment failure, particularly broken steps, accounts for some accidents. Constantly inspect gear for weak points. The most dangerous moments come as you're hanging from or climbing into a stand, or trimming limbs. To free your hands for securing a stand, hang the stand on a step screwed into the tree. And never climb up into a stand. Instead, place your steps at least as high as, or higher than, the stand and step down onto the platform.

Always wear a safety belt as you climb and prepare your stand. Several companies make climbing belts that double as safety belts once you're on stand. A climbing belt not only protects you from falling as you climb—with both climbing stands and steps—but also relieves strain as you install steps, hang stands, and trim limbs.

Although arrows pose a greater threat climbing into or descending from a tree stand, always be sure to unload your firearm.

Tree Stand Safety

Every year, hunters are seriously injured in tree stand accidents. Take these safety precautions whenever you use a tree stand:

- Always make sure the stand, ladder, or climbing steps are secure before using them.

- Wear a safety harness whenever you are in a tree stand.

- Unload firearms or secure hunting arrows before climbing into a tree stand. You can use a rope to pull an unloaded gun or a bow into the tree.

- If you feel drowsy, climb down from the stand.

- Perform regular safety checks on all tree stands for deterioration or damage.

- Do not place stands in dead or diseased trees.

- Snow, ice, or rain makes steps and platforms slippery. Use extra caution during inclement weather.

- Be sure that someone knows where your stands are located and when you'll be hunting from them.

Always unload firearms or secure arrows when climbing a deer stand. Use a rope to haul any materials into the tree, and perform regular inspections of the durability of the stand and the tree.

Most stand hunters take their deer in full daylight, but this requires getting to the stand early in the morning. Be sure to take a practice walk to a new stand when the sun is down to ensure you can find it when it counts. Stay alert—you may just find a buck waiting for you when you get there, inspecting a newer stand!

Amacker makes one with two loops for use with the Hook. As you go around limbs, you attach a loop above the limb before releasing the one below so you're always protected against falling.

The need for safety belts has been so belabored that it hardly seems worth repeating. But some people won't learn. You wear a safety belt not just to catch you if you fall, but also to prevent your falling. Some belts have no adjusters, just loops at each end, which leaves 2 to 3 feet of slack between you and the tree. Bad scene. Use an adjustable belt that eliminates slack.

HUNTING FROM A STAND

For stand hunters, patience is a virtue. Novices often find it is difficult to sit still for long periods of time. Wear enough clothes so you'll be warm and comfortable. In cold weather, carry extra clothes and put them on when you get to the stand, so you don't become overheated while walking. Bring snacks, a lunch, and something to drink. Have a cushion to sit on.

When is the best time to go to a stand? In the morning, you want to be ready to hunt at the start of legal shooting time. This may mean walking to your stand in darkness. Have a well-marked route that you can follow with a flashlight. In late afternoon, go to your stand at least two hours before sunset to make the most of evening deer activity. Remember that you may see deer from a stand at any time of day. During gun season, it is a good idea to sit in your stand at noon when other hunters are leaving for lunch. They may push a deer past you.

Always walk upwind to reach a stand, so that your scent doesn't alert deer before you get there. Try not to walk through prime deer cover on your way to the stand. Don't cross fields or other openings that will allow the deer to see you from a distance. If you must go around a field, stay within the edge of the woods so you can't be seen. When you reach the stand, climb into it quietly. Don't make metallic, clinking noises that carry a long distance and are obviously human in origin. Prepare your gear in advance so you can settle in to hunt with a minimum of fidgeting.

Stay alert and watchful. Deer often seem to just materialize within your field of vision. A moment of inattention can mean a missed opportunity. Listen for footsteps, a breaking branch, or other sounds. Watch not only where you expect the deer to appear, but all around you. Keep your movements to a minimum, slowly turning your head and searching with your eyes. Be silent.

When you see a deer, remain calm. Keep your actions slow and deliberate. Carefully, with a minimum of noise and motion, shift into a shooting position, preferably when the head of the deer is blocked from view by tree trunks or cover. Even a faint, unnatural sound, such as the metallic click of a gun safety, may alarm a deer. Pick a clear opening where you expect the deer to step out, and wait for it to do so. Carefully aim and shoot when you've confirmed that the deer is a legal animal.

After the shot, watch the deer. Even if it goes down, don't leave the stand. Sometimes a wounded animal may get up again. Gun hunters should wait at least a couple of minutes before going to the downed deer or following an animal that went beyond their field of vision. Bowhunters may wait an hour or more depending on the hit. Walk slowly and quietly in case you are approaching a wounded animal.

CHANGING STAND LOCATIONS

If you hunt from the same stand for several days or happen to spook a deer from the site, whitetails may shift their habits to stay away from your location. Use more than one stand to avoid "burning out" a site. Be careful not to disturb the area around your stand. Enter and exit quietly. If you have a hot spot, hunt there during weather conditions or at times of day when you are most likely to encounter deer.

Many hunters have favorite stands they use from year to year and consistently see deer. Often these stands are located along trails or habitat edges used by deer traveling from one place to another. During the rut, you are likely to see bucks using such trails. In Northern climates where deer migrate to wintering areas, different family groups of deer will use the same travelways from year to year. If you find one of these locations, by all means hunt it. But don't become so set in your ways that you refuse to try other stands.

You may decide to change stands during the course of a hunt if the wind changes direction or you think another location is better based on present conditions. Some hunters use a strategy where they sit for a while and then move to another stand. If you happen upon a fresh scrape or other sign, sit down on a nearby stump and wait. The rutting buck may be close at hand.

STILL-HUNTING

Still-hunting sounds deceptively like a simple method, but it is really a very difficult way to kill a whitetail. The name for this hunting method is a misnomer, because the still-hunter actually sneaks through the woods, hoping to encounter a deer. To be successful, the hunter must avoid detection by sight, sound, or scent. Still-hunting is typically a big-woods method because you need room to move around without encountering other hunters. However, you can sneak into any deer habitat under the right conditions.

Movement

Still-hunters use the wind to their advantage, always moving upwind or crosswind so the breeze doesn't deliver their scents to the deer. Weather conditions and terrain often cause shifts in wind direction, so you must

Still-hunting is anything but still—it is a time-consuming, energy-sapping process, but one that some hunters favor. Still-hunters use wind direction to their advantage, and are slow and deliberate in all movements.

Quick Tips: Still-Hunting

Still-hunting is both an art and a science. There are, of course, more efficient ways to harvest a buck, but none offer the deer hunter more pride and sense of accomplishment than still-hunting. These tips cannot guarantee you success, as there is no magic formula to bagging a buck.

- Use total camouflage. That means all outer clothing, exposed skin, and equipment must be dulled with earth-tone colors—unless you're hunting in the snow.

- Use a cold cream–based camouflage cream to cover your entire face, including ears, neck, forehead, and eyelids. A camo handkerchief also covers your neck and helps keep you warm when temperatures dip below freezing.

- Avoid wearing head nets because they invariably obscure your peripheral vision, muffle woodland sounds, and impair your ability to detect subtle changes in wind direction.

- Learn to mix and match your camo for ideal concealment in a variety of situations. A good rule of thumb is to match your upper body with what's above the forest floor, and your lower body to what is on the forest floor.

Early season still-hunting can be particularly challenging because the ability to still-hunt is diminished by all the crunchy leaves underfoot. It's best to make your noise early on the way to a stand and wait for the deer to come to you.

always adjust your strategy to hunt into the wind. A stiff breeze is beneficial because it masks your sounds and movements. However, deer may be especially wary when winds are strong.

Unlike the stander, who waits for deer to come to a specific place or pass by along a trail, the still-hunter goes where deer are most likely to be. Slow and deliberate movements are necessary to approach whitetails. Take a step or two and then stand still, looking and listening for deer. Don't move again until you are certain no deer are nearby. Every step changes your view of the surroundings. Stop often.

Wet or snowy weather creates prime still-hunting conditions because you can move quietly in the woods.

Take careful steps to avoid breaking sticks or making other sounds. Wear wool or similar soft clothing to minimize noise when you brush against vegetation. If possible, follow logging roads or pathways to walk quietly. Often, it is difficult to move without making sounds, but you should avoid the slow, steady footsteps that characterize a person walking.

Always use available cover to your advantage. Avoid unnecessary motions. Never step into openings; walk around the edge instead. Stand beside trees or behind brush and windfalls. Do not "skyline" yourself on hilltops. Sneak over the crest of ridges and carefully scrutinize new terrain before your body comes into full view.

Still-Hunting Tips

Learning to still-hunt takes time—and patience. Hone your skills every chance you get. Soon you'll be seeing fewer "flags" and getting more shots.

Never "skyline" yourself by walking over a ridge in an upright position. Instead sneak or peek over the top and use whatever available trees or brush there is to hide your movement.

By yelping on a turkey call, you may be able to convince a deer that the sound of your movement came from a turkey. Use this tactic only when the turkey season is closed.

Sight

The point of still-hunting is to get the drop on an unsuspecting whitetail. You must hear, see, or even smell the deer first. Experienced still-hunters learn to look for a piece of a deer—an ear, a leg, or the back line—that reveals an animal standing behind a screen of underbrush. Always look to the far edge of your field of vision because that is where a deer is most likely to be. If a whitetail detects your presence, but cannot catch your scent, it will often stand motionless until it can visually identify you as a human.

You should use binoculars to look for deer. Magnification makes it easier to spot deer screened by brush. While hunting, keep your scope magnification at 4X or less, so it will be easier to see a deer if you must make a quick shot.

Deer can show up at anytime, anywhere, no matter how sure you are that you're alone. Being ready for surprise appearances is often the difference between the thrill of a trophy buck and the remorse of seeing him run away.

Be sure to map out your still-hunting or driving strategy well before entering the woods. Nothing ruins a good hunt like walking in the wrong direction or wandering onto private land.

Sound

If you hear a deer, stop and get ready. If possible, lean against a tree or use cover to break your outline. The animal may be very close when you actually see it. Use a grunt or doe call to attract deer that may not otherwise come in your direction. If hunting conditions are quiet, you may be able to move and position yourself to intercept a deer that you can hear.

When still-hunting, you may hear a deer blow or make a sharp exhalation in alarm. The deer has heard or perhaps seen you, but hasn't identified you as a human. Very likely, it is just beyond your range of vision. Stop and scan the cover with your optics in the direction where you heard the deer. It probably won't approach any closer, but you may be able to pick it out in the brush. Respond to the deer with a couple of soft grunts. Often it will blow again and again before eventually

walking off. Some hunters believe does are most likely to blow, but bucks do, too. You may be able to move closer by taking quick steps that sound like a walking deer. Getting a shot is difficult because the animal will bound off when it determines that you are not a deer.

When you spook a deer while still-hunting, it may bound a short distance and stop until it determines if you are following. Often, deer will walk away from an approaching still-hunter or simply move out of your line of travel. Deer do only what is necessary to avoid danger. Rarely will a deer run a long distance to get away from a lone hunter.

Options

Two hunters can still-hunt as a team. Agree upon a strategy before you begin hunting. Separate and move

The Still-Hunting Advantage

The buck never knew I was there. I had been pussyfooting down an old logging trail, pausing every 5 yards or so, stopping every 20. I was standing next to a large hemlock, my body partially obscured by branches, watching the road in front of me, when I saw movement off to the right. A deer was moving down a trail that intersected the logging road 40 yards ahead.

Head down, nose to the ground, the buck was obviously following the scent of a doe. Caution was the last thing on his mind. When he reached the logging road, he skidded to a stop, turned, and looked right at me. Too late. I took him with one shot.

Still-hunting. It's a highly effective way of hunting deer, especially if you do it at the right time, in the right place, the right way.

When

Much depends upon the weather. On still days, with crunchy leaves or icy snow covering the ground, still-hunting is out of the question. No matter how quiet you try to be, you'll still make too much noise and spook any deer way before you can get within gun range. Better to remain in a tree stand on still days, and still-hunt on windy days, when gusts conceal your leaf crunching, or on damp or rainy days, when ground cover is wet and won't make noise when stepped on. Deer also tend to bed down on rainy and especially windy days, so your best chance of getting a shot at a buck under such conditions is to go find one, on foot, quietly.

Where

No matter what the weather, I like to still-hunt when I'm in new territory. While I prefer a tree stand when the situation is right, I don't have a clue where to put up a stand when I'm in unfamiliar country. Still-hunting lets me learn the property, plus it gives me a better chance at a deer than just putting up a stand in any old tree.

In damp or windy conditions, when deer are probably bedded down, I head to the thickest cover I can find. Rhododendron stands, hemlock groves, cedar swamps, thickets, steep ledges; anyplace a buck is likely to bed down is where I'll go. When hunting such spots, wear camo if the law allows, and move slower than slow. Deer pick these spots not only because they're sheltered, but also because they can watch for approaching danger.

Sometimes the deer find you, and sometimes you have to find the deer. On windy days, bucks like to bed down and wait until the wind dies so they can hear what's going on around them. These are good days to still-hunt, as you spook a buck into a favorable shooting lane.

When hunting tough-to-reach cover, pay special attention to the wind. Even if you're wearing a cover scent that's consistent with the area's vegetation, moving into an area with the wind at your back dictates that you stop and figure an alternative route. The brush may be ridiculously thick, or the ledges perilously steep, but common sense says you should try to circle around and approach from downwind. Being lazy and just barging ahead anyway will only ensure that you won't see deer.

How

This may sound like a cliché, but it's true: If you think you're going too fast, you are. Serious still-hunting means going painfully slow, so slow that it's almost boring. But you're doing this for a number of reasons. With each step you take, you have a different perspective of the woods. A bedded buck can come into view with just one or two steps. Take five or six, and that buck will detect your movement and be history before you even know he's there.

You're also moving slowly because you want to be quiet. Take each step carefully. Watch where you're putting your feet. If you suspect there might be a stick under the wet leaves you're about to step on, put your foot down slowly. Gradually increase the pressure, putting your weight first on your heel, then on the rest of your foot. As you go, if you can put your foot on a rock that won't tip, on moss, on snow—anything that you're certain won't make noise—do it. If you're in an area where you know your footsteps will be silent, then don't watch your feet. Instead, watch the woods in front of you and around you. I'm not talking woods that are 25 yards in front of you, either; rather, 100 yards or more. That's where you're likely to see a buck, not close up. Train yourself to look as far as you can see, and you'll start spotting deer you wouldn't have seen otherwise.

As you move through a given patch of woods, be aware of where the large, silhouette-breaking trees are located. Pause by them. The last thing you want to do is pause out in the open, because that's exactly when a buck is going to come walking into view and see you. Pause by trees, as I did on that logging road, boulders, blow downs, anything to break up your silhouette. And do it no matter where you are; even if you think you're in an area where you know a buck won't be, still-hunt carefully, and pause by large objects.

Be Ready

Three years ago I was hunting in New York's Catskill Mountains. I was way down the mountain, hunting virtually inaccessible ledges. With a lot of hunting pressure up top, I figured deer would be down low, away from the crowds. It was nearing the end of the season, there was snow on the ground, and it was late afternoon. The snow was somewhat crunchy, so I was moving extra carefully, placing my feet on rocks whenever feasible.

Dropping down to another ledge, I stopped next to a boulder. Generally when I stop, I don't move for at least five minutes, usually 10. Just as I was about to end my break and move another 25 yards or so, I heard something crunching off to my right. Sure enough, a doe and yearling appeared, moving along my ledge. To my surprise, they came to within 10 yards of me, then stopped and started to paw the ground, looking for food. They didn't see me at all. And while I was tempted to quietly say Boo, I stayed silent and motionless. I wanted to see what would happen.

What happened was that I heard more crunching off to my right. Now antlers came up over the lip of the ledge. It was a 7-pointer, just 30 yards away. He looked at the does and then froze, his widening eyes

riveted on me. He had me, but he didn't move; obviously the presence of the does so close to me had him confused. What would he do? I figured I'd better do something, because he'd probably bolt any second. Ever so slowly, I started to raise my rifle. If I could get it just halfway up to my shoulder, I could take a snap-shot and maybe get him.

Naturally, it didn't work that way. The retractable scope cap snapped on the zipper of my camo jacket. Both the doe and yearling heard it and looked right at me; then all hell broke loose. Throwing the gun to my shoulder, I looked through the scope and immediately saw brown. But it wasn't the buck! It was the yearling, running to my left, blocking my view of the buck. And within seconds it was over, as all three deer disappeared over the edge of the ledge. I took no shot at the buck, as the only shot I had, at the last split second, was a running kidney shot. Too risky, in that situation.

Lesson learned? Whenever I stop somewhere now, I never, never, hold my gun low on my body, no matter how tired I am. Port arms is always my rule now. And so is that time-honored piece of advice: Always be ready, because you never know.

—Jay Cassell, professional hunter and *Outdoor Life* contributor

Sloppy hunting techniques often lead to this—a whitetail diminishing in the distance. Not only have you lost the deer you were after, but their fleeing may have alerted other deer in the area.

Driving slowly toward known bedding areas is a surefire way to spook the deer, especially if the weather conditions are right.

through the cover, staying 100 yards or more apart. Move slowly and pause frequently. One hunter may rattle or call. A pair of hunters is more likely to see a deer that investigates the sounds.

Opportunities to kill a deer when still-hunting often occur quickly and at close range. Unlike the stand hunter, who is hidden in ambush, a still-hunter usually has just a few seconds to shoot after a deer comes into view.

Once you identify your target, you must get into a shooting position without being seen or heard by the deer. Wait to move until the animal turns or steps behind cover. Keep your motions slow and minimal. Make no noise when clicking a safety or drawing an arrow. Take the first available clear shot at the vitals once you've determined that the deer is of legal size and/or sex. If you wait for the "perfect shot," the deer may become aware of your presence and get away.

DRIVING

Deer drives are a team effort where a group of hunters are organized to walk through an area and push deer to other hunters posted on stands. An effective drive can be made by two hunters, or more than dozen. The key to success is knowing the whitetails' likely escape routes and placing standers to watch them. Driving is best used to roust deer from cover that is difficult to hunt by other methods.

Every deer drive begins with a plan and a leader to carry it out. When you are planning deer drives, a general rule of thumb is to not "bite off more than you can chew." The larger the area, the more likely whitetails will elude the hunters. Drives work best in patches of cover with definite boundaries—roads, field edges, creeks, or fencelines. This makes it easier to determine

Quick Tips for Driving

A deer drive's success depends on good organization. A group of hunters wandering haphazardly through the woods has little hope of shooting deer.

Every drive should have a leader who is familiar with the terrain. Before the drive, the leader gives clear instructions to each hunter. Posters take their stands first; each should wait in a spot with a good view, preferably from an elevated stand. Drivers synchronize their watches, then spread out across the upwind side of cover. Distance between the drives may be only 15 yards in dense cover or more than 50 yards if cover is sparse.

At the appointed time, drivers begin walking downwind. Deer soon detect the hunters' scents. They flush closer if drivers move quietly. Some deer move ahead, some double back, and others remain bedded down.

Driving can work anytime deer are in cover. But if you drive a block of cover too large, deer slip to the side and let the drivers pass.

Though effective, deer drives can be dangerous—limit the number of hunters so you can keep track of everyone's location. Posters in elevated stands also make a drive safer. Their shots angle toward the ground and they are above the normal shooting plane of the drivers.

- Watch closely for whitetails doubling back through the driving line. Deer may sneak back even though drivers are visible on both sides. As drivers approach posters, deer must double back or break into the open.

- Keep adjacent drivers in sight at all times. This prevents a hunter from moving too far ahead of the others and into the firing zone.

- Post near a known escape route. Deer often move from one block of woods to another by sneaking through a connecting patch of lighter cover.

When driving downwind from deer, it won't be long until they pick up the hunters' scents—this doe isn't fooled. The question is, what will she do, and will the hunters be prepared for it?

Some deer are simply nonplussed by drives, and remain bedded or hidden. This wily buck settles into the tall grass, hoping the hunters walk right by or around him.

where the deer are likely to be and helps keep the drive organized. For a deer drive to be effective and safe, every participant must understand his or her task and follow instructions.

You can make drives in all kinds of whitetail cover. Look for places the deer use as bedding areas or refuge. In the Northwoods, hunters make drives in conifer thickets or places where deer can be pushed to a forest trail or a clear-cut. Woodlots and cornfields are frequently driven in agricultural areas. Creek bottoms, set-aside fields, and brushy draws are prime locations in open country. In the South, hunters sometimes use dogs to drive deer from thick cover.

The drive leader must consider several factors when planning a drive. What direction is the wind blowing? What escape routes are deer likely to use? How many standers are needed to cover those escape routes? Can they move into position without spooking the deer?

Standers should be placed in locations where their scent will not be carried to deer fleeing ahead of the drivers.

The drive leader decides who walks and who posts. Generally, the most experienced hunters and best shots should take stands. Less experienced hunters can be drivers, provided they have a good sense of direction. Drives work best when the group has previously hunted together and most of the hunters are familiar with the land.

Making the Drive

Standers quietly move into their positions. Park vehicles away from the hunting area. Sneak along without talking. Whenever possible, place standers in elevated positions, such as in tree stands. This makes it easier to see deer and puts the line of fire toward the ground, which is safer. Standers must clearly understand where

Making a drive is not as easy as it looks. It requires patience and skill, and a good driver knows when to take the shot, and when to back off.

Types of Drives

Hunters with knowledge of whitetail behavior can successfully drive the animals toward waiting standers posted strategically along escape routes.

Different terrains require different methods. Here are some tried-and-true setups that are sure to increase your odds:

Funnel drives take advantage of funnels through which deer are forced by drivers. Funnel drives require fewer standers than drives through wider expanses of cover. To prevent deer from slipping back through drivers in heavy cover, a middle driver drops out and takes a stand as the drive passes the narrowest area and continues.

Ravine drives also work well with two hunters, but wide ravines require more drivers. Select a ravine where the wind is blowing parallel to it and toward its head. Hunter A starts at the bottom of the ravine and begins walking uphill. Hunter B is on stand near the head, but about 75 yards in from the tip, for shots at slow-moving deer.

Hopscotch drives are ideal for two hunters. They begin the drive from opposite ends of the cover. Hunter A moves slowly toward hunter B for about half an hour; A then sits quietly for about half an hour as B closes the gap. Because each hunter alternates between driving and posting, both have an equal chance of seeing deer.

A good drive often covers many different forms of habitat, including man-made roads and other structures.

other standers are located and where the drivers will appear, and not take shots in those directions.

The drive leader arranges the drivers on the other side of the cover, keeping noise and commotion to a minimum. The distance between drivers is determined by the terrain and vegetation. In most situations, the drivers should be close enough to occasionally see one another as they make the drive. The drive leader can give each driver a compass bearing to help him or her stay on course. In some hunting parties, drivers are unarmed. If the drivers carry firearms, firm rules should be established to ensure only safe shots are taken.

A signal from the drive leader begins the drive. The drivers should move forward at an agreed-upon pace, typically a slow walk. Making excessive noise is unnecessary because the deer will sense the presence of drivers and move ahead of them. It is more important that drivers go through heavy cover where deer may try to hide and let them pass by. Watch for whitetails that try to double back and sneak between the drivers or cut out from the flanks.

You don't need a gang of hunters to make a drive. Often, two or three hunters working in concert are more effective. Small drives are most often a combination of stand and still-hunting. While one hunter waits in an elevated stand or ground blind, the other hunter sneaks through likely cover and tries to push a deer toward the stander. This is an excellent midmorning tactic because

Driving Safety

Drives inherently have more safety risks than other hunting methods because the deer may go between hunters. It is imperative that every hunter participating in a drive puts safety first. To prevent accidents, consider the following:

- Always follow the drive leader's instructions.

- Never shoot in the direction of other hunters, even if they are out of sight.

- When walking, don't get ahead of the other hunters on the drive.

- When taking a stand, consider the directions where you can safely shoot. When you see a deer, make sure it is within one of your safe shooting windows before pulling the trigger.

- Only shoot at deer running across open fields if you have a safe backstop.

- If you are uncomfortable with the safety skills of another hunter in the party, quietly voice your concerns to the drive leader.

- Be aware that other hunters who are not members of your party may be in the drive area.

both hunters can sit during the prime early hours and then one can make a push to the other.

Two or three hunters can also move deer from small islands of cover in agricultural areas. Whitetails, especially bucks, will hide in a weedy patch, a fencerow, or a cattail slough where most hunters are unlikely to look for them. Try to stealthily approach small covers from opposite directions. Expect fast shots at running deer.

With snow, sometimes you'll happen upon fresh deer tracks and be able to predict where the whitetail is likely to go. One hunter follows the tracks while one or two other hunters, circle around, and post in likely locations. The tracker must be patient and give the standers sufficient time to get into position before going after the deer.

GLASSING AND STALKING

Hunting an animal you've sighted is called stalking and is an exceptionally challenging way to kill a deer. While in some instances, particularly in the West, you may stalk deer while hunting with a gun, most often the technique is used by experienced bowhunters. To sneak within

Veteran hunters often serve as the drive leaders. They know the land, the habits, and sometimes even the tricks of local bucks. They can be depended upon to set the pace of the drive, when and where to stop, and when it's time to switch tactics.

One advantage of making a drive in the winter is the ability to stalk a deer using its tracks in the snow. Savvy hunters know that the same rules apply, however—walk slowly, stop often, and keep your eyes and ears open.

archery range of a whitetail is among hunting's greatest accomplishments. Glassing is a term often found hand-in-hand with stalking; it merely refers to using enhanced optics, such as binoculars or a spotting scope, to aid your hunt.

Glassing and stalking is a good method to use on whitetails in any open country, including agricultural areas mixed with sloughs, woods and draws, mountain foothills, and canyons and broken country in the West, where whitetails live along wooded creeks and rivers. Watching from a high point with binoculars or spotting scope to locate deer feeding, bedded, or moving about may be the only option for whitetail hunting in the rugged hill country of Texas. Coues deer in southern Arizona and New Mexico are usually spotted from a long distance, then stalked to within gun range. Any place in whitetail range where there are wide-open spaces and vantage points high enough to see down into cover is good for glassing and stalking.

Study your hunting area to see if you're missing a bet by not using this method. If there are ridges, hilltops, rimrock, or points that overlook feeding locations, bedding areas, trails, travel corridors, funnels, or cover edges, you've got possibilities. If the terrain allows either shooting from the vantage points or planned stalks to within range, you've got to add this method to your repertoire of hunting techniques.

By glassing and stalking, you can hunt large areas with a small expense of energy and you can cover heavy deer-use areas with only your eyes, leaving no scent or other sign of your intrusion. You can also observe deer that are usually undisturbed and map their patterns even when a stalk or shot won't work at the moment. Glass-and-stalk can lead you to use other techniques. If you repeatedly observe a big buck feeding at dawn in the edge of a crop field, set up a stand or blind there and he's likely to come by the next morning. Glassing and stalking when deer activity increases during the rut can also create some opportunities at big bucks.

Top-quality optics are essential to effective glassing and stalking. The basic tools are binoculars, a spotting scope, and rifle scope. Binoculars are generally used to cover wide expanses of territory. The best binoculars for this technique are full-sized models that can be worn comfortably around the neck in the 7x35 to 10x40 range. More powerful binoculars are too hard to hold still for

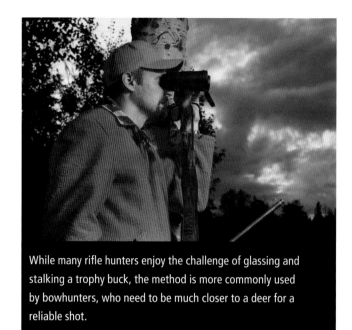

While many rifle hunters enjoy the challenge of glassing and stalking a trophy buck, the method is more commonly used by bowhunters, who need to be much closer to a deer for a reliable shot.

Magnification isn't limited to only binoculars while hunting—many hunters use high-powered spotting scopes before the season to learn where and how deer move through a particular area. Intimate knowledge of the land you'll be hunting will prove invaluable when the season arrives.

effective glassing. Pocket-sized binoculars are popular because of their light weight, but most of these models do not perform well under low-light conditions, such as those found at dawn and dusk.

A spotting scope has a longer optical reach, which helps you zero in on a buck you've found with the glasses. Using the extra power of the scope, you can size up his trophy potential by counting points, estimating the mass and horn spread. Always use a tripod on a spotting scope; you simply cannot hold a high-power optic still enough to zero in on game. A 20x, 30x, or 40x fixed-power scope works well for most deer-hunting situations; however, a zoom or variable-power scope has some advantages. With the zoom, you can scope a wide area at low power, then increase the magnification for a closer look.

Sometimes glass-and-stalk becomes glass-and-shoot because the terrain or cover will not permit a stalk to closer range. The unseen steep canyon or open field may necessitate that the shot be taken from there or passed. In these circumstances, a scoped, flat-shooting rifle sighted in for long-range shots is a must. A variable-power scope providing a bright, sharp sight picture complements a rifle with long-range capability. Shots through a hole in brush at 100 yards or a 300-yard shot across a canyon may be necessary. A variable-power

Shooting an arrow requires strength of body and strength of mind—you must be patient enough to not only get near the deer, but patient to raise the bow without being seen, patient to draw the bowstring and arrow back, and patient to finally release the arrow when a favorable shot arises. Bowhunting is a lot of things, but it's not easy.

Glassing and stalking pits your ears and eyes against the deer's ears and eyes, and represents a considerable challenge (with considerable bragging rights). The moment a whitetail is spooked is often the moment it runs.

Hunting Mature Bucks

According to Toby Bridges, a dedicated muzzleloader and trophy whitetail hunter, "The key to tagging a certified trophy buck, one of those heavy, old bruisers with the rocking-chair rack everybody dreams of, is to hunt where one lives." He adds, "That sounds obvious, but it's the ultimate reality of trophy hunting. You can have the best equipment and the best tactics in the world. You can have the sharpest eyes and be the best stalker since Daniel Boone. But if there aren't any old bucks living where you hunt, the only thing you'll get is disappointment."

Toby is right, of course. The most important part of any trophy whitetail hunt is finding an area where bucks have survived long enough to grow large antlers. Trophy bucks are almost always old bucks.

Preparation Basics

Hunting for large, mature bucks is most successful in areas with light hunting pressure, low to moderate deer densities, and buck-to-doe ratios of 1:2 or 1:3. Wildlife management agencies can provide you with these statistics. Don't be concerned if hunter-success statistics are low. High hunter success generally means only that large numbers of immature bucks are being taken each year.

As a rule, areas with high deer densities are hunted so heavily that bucks rarely live past 3½ years. In some places, 90 percent of all antlered bucks are killed each season. And if there is a high ratio of females to bucks, the males don't engage in normal, competitive rutting behavior and are therefore difficult to lure with rattling, calling, decoying, or scrape-hunting strategies.

Here are a few things you can do to up your odds of learning where the big bucks live:

- Study topographical maps and aerial photos to find isolated habitat where few hunters penetrate.
- Talk to rural mail carriers, UPS drivers, and farmers who may have seen large bucks.
- If possible, scour the winter range after snow melt, looking for shed antlers.
- Drive area roads at dawn and dusk, and watch feed fields with binoculars.
- Visit local taxidermists and learn what the trophy potential is for the area. What's the usual rack size? How many recordbook bucks are taken each year?

When you've discovered a suitable hunting area, begin narrowing your search. Your goal is to locate at least three trophy bucks so you'll have hunting opportunities throughout the season, even if someone else kills one of "your" bucks. If you actually spot the bucks, great; but it's likely you'll have to settle for second-hand evidence, such as finding large tracks or big shed antlers, or a description from an eyewitness. Try to get permission to hunt as much land as possible. Your chances of harvesting a buck will be greatest if you have permission to hunt the land around his bedding area, because this is where he spends most of his time.

How to Hunt for Trophies

Once you've confirmed the existence of a mature buck, the hard part is over and the fun begins. Forget the old myths about superbucks. There is nothing supernatural about a trophy buck, and no reason for you to feel intimidated. A stupendous set of antlers simply means the buck is old, and the main reason he's old is probably because hunting pressure has been light in his territory. The argument about whether an old buck is more intelligent than other deer will probably never be resolved, but one thing is certain: During the rut your buck will be susceptible to the same strategies that work with younger bucks—rattling, decoying, calling, and using scents.

But there's no denying that the trophy buck is a special animal that requires a special hunter with unusual dedication, patience, and restraint. For one thing, a mature trophy buck is calmer and less energetic than the young guys. Rather than dashing about and exposing himself to hunters, he's learned to lay low and watch carefully, knowing that most humans will overlook him. As a veteran of many seasons, he's used to seeing, smelling, and hearing hunters at dawn and dusk, so he generally waits until night to move about.

The old buck is a creature of leisure and habit, with periodic moments of energy. He lies resting most of the daylight hours, and often chooses the shortest distances possible between food, water, and bed. If he found refuge on an island during one hunting season, he'll remember to seek out the same island in following seasons. Only during the rut does the old boy rouse himself for frenzied action—this is your best chance for taking him.

Seasoned trophy hunters know that information is power. Learn as much as possible about your quarry: Where, when, and what does your buck eat? Where does he drink? Where does he sleep, walk, rub, scrape, and chase females? Where does he hide when hunting pressure gets intense? It may take several years to piece together such a profile, but once you know your buck this well, you're ready for the most memorable hunt of your life.

Fresh tracks like this one have well-defined edges. Remember that the landscape itself can tell you whether a track is old or new—tracks in snow will freeze after some time, but be soft and supple if a deer recently made them.

scope set at 8 or 9x helps increase the chances of a good shot.

The glass-and-stalk hunter using a bow, shotgun, or muzzleloader accepts the challenge of stalking to within the limited range of the weapon. The stalk must be carefully planned and executed to be successful. Quiet clothing, soft, padded shoes, or sneakers and as much outer-camo as the law allows can help in the final stages of a close-in sneak.

How to Glass-and-Stalk

Tony Oliva, a former Minnesota Twins player, had a simple approach to hitting: "See ball, hit ball." Glass-and-stalk appears as simple: see buck, sneak in, shoot buck. This is easier said than done, however. Much easier!

First, select one or more vantage points on hilltops, ridges, canyon rims, or points overlooking areas frequently used by deer. Elevation is key; the higher the better, since you want to be able to see down into cover. Plan your stalk to approach from downwind. Even if your vantage point is a long way from the deer, stay out of sight as you move into position to begin the stalk. Go as quickly as you can.

Do not skyline yourself; use available natural cover or terrain as a background. Keep movement slow and minimal. Be on your first vantage point at first light. Scan the entire area, but concentrate first on crop fields and other open feeding areas. On subsequent scans, as the light improves, check field edges, fencerows, ravines, and other shadowed places. You may see deer feeding in fields or clear-cuts. Scan sunny ridges for bedded whitetails. When you see a deer, look for a landmark so you can get a fix on its position. Be sure to pick a landmark that will be visible as you move closer and from different angles.

If you have more than one vantage point, change locations as soon as you have thoroughly looked over an area. Move to another place along the most concealed, quietest route. Again, do not move along the skyline. Change locations slightly to get a different sight angle into the cover. Bedded deer are especially hard to see. However, a buck will occasionally get up, urinate, and move to another bedding location.

You will only see an entire deer when one is standing in a wide-open place, such as a field or clearing. At most times you will be looking for a piece of a deer—the horizontal line of a back, wag of a tail, flick of an ear, or slight head movement. Sun glinting off an antler tip should really get your attention. Concentrate on any spot that shows even the slightest movement until you're certain it is not a deer. Birds, rabbits, and other animals can be deceptive; make sure not to overlook any possibility.

Wet or snowy conditions are best for stalking because you'll make the least amount of noise. Stay out of sight as long as possible. Crouch like a cat stalking a songbird in your backyard. The closer you get to the deer, the more difficult the stalk becomes. Never move when the animal is alert and studying its surroundings, even if it isn't looking at you. Avert your eyes if the deer is looking in your direction. You don't want to make eye contact. If the deer is feeding or walking, it may be easier to sneak to a position where the deer will come closer to you.

Sometimes, the deer will hear you make a noise or somehow sense your presence. It may look your way, perhaps even staring to try to discern what you are. If it can't smell you or detect movement, it may eventually look away and show little concern. Be aware, though, that deer quickly notice something out of the ordinary. Even if you are camouflaged, a whitetail may identify you as an object it hasn't seen before. If it does, you'll have a tough time getting any closer to it.

If he's bedded, reference the spot by some physical landmark. If the deer is moving, try to determine his speed and travel direction and pick a likely ambush spot. Plan the stalk along a route where you can be completely concealed by terrain features or cover. Be aware of wind direction; take pains to stay downwind from the target's approach. Reference your planned route by landmarks and physical features, recognizing that the terrain will look different up close than it did from above. Be prepared to crawl to reach a shooting range and position.

Once your target is in sight, get into a solid, comfortable shooting position. Use a tree, rock, or other object that will provide a solid rest. Some hunters have a bipod installed on the rifle's fore-end; others carry crossed sticks to make a rest. When the target is within your shooting-confidence range, align the sights, and place the shot.

Glass-and-stalk isn't for everyone—some enjoy the quiet peace and relative invisibility of the tree stand to the feeling of being exposed in the woods, even when covered in camo. The feeling of successfully stalking a trophy whitetail is second to none, however, and will garner serious bragging rights at deer camp for years to come.

Because bucks are so active during the rut, it is not rare to come across one or multiple paths of wandering bucks. Use the signs around you to find a trophy buck!

A deer relies on its sense of smell to survive from the day it is born. It is much easier for a buck to disregard danger he sees or hears than if he smells something that alarms him.

Stalking in Standing Corn

A version of the stalk is to sneak from row to row through a standing cornfield. Whitetails frequently use corn as secure feeding and bedding areas. From a downwind or crosswind position, sneak through the field perpendicular to the rows. The sound of a breeze rustling the stalks will help conceal any noise you make. Look down a row before you step into it.

Taking the Shot

Deer killed by stalking are often taken at close range, especially if you are bowhunting. Slow movements and patience have put you in a shooting position. Now you must move even slower. If at all possible, wait until the deer's head is behind a tree or some other object before lifting your gun or drawing your bow. Otherwise, make your movements so slow that they are imperceptible. It may take minutes to get into a shooting position.

TRACKING

Tracks provide evidence that deer are living and traveling in specific areas. The clues left by tracks can often lead to more confusion than information, however. For instance, finding a single deep track that shows the dew claws only means you have discovered the track of a heavy deer—buck or doe. Beyond that, and despite what many old-timers might say, most biologists agree that it is impossible to definitely identify the sex of the deer from its tracks.

There are dependable indications left by tracks, however, which will help a hunter make a more educated determination as to the probable sex of the deer. For example, tracks that show the spreading of the toes on a hoof and do not appear to be pigeon-toed generally belong to a buck. If you are following tracks that meander throughout the woods, you can bet you are on the trail of a doe. Bucks walk with a purpose. Their tracks will often move from point A to point B while taking the path of least resistance. When a buck meets an obstacle, he will often walk around it (unlike a doe, which will often

Prevailing winds and differing currents play a daily role in the savvy hunter's season. By paying attention to how and where winds are moving, a hunter can position himself on the ground or in a stand to minimize his scent and maximize his chances of seeing a buck.

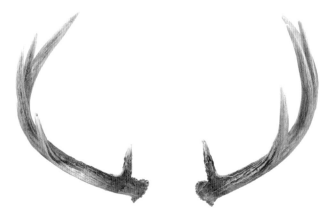

A pair of rattling antlers is a valuable tool in your arsenal. Some hunters swear by the real thing, using only fallen antlers from real deer, while others are happy with artificial antlers. Either way, there is no denying that if you rattle well, bucks will hear you…and maybe come calling.

Besides rattling antlers, a buck call is a common tool for the whitetail hunter. Snorts, bleats, and grunts can all be replicated, and knowing when and how to grunt is another ability developed over time. Using tools like these is one way to make the deer come to you instead of the other way around.

walk under it) and then resume his line of direction. In addition, when a buck urinates, he drips urine into his tracks. A doe squats and urinates in one place.

The ability to follow deer tracks in a variety of conditions is the mark of a good hunter. Tracking skills are essential to following a deer after you make a shot. A print in the soil, a turned-over leaf, or a broken twig may be your clues to finding a mortally wounded deer. Such tracking skills are acquired only through experience.

Another set of skills is needed to track deer as part of your hunting strategy, a method typically used when snow blankets the ground. You must be able to recognize fresh deer tracks, have a general idea where the animal is headed, and then follow them quickly and quietly so you can close the distance for a shot. Hunters often track deer in North Country areas with a low deer density, where stand hunting is unproductive.

About Tracks

Generally, fresh deer tracks have well-defined edges. With very fresh tracks, you may find muddy water where the deer walked through a puddle or even see water oozing into muddy tracks. Older tracks have crumbling edges and are hard to the touch. In snow, fresh tracks will be soft when you touch them. Old tracks have frozen edges.

Tracking Strategy

The best tracking conditions are soft, fresh snow, because you can follow tracks with less likelihood of becoming confused by the tracks of other deer, especially on well-trodden trails. Fresh snow is quiet underfoot, so you can walk without making noise. Often deer are on the move during and after snowfalls.

Tracking is rarely a matter of finding tracks and following them until you catch up with the deer. Most of the time, the deer will become aware of your presence before you see it and bound away. If the animal beds, it will be watching its backtrail. Also, deer have a tendency to go through thickets and tangles that most hunters would rather avoid. If you try to stay on the tracks, most likely you'll make noise in the heavy cover.

A better strategy is to think like a deer. Follow the tracks far enough to get a sense of where the deer is headed. Pay keen attention to wind direction because the deer will walk upwind or crosswind. Then plan your course. Perhaps you can walk parallel to the tracks and watch for the deer out ahead. In hilly terrain, you may find a vista where you can watch for the deer crossing a ridge or valley. Often, the best strategy is to guess where the deer is going and then try to intercept it.

Tracking with a Partner

Two hunters can track better than one. Working as a team, one hunter closely follows the tracks, while the other still-hunts on a parallel course. By staying slightly ahead of the tracker, the still-hunter may be able to get into a position for a shot.

Sometimes, in a variety of conditions, you may encounter very fresh deer tracks. Immediately begin to hunt as if the deer is close at hand. Often, it is. Stand still, watch and listen. If you know the country, you may be able to head off the deer. Hustle (quietly) to your ambush point and wait. If the deer doesn't appear, still-hunt toward the place where you first saw its tracks.

Go for Bucks

Tracking is a good way to hunt bucks, especially when they are active during the rut. It is easy to recognize their large, solitary tracks. Bucks are built differently at the hips than does, and sway and rock slightly side-to-side when they walk. This gives a buck the tendency to drag his feet, especially in the snow. A buck will drag his hooves rather than daintily lift them as a doe will.

A track accompanied by a drag mark will most likely belong to a buck. The deeper and longer the drag mark, the older and heavier the buck. To further confirm your findings, measure the size of the track. Generally, tracks that measure 4 to 5 inches long belong to 2-year-old bucks. You can bet that tracks larger than 5 inches long are from mature bucks (3 to 6 years old).

Remember that bucks usually appear to be going someplace, headed on a straight course. Does are more likely to meander. A good strategy is to cut away from the tracks and try to beat the buck to his destination.

If you follow a buck, it will likely lead you to other deer. A rutting buck will be looking for does or it may associate with local family groups. Tracking gets tricky when you run into other deer because it may be hard to follow the original set of tracks. Also, you are more likely to startle a deer, which may alarm others.

If you're hunting an area where you've noted does before, consider using a bleat call to attract an overprotective doe; hot on her tail could be a buck.

Some hunters employ old-fashioned scent with modern technology. This bowhunter is checking a trail cam, a device that photographs wandering wildlife. By scenting around an area and checking the video from the trail cam, he can determine if his strategic scenting is successful.

RATTLING, CALLING, AND USING SCENTS

Serious hunters know that whitetails depend on their senses of hearing, sight, and smell to survive. They also know how to manipulate those senses to their advantage.

Nothing plays a more important role in a buck's daily existence and survival than his sense of smell. He may occasionally ignore danger signals he sees or hears, but he will never disregard those he smells. White-tailed deer depend on their sense of smell, and use even the slightest air currents to pinpoint danger, water, and food sources

and estrous does. Therefore, the hunter who pays attention to wind direction is the one who will see, and ultimately shoot, the most deer.

Whitetails can be attracted to sounds they expect to be made by other deer. The clatter of antlers, guttural grunts of a rutting buck, and distress bleats are sounds you can make to draw deer out of the cover. Though effective, noise-making strategies require confidence because they seem counter to the silent approach that typifies whitetail hunting.

Various scents are used to attract deer, too. A whitetail uses its keen nose not only to detect danger, but to find food and other deer. A variety of commercial and natural scents can be used to lure deer or to cover up your human scent.

Meteorologists define wind as air in horizontal motion relative to the surface of the earth. It can be broken down further into ascending and descending currents. Wind normally picks up during the day, as the temperature increases, and slows in the late afternoon around sunset. If it doesn't slow at sunset, the barometric pressure is going to change and deer will be moving about more than usual.

If the weather is stable, deer will stick to their normal routines. This is when you should pay close attention to prevailing winds, and convection and thermal currents.

PREVAILING WINDS

These are regional currents that blow in the same direction nearly every day. (When they don't, it's usually because of changes in barometric pressure.) Such predictability makes them an important factor in choosing a stand location, especially when you're going to post in a field, bottleneck, or ravine.

To determine the direction of the prevailing wind in a specific area, post there several times and keep track of where the wind comes from, and where it goes. Write down your findings! After you've done this a number of times, you'll have a good idea of the area's currents, and can then put up your stand in a spot where your scent won't be carried to where deer are likely to appear. Keep in mind that major airflow in much of the United States is from slightly southwest to slightly northeast.

CONVECTION CURRENTS

Convection currents are caused by heat rising off large objects, such as boulders, or wind deflected off trees, rocks, and other terrain features. They are indigenous to a particular terrain, often blow in an entirely different direction from the prevailing wind, and can cause you a lot of problems if you don't know how to read them.

Be aware that a convection current may be present in your area, and adjust your location accordingly. To detect one, hang a strand of thread from a branch and observe how it blows in relation to the prevailing wind. At times, you'll be amazed to see it flag contrary to the direction of the prevailing wind; other times, it will conform to it.

THERMAL CURRENTS

Hunters should pay special attention to thermal currents in early morning and late afternoon. At dawn, as the temperature normally begins to rise, thermal currents flow upward. Conversely, as evening approaches and the temperature begins to drop, thermal currents flow downward. A hunter who takes a stand at dawn should position himself above the area where he expects to

Grunt Work

A deep, guttural vocalization made through a tube call imitates the sound bucks make when they're either with a hot doe or actively looking for one. I've seen and heard bucks grunt throughout all stages of the rut. Unfortunately, although I've used the call during that period, I've had limited success. I have come to the conclusion that with all those hunters in the woods blowing on grunt calls, many deer now associate the sound with the presence of a human being and have therefore learned to avoid it. This is true especially at the beginning of the season, when the woods are full of grunting hunters, so in the past few years I've remained quiet at this time, during the gun season in particular.

In the early bow season, or in the latter half of the gun season, I use the grunt call fairly often. And while I've spooked deer with the call—they either figured out that I was a human grunter, or else thought I was a larger buck that they didn't want to mess with—I have also called a few bucks in. It really seems to depend upon the individual buck. If a buck is hot after a doe and hears a grunt, he's more likely to investigate than if he were just going about his daily routines. Sometimes rattling antlers in conjunction with grunt calling has worked, too.

—Jay Cassell, professional hunter and *Outdoor Life* contributor see deer. By doing so, his scent will rise. The same stand should be avoided in the evening, however, because his scent will be carried downhill.

You can beat thermal, convection, and prevailing wind currents by reacting like a buck. A buck who has survived a couple of seasons has learned how to keep the prevailing winds blowing in his face, and therefore has alternate routes leading to and from bedding areas. Likewise, when you set up your stand, you should have alternate approach routes to use as wind currents dictate.

RATTLING

Rattling may not bring in a buck every time, but it's so effective when done correctly that every hunter should know how to do it. Before, during, and after the rut, you can mimic the sounds of fighting whitetails to attract bucks, and some hunters swear no other tactic can beat it— where there's rattlin' bucks, there's a doe nearby. Maybe your trophy buck is hoping for a fight!

Rattling is a hunting technique that originated in Texas, but is used successfully wherever whitetails are found. It is one of the best ways to overcome the innate wariness of an adult buck and make it come to you. Veteran deer hunters consider rattling one of the most exciting hunting methods. However, rattling is generally inefficient during firearms seasons in areas with heavy hunting pressure.

To rattle, all you need is a pair of antlers not attached to the skull plate. You can use shed antlers or saw the antlers from an intact rack. Each antler should have three or four tines. Saw off the brow tines to make it easier to hold the antlers. If you don't have real deer antlers, commercial substitutes are available, including synthetic antlers and various rattling bags or calls. Some commercial products are more convenient to carry in the field than the real thing.

First, the terminology. There are two basic rattling techniques: ticking (or tickling) and aggressive rattling, and each has distinct sounds and meanings. Confuse the two and you'll be wasting your hunting time. Ticking is done by lightly clicking the tips of your rattling antlers to imitate the sounds of two bucks sparring. Aggressive rattling starts with a slight ticking and builds to a crescendo of noisy, violent clashing that sounds like two bucks engaged in an all-out fight.

Ticking can be used throughout the breeding season, when bucks are just pushing each other around, not seriously fighting. Bucks that respond to ticking generally do so quite cautiously. As the rut progresses and sex-crazed bucks have zero tolerance for other males—especially transient ones that have moved into the area, searching for estrous does—more serious fights start to break out. Full-scale rattling works best now, and attracts more aggressive, bigger bucks that are generally less cautious than usual. Other times to use it are during periods of significant buck movement, intense scraping, and rubbing activity, and when lone estrous does are on the move.

There are several ideal times to rattle. Each one lasts two to three days and coincides with one of the three different rut cycles (false rut, primary rut, and post-rut). Some hunters swear that the last week of October is the prime time to draw bucks in by ticking. By this time, bucks start becoming belligerent and spend a lot of time chasing competitors (as well as potential estrous does) and sparring with them. Bachelor groups begin to disperse at this time, with bucks moving out of their own territory in search of receptive does.

The best time to draw in a big buck with aggressive rattling is November 10 to 13. Bucks are ranging far and wide now, and are sexually frustrated enough to be in a perpetually nasty mood. They will respond quickly and enthusiastically to the sounds of a full-scale fight during this period. Using a buck decoy can be especially effective at this time.

The final prime time for rattling is during the late rut in December, usually from the 13th to the 15th. Does that have not been bred enter another estrous cycle during this phase of the rut. They attract a lot of buck attention, as there aren't many of them to go around. Once again, bucks from surrounding areas enter the turf of resident bucks, with many skirmishes the end result.

The best time to rattle or tick is usually between 10:00 a.m. and 1:00 p.m., when the woods are quiet and generally free of hunters. Bucks often move during these off-hours, seeking does and checking and freshening scrapes. Dawn and dusk are also good times, although low-light conditions may hamper your ability to see incoming bucks, especially ones in thick cover.

Scents and Glands

Savvy hunters know whitetails have external scent glands that play a significant role in their communication and behavior; different odors serve to alert, calm, attract, frighten, or identify one another, even establish a deer's rank within the herd. By knowing precisely which glands the animals use, when they use them and why, you can employ scents to elicit a variety of responses and create opportunities that wouldn't exist otherwise.

Whitetails have powerful olfactory senses that allow them to communicate, find food, and avoid predators. Deer usually walk upwind or crosswind so they can use their nose to determine what lies ahead. Hunters take advantage of this trait when they employ scent strategies.

Hunters typically use deer urine, scents derived from whitetail glands, food attractors, or scents intended to cover human odor. Dozens of commercial scent products are available. Some hunters use glands taken from deer.

Tarsal A true external gland, the tarsal is located on the inner part of the hind legs of all deer. This tan gland turns almost black as bucks urinate on it throughout the rut. Deer use tarsal gland pheromones (a type of animal chemical) several ways: as a visual and olfactory signal of a mature buck; as an alarm; as an i.d. for individual deer; and, in a mature deer in rut, as an indicator that an individual is ready to breed. When a buck is aroused, the hairs on the tarsal gland stand erect and can be seen from quite a distance by other deer. All deer urinate on the tarsal gland, contributing to its pungent odor. Some hunters cut the tarsal gland from a freshly killed buck to use on subsequent hunts.

To get a response during the rut, put several drops of commercial tarsal scent on a boot pad and hang the pad from a branch near your position. The odor will permeate the area and act as a deer attractant or agitator. Don't place it on your clothing, as you don't want deer focusing on you.

Metatarsal The function of the metatarsal gland, located in a white tuft of hair on the outer portion of the hind legs just above the dewclaws, is unclear. Some biologists believe it is atrophying and has no purpose. Others believe it emits a pheromone that deer use to identify and warn one another of danger. In any event, when you use metatarsal scent, use it sparingly, and be ready for anything.

Preorbital This gland lies just below the inner corner of the eye, where it acts mainly as a tear duct, though deer will also rub it on bushes, branches, and limbs, especially during the rut. Biologists speculate the gland secretes a pheromone that deer use to mark certain areas and to help identify one another. Hunters can achieve best results by placing a small amount of the scent on a branch directly above a mock scrape.

Interdigital The offensive, potent odor of the yellow waxy substance produced by the interdigital gland is like a human fingerprint, individual to each deer. Used sparingly, interdigital scent both attracts and calms whitetails; large quantities of it, however, will do the opposite, since it signals danger. The gland is located in the cleft of the hoof, and all deer leave minute amounts of the scent as they walk. Other deer will follow a trail marked with a normal amount of it. When hunting, put only one or two drops of this commercial scent on a boot pad.

"New" Glands Research has discovered additional glands that deer may use in breeding activities. According to Dr. Karl Miller, of the University of Georgia, an expert on the physiology of whitetails, three glands in particular seem to be of importance. The first, at the base of each antler, is called the forehead gland (and is sometimes referred to as the orbital gland). During the rut, the thick hairs covering the gland swell and produce a scent, specific to that buck, which he deposits on trees as he is rubbing. Other bucks and does inspecting the area will smell and lick the rubs.

The Nasal Gland Inside a deer's nostrils, this gland consists of two almond-shaped sacs. Scientists speculate that bucks use this gland to mark overhead branches when making a scrape.

The Preputial Gland Located inside the buck's penile sheath, it is still being studied. Research shows that this gland doesn't play a significant role in producing the rutting odor of bucks during the breeding season.

Good rattling goes hand in hand with bad weather. A cold, overcast day with drizzling rain or spitting snow, or a forecast of precipitation, is perfect. If it has rained or snowed heavily, the following morning will also be prime. A steady breeze or wind is okay for rattling, but if there are heavy gusts, forget it, as deer are reluctant to move when they can't hear above the wind. A warm, bluebird day, when deer are apt to bed down, also means that rattling will probably be a waste of time.

The spot you choose to rattle from plays only a minor role. If a buck wants to respond to your rattling or ticking, he will. The important thing about location is cover. When you rattle and tick, you move a lot. You can't help it. But what you can do is break up your outline with surrounding cover. If you don't get a response to your rattling within an hour or so, consider changing locations. Some hunters believe the key to successful rattling is to be constantly on the move. These guys never stay in one spot for more than an hour unless they get a response.

Ultimately, the decision on whether to move from a spot or stay there rests with you. If you have a good feeling about it, and suspect that a buck is eventually going to show up, then it makes sense to stick around for a while. It's all a matter of timing.

Rattling Tips

Quietly approach your rattling site, taking care not to spook the deer with human sounds or scent. Remember, the deer must be within earshot of your location to be attracted to the sound. You can set up in a ground blind or tree stand, so long as you have a good view—especially downwind. Two hunters can take separate positions.

You can use a cover scent to disguise your scent and place an attractor scent downwind and to the side of your location. However, the more you move around, the more likely you are to alert whitetails to your presence. Make sure your gun or bow is positioned so you can pick it up with minimal movement. A buck may appear at any time once you begin rattling.

Start out by clicking the tines gently a few times, then pause for a few minutes. Rattle more loudly the second time. Make it sound as though two bucks are clashing and then stepping back. Keep your rattling

time short—a couple of minutes is about right. Pause for several minutes and then rattle again. The entire sequence should take 15 or 20 minutes. When you are done, wait patiently for approaching deer because a big buck may take his time.

You can add realism to your rattling by incorporating other sounds. Start your sequence with a few soft grunts. Rake the antlers in the brush or leaf litter. Break sticks or stamp your feet to make the sounds of a fight.

CALLING

Take a look at almost any deer hunter and chances are he has a grunt call hanging around his neck. Do these devices really work, or are hunters wasting their time snorting and grunting as they make their way through the woods?

Deer make three basic calls—the snort, the bleat, and the grunt. We've all heard deer snort. You're tiptoeing through the woods, trying to get close to some heavy brush, and all of a sudden you hear a loud wheezing sound; a second later you see a white flag go bounding off through the trees. That sound is the snort, which deer make when alarmed and to alert each other to danger. For the hunter, making a snort on a deer call is of little practical use.

On the other hand, the bleat, made mostly by fawns and does, can be used to advantage. A hunter calling in an area that does frequent can usually bring in a doe by making a pleading, crying bleat. "You have to put feeling into it," says Jim Strelec of Knight & Hale Game Calls. "A lot of hunters just blow into the call and produce a dull, boring bleat. That's not going to attract any deer's attention. For a bleat call to work, you have to make it sound as if a fawn is really in distress. Cry through that call and you'll see the difference. Does will practically come running."

And following the does, one hopes, is a buck.

An array of calls is commercially available. Calling is effective throughout the whitetail range, but is best used in conjunction with other hunting strategies. The most commonly used call is the grunt made by rutting bucks, either when alone or accompanying a doe. Bucks are attracted to grunts because they expect a doe to be in the vicinity. When using a commercial call, take

When Not to Call

- Do not keep calling if the buck does not respond in a timely manner. He may simply not want to come over for a look-see, so let him go for another day. The last thing you want to do is educate him to your imitation grunts and bleats.

- Do not call again if the buck appears to have heard your call and is already working his way toward your position. Additional grunts or bleats may only serve to confuse him, or worse, alert him to the fact that you are not a deer.

- Don't call if the buck is already in range or looking at you from out of range. If he pegs you, the game is already over. Instead, hold your ground and let him make the next move. If he turns to walk away, hit him with another note. This is another case where a decoy, buck or doe, can help, as the buck's attention will be riveted on the decoy.

care not to blow too loudly. Start with soft grunts and increase volume as necessary. Blow a short series of grunts and then wait. Use the call sparingly and when you think a buck is nearby.

A fawn separated from its mother will bleat. You can use a bleat call to attract a doe or, occasionally, a buck. Bleat three or four times, spaced a few seconds apart.

Sometimes you can make a deer pause or look in your direction by whistling. Some hunters have the blows, snorts, and wheezes that are part of whitetail alarm and breeding vocalizations in their calling repertoire. However, these calls are on the periphery of hunting strategies.

Is Calling Worth It?

It can be—there will be times when you spook deer with grunt calls or bleats. And there will be times when deer pay you absolutely no attention. But there will also be times when the call will either draw a buck into range or make him stop in his tracks, giving you an opportunity for a shot.

In short, calling is not a panacea but merely another tool in a deer hunter's arsenal. Don't expect too much from calls, and use them at the appropriate times.

URINE

Whitetail urine is commonly used as an attractor. Doe-in-estrus urine is used to attract bucks. You can apply the scent to your boots as you walk to your stand, place urine-soaked rags or cottonballs in locations that will draw deer to your stand, or make a mock scrape and use a drip dispenser to slowly release urine. When setting up attractor scent stations, be careful to place them so the deer won't smell you as they approach.

SCENT STRATEGIES

Scents smelling like apples, acorns, persimmons, or other deer foods are used to lure deer. While deer will investigate these smells, they are unlikely to travel any distance to do so. You can place food scents near your stand to distract deer or get them to pause for a shot.

Bowhunters in particular go to great lengths to mask their human odors because they must get very close to whitetails in order to get a shot. Strong natural cover scents, such as skunk musk and fox urine, were once popular. Some hunters rub their clothing with freshly crushed pine or cedar branches. Remember, the best way to keep a deer from smelling you is to use the wind to your advantage.

When mixing scents, especially those from glands, make sure you choose ones that don't conflict. For example, don't use a large quantity of interdigital scent with an attractant scent. Excess interdigital scent is meant to warn deer of danger, not attract them. You can, however, use just one or two drops of it with an estrous scent, as both serve to attract.

If you use gland scents collected from recently harvested deer, use less than you would of the commercial variety, as real scent is much more potent.

Gland scents, or even the urine from bladders, can be overused and lead to problems.

Dedicated trophy hunters use a scent-control system that utilizes deodorizing chemicals combined with special odor-containment clothing to eliminate human scent. Soda-based and oxidizing liquids and powders are available that will neutralize human smells, which are produced by bacteria, body oils, and perspiration. With meticulous attention to detail, you can control human scent enough so that a deer approaching from downwind will be less likely to detect you.

All clothing should be washed with scent-free detergents and stored outdoors or in scent-free containers. On the day of the hunt, you should wash with scent-free soap and shampoo. The neutralizing chemicals are applied to your body, all clothing, and hunting gear prior to the hunt. A scent-containment suit is worn under your outer layer of clothing. Special coveralls are worn over your hunting clothes while traveling to the hunting area to avoid scent contamination. Wear rubber boots (leather holds scents) and walk slowly to your hunting site to prevent scent-producing perspiration. Proper preparation will allow you to remain scent-free during the hunt.

USING DECOYS

The use of deer decoys is a relatively new advancement in deer hunting. Whitetails approach decoys for two reasons. The first is curiosity; deer are naturally gregarious and want to identify the stranger. The second reason is the estrus-induced mania bucks experience during the rut. When combined with with rattling, calling, or the use of scent(s), decoys can be powerful allies in the search for the trophy buck.

While a doe decoy will attract bucks, a buck decoy represents a rival challenger during the rut. Male deer in an area know each other on sight. Except during the rut, they stay together throughout the year in bachelor groups, so when a dominant buck spots a stranger in his territory, he'll be more than ready to put the trespasser in his place. If you use a buck decoy and combine it with rattling and calling—in effect setting up a mock battle between two bucks—your chances of drawing in a real one are quite good.

For safety reasons, decoying is primarily a bowhunting strategy. Don't use decoys when gun seasons are open, or in places where you are likely to run into other hunters. When carrying a decoy, be sure you are wearing at least a blaze-orange hat. Tie some orange material to the decoy or carry it in an orange bag.

The advantage of using a decoy is that it gives an approaching deer a visual focus, which means the deer is less likely to see you hiding nearby. There are three basic types of deer decoys. Lightweight three-dimensional foam models resemble bedded deer. Rolled up and placed in a plastic bag, they are easy to carry. Hinged two-dimensional plastic decoys collapse for easy carrying, but they look realistic only when viewed from the front. Hard-plastic full-bodied decoys are bulky to carry but present the most realistic impression from all angles. On most models, antlers can be added to convert a doe to a buck. Some have adjustable ears and tail to indicate whitetail mood.

Decoy Strategies

Decoys are often used in situations where deer can see them from a distance, such as fields or forest openings. Place the decoy along a buck's travel corridor, near a feeding area, or along a rub-line near his sanctuary. They are most effective when used early or late in the day, when deer are more likely to be on the move, so set up before daylight for early-morning hunts or in the afternoon for evening hunts.

The trick is to place the decoy without being seen by the deer. Wind direction, decoy placement, and stand or blind location must all be coordinated well. Also be sure that your decoy remains clear of all shooting lanes and that you know the yardages to different points in the setup. Once a buck has sighted the decoy, he will usually circle around and approach from the downwind side. Be in position to shoot as he circles toward the downwind side or as he moves toward the decoy. Shoot at the first good opportunity. If his attention is focused on the decoy, he may not see you draw.

Use a scent blocker to rid the decoy of human smells and attractor scents to lure deer. Position yourself downwind of the decoy, taking care to ensure a whitetail won't smell you as it approaches. If you rattle or call to simulate a fight, stop when you spot a deer

Some hunters lure bucks into range by placing decoy bucks in their hunting area. Deer are naturally curious, and will readily investigate a decoy in an effort to identify a buck or doe they don't recognize. Combining a reliable decoy with effective calling or rattling techniques is a powerful tool in your whitetail arsenal.

coming in. You want him to think a stranger is with one of his does, or he may pinpoint you as the source of the sound.

During the rut, a buck may appear at any time of the day, so set up a decoy near scrapes or where buck activity is evident. Use doe-in-estrus or gland-based scents that will attract a buck in rut. A buck in full rut may approach the decoy quickly and physically interact with it—trying to mate or fight with it. To fool especially wary old bucks, you may find success using more than one decoy, such as a buck and a doe.

Look for ways to add movement to your decoy setup. Some hunters tie a white cloth to the tail so it flickers in the breeze. You can tie a fishing line to the cloth and pull to make it move in calm conditions. Fishing line can

also be used to rustle brush near the decoy, creating movement and sound to catch a buck's attention. Check state regulations before using real deer parts or mechanized moving parts on a decoy.

Depending on the situation, a deer may walk right into a decoy or circle cautiously; wary bucks walk around the decoy to size it up. Don't expect the decoy to be foolproof. Big antlers on a decoy can intimidate smaller bucks. The decoy's antlers should be just big enough to represent a challenge to the dominant trophy buck, but the longer he watches it, the more likely he will decide the motionless dummy is a fake. However, a deer preoccupied with the decoy may come close enough to you to present an opportunity for a shot—which you should take without hesitation!

CHAPTER FIVE

REGIONAL DIFFERENCES

The white-tailed deer has such a wide range in North America that you can hunt it in ecosystems ranging from boreal forests to subtropical jungles to western deserts. While the habits of deer remain largely the same, hunting tactics vary with the habitat, climate and local customs. Traveling deer hunters find these regional differences add to the challenge and charm of the hunt.

Deer are extremely adaptable creatures, and have made the majority of North America their home. No matter where you are, you can bet there's a whitetail somewhere nearby.

State and provincial hunting seasons and regulations vary, too. Generally, they are based on the science of deer population management, safety considerations, and social traditions. Land access and ownership affect the hunt as well. Some places have large tracts of public hunting land, while in others hunting access is controlled by private landowners. Leasing land for hunting has become prevalent in recent years as deer hunting has become increasingly popular. It is difficult to find places where a knock on the landowner's door and a handshake will gain you permission to hunt.

In many areas, you can seek the services of a deer-hunting guide or outfitter. For a price, you will get a place to hunt, likely with pre-placed stands. Some outfitters have access to extensive property and specialize in trophy bucks. A hunt with a trophy outfitter in Canada or Texas is a dream trip for many hunters.

THE HEARTLAND

Most North American deer hunting occurs in the eastern half of the continent, in habitat that is a mix of hardwood forest and agricultural fields. This type of cover is found from the Eastern Seaboard to the Midwest and represents the heartland of whitetail hunting. Deer populations are abundant across this landscape, and most states allow hunters to kill more than one deer, usually through a permit system. Some heartland states, particularly in the Midwest, have the combination of limited hunting access, fertile soils, and good genetics that make them consistent producers of record-book bucks. Most heartland deer can feed in farm crops, although in hilly or mountainous regions they may rely on mast crops such as acorns.

Wildlife management areas and publicly owned forests are scattered throughout the heartland. Public areas are usually heavily hunted, but with careful scouting you can have a successful hunt. Many heartland hunters prefer to hunt on private land. Due to deer hunting's popularity, it is necessary to secure landowner permission to hunt long before the season begins. Many properties are hunted year after year by the family and friends of the landowner. Leasing of private lands for hunting is increasingly common, especially in areas that produce trophy bucks.

Firearms seasons attract the greatest numbers of hunters and account for most of the annual deer harvest. The firearms season is an unofficial holiday in some rural locales, with large numbers of hunters taking time off from work or school to go hunting. In many agricultural areas within the heartland, firearms hunters are restricted to using shotguns with slugs. To beat the crowds, many heartland hunters take up bowhunting, which gives them longer hunting seasons and better opportunities to get permission to hunt on private property. Late-season muzzleloader hunts continue to gain fans, especially among hunters seeking less hunting pressure and a challenging hunt.

No matter where you hunt, there are whitetails all around (even if you don't see them).

Open prairies, thick forests, and few people equal large bucks for those lucky enough to hunt in the central Canadian prairies.

Stand hunting is the preferred heartland hunting tactic, because hunters generally have limited land access or, especially during firearms hunting seasons, must contend with heavy hunting pressure. Heartland bowhunters employ all the modern tactics and have been pioneers in the use of scents, calls, and decoys. The archers take advantage of increased whitetail activity during the pre-rut and rut periods, which in some heartland states occur prior to the start of gun seasons. Late-season hunters often key-in on food sources, such as unharvested crops or crop residues.

THE NORTHWOODS

The northern forests of the Upper Great Lakes, the Northeast, and eastern Canada have deep-rooted deer-hunting traditions. Whitetails proliferated in the Northwoods a century ago when logging activity and large fires created an abundance of young forest habitat. This is big country, typified by large expanses of unbroken forest and minimal agricultural activity. In winter, Northwoods deer migrate to yarding areas, usually cedar swamps or similar coniferous cover, where

Though food sources are bountiful, hunting land in the South is more limited than in the North, meaning hunters have to do a little more legwork to find the prime hunting areas. When they do, however, they are often rewarded with bucks such as this one.

they find shelter from cold temperatures and deep snows. Mortality caused by severe winter weather can decimate a Northwoods deer population.

Low deer population densities make Northwoods hunting challenging. Hunters often set up stands along deer trails or near forest openings, such as recently logged areas, where there is an abundance of browse and other natural foods. Still-hunting and tracking are effective, especially when there is snow on the ground. Firearms hunting is the traditional method, with seasons generally occurring during the rut. October archery hunting is excellent.

Most Northwoods hunting occurs on public land or large private tracts, such as paper company holdings. Many hunters have deer camps where they gather annually with family and friends during the firearms deer season. The social traditions associated with a Northwoods deer camp are often as important to the hunters as the hunt itself. Hunting pressure can range from minimal in remote areas to heavy in more settled regions. Across most of the North, enough bucks elude hunters and survive the winters to reach trophy sizes.

THE SUBURBS

Whitetail hunters who live in metropolitan areas don't need to travel far to find good hunting. Suburban deer populations have exploded throughout the whitetail range. Parks, undeveloped properties, stream corridors, and even residential neighborhoods create habitat conditions suitable for whitetails.

Local ordinances often prohibit or restrict hunting, so deer numbers grow unchecked. Human perceptions of suburban whitetails go from novelty to nuisance when vehicle collisions, damage to shrubs and gardens, and the threat of Lyme disease escalate. In such situations, hunting is a practical means to control the deer population.

Special hunts or seasons, often with liberal antlerless deer limits, are used by game managers to reduce suburban whitetail numbers. Bowhunting is the preferred management method because it is quiet and unobtrusive.

In densely populated areas, hunters may be restricted to public parks or similar green spaces, which are closed to other uses during the hunt. If the municipality contains a fair amount of undeveloped land, hunters may be allowed to access properties where they have permission to hunt. In some metropolitan areas, responsible local bowhunters have formed organizations that specialize in suburban hunts.

Often in the suburbs, hunters are confined to small woodlots or vacant lands in the midst of development. The sounds of traffic, children playing, and other human activity form the backdrop for the hunt. Stand hunting is the safest, most practical tactic for suburban deer. A good suburban hunter is mostly unnoticed and makes minimal disruptions for the people who live nearby.

Precise shot placement and prompt recovery of downed animals is of utmost importance. Harvested deer should be moved discreetly from the hunting area. Suburban hunting has unique challenges, but offers many hunters the opportunity to hunt close to home.

CENTRAL CANADIAN PRAIRIES

The prairies and transitional forests of Manitoba, Saskatchewan, and Alberta have produced some of the largest white-tailed bucks on the continent, including the present world-record typical, killed in 1993 by local farmer Milo Hansen in Biggar, Saskatchewan.

For many U.S. hunters, a Canadian whitetail hunt is a dream trip. Numerous hunting outfitters exist to fulfill that dream. Hunting occurs on prairie farms, as well as in the northern forest, where bait piles are sometimes used to attract deer. Biting cold and snow are normal hunting conditions. Nevertheless, the opportunity to kill the buck of a lifetime lures thousands of American hunters north of the border every year.

THE WEST

Whitetails thrive on the open prairie and plains west of the Mississippi River, as well as in mountain and desert regions. Western whitetails are not widely distributed across the western landscape, but are mostly found in association with row crop agriculture, stream corridors, or dense woody cover. They are often abundant in good habitat, although western deer are susceptible to occasional die-offs from severe weather or diseases such as EHD (epizootic hemorrhagic disease). Whitetail hunting, particularly for trophy bucks, has become more popular in the West, but often they receive less attention from hunters than other big-game species.

Most western whitetail hunting occurs on private lands, although good public hunting opportunities are available. In situations where whitetails are abundant and lightly hunted, you may easily gain permission to hunt private farms and ranches. In many regions, ranchers charge an access fee. In top trophy areas, the best ranches are leased or controlled by hunting outfitters. An outfitted hunt with a reputable guide is the surest way to kill a trophy western whitetail.

Western whitetails typically spend their time in the heaviest cover available, where they can be hunted at close range by archers or black powder hunters using traditional tactics. Rifle hunters often place stands near feeding fields early and late in the day, where shots of 100 to 300 yards are not uncommon. During the day, they still-hunt or stalk in breaks and bottoms the deer use as refuge and bedding areas.

BRUSH COUNTRY

The brush country of South Texas and northern Mexico has long been a popular deer-hunting destination. Although the bucks are small in stature, mature animals often sport trophy-size antlers. The best hunting occurs on private ranches, which charge hefty fees for hunting access. Some large ranches are surrounded by high fences to contain the deer.

Brush-country hunters often use platform towers to see over the dense brush. They use rifles chambered for long-range cartridges and quality optics to make challenging, distant shots. However, not all brush-country hunting is a far-off affair. The close-range tactic of rattling was perfected by Texans.

THE SOUTH

The South has abundant deer populations and deep-rooted hunting traditions. Excellent deer habitat and a warm climate allow some southern states to offer long hunting seasons and generous bag limits. Hunting terrain ranges from forested mountain ridges to semi-tropical swamps, but much of the hunting occurs in rural areas with a mix of agricultural and forested lands. In some areas, extensive private timberlands offer hunting opportunities.

In most southern states, finding places to hunt requires some legwork, because public hunting areas generally are limited. Many hunters choose to lease private land or join a hunting club to gain access. In recent years, increasing numbers of landowners and lessees have begun managing their property for deer. This management often includes the development of food plots or whitetail habitat. Hunters on the property are encouraged to practice selective harvest, which typically is focused on achieving an adequate doe kill and not harvesting young bucks. The management intent is to balance the ratio of does and bucks, and to improve the herd's age structure. An effective management strategy may increase the number of mature bucks in the vicinity.

Southern whitetails generally are smaller than their northern kin. The rut begins later and lasts longer than in the North, though the peak rutting activity is generally less intense. Hunting from stands is a common tactic in the South and in better areas hunters may see several deer in the course of a day's hunt. To drive deer from dense cover, some southern states allow hunters to use dogs.

Big City Bucks

As suburbs have crept into the countryside and more and more people have built homes in the heart of deer habitat, whitetails have adapted to city life. In fact, urban deer populations may contain more big bucks than herds in more traditional deer habitat. Large homes built on several acres are often closed to hunting. Deer thrive in these situations as long as there is cover, some browse, and good bedding sites. With little or no hunting, good food and cover, bucks grow to older ages and trophy size.

In many of these areas, whitetail populations get out of hand. Residents who started out with an affection for the brown-eyed doe in the backyard often change their minds when hoards of deer eat every shrub, flower, and vegetable on their property. Whitetails are hosts to Lyme disease, a serious human ailment, and collisions between deer and autos are costly and potentially dangerous. More and more communities are facing the problem of too many deer.

One solution to the urban deer problem is to allow bowhunting in town. Bowhunting poses few hazards to hunters or nearby nonhunters; it's quiet and unobtrusive, and it can control a deer population.

Of course, getting permission to hunt is important for any deer hunter, but it's absolutely critical for the urban hunter. In many eastern communities with urban deer problems, groups of experienced, ethical bowhunters have formed informal clubs that landowners and home owners can contact when they want deer removed.

These clubs have membership qualifications and ethics rules that are strictly enforced. Members must meet with landowners and become acquainted with their concerns.

Once a bowhunter has permission to hunt in a suburb, he (or she) should make an extraordinary effort to keep landowners in the area happy. If he arrives before daylight, he should avoid making noise that might disturb the residents. He should do his best to maintain a friendly one-to-one relationship with people in the neighborhood. A little courtesy helps keep the backyards open for hunting the next fall.

Municipalities initiate controlled bowhunts to reduce deer numbers, That means harvesting female deer is critical. While most hunters want to kill bucks, they will do more to control the herd by taking does. Once the meat gets to the table, nobody will know the difference. Of course, when that once-in-a-lifetime trophy walks into range, there's generally time to make an exception.

A bowhunter in the suburbs can better his or her chances by hunting strips of timber (the thicker the cover, the better) used as travel corridors by deer. Heavily used trails, lines of tree rubs, and scrapes during the fall rut mark these corridors. A hunter using a stand should get settled well before daylight to avoid disturbing deer moving through the corridors to their bedding sites in early morning. It's smart to approach the stand from a different direction each day to disperse human scent and prevent deer from identifying a pattern of human use.

As rising human populations swell cities into countryside suburbs, deer populations rise too. Though it may seem beneficial to have a large deer population nearby, oversize herds are more prone to spreading disease, and their massive numbers tend to weaken, not strengthen, the overall health status of the herd.

Sights like this are becoming more and more common as deer are forced from the countryside into suburban areas and settlements.

CHAPTER SIX

AFTER THE HUNT

Let's assume you've been successful to this point in your deer hunt. You prepared in advance of the hunt by scouting, practicing with your firearm or bow, and learning which techniques to use in your particular hunting area. Now you stand watching the spot where the deer was standing before you fired your weapon. What happens now?

A good shot at a large buck is only half the effort of a dedicated whitetail hunter— finding him and collecting him is the other.

TRAILING WOUNDED DEER

Hunters may buy expensive equipment, travel great distances, and spend countless hours hunting, only to lose a deer because they didn't know how to trail it after the shot.

The trailing process starts when you squeeze the trigger or release the arrow. Watch carefully to spot an entrance wound or protruding shaft. Deer hit in a vital area with a single, well-placed shot won't run far and are usually easy to recover. Remembering the details of the shot will help you find a deer that requires trailing.

Before trailing the deer, mark the location from which you shot. This way, you can easily find it again should you need to backtrack. Walk along the line your bullet or arrow traveled; if you find nicks or gouges in vegetation, your shot may have deflected enough to miss the deer.

DEER BEHAVIOR

As you shoot, watch the deer through your sights and study its reactions.

- A leg, rib, or grazing shot usually makes a deer jump and run.

- A heart or lung shot may produce similar reactions, or the deer may show no immediate response, then bolt away at full speed. But it will seldom go more than 200 yards.

- A gut-shot deer often holds its tail down and hunches up as it runs.

- A brain or spinal-column shot will drop a deer in its tracks.

Tracking deer is an art form unto itself. Remember to take your time, think logically, and don't be afraid to backtrack—retracing your steps will often reveal a broken twig, a spot of blood that you may have missed.

Though rare, some states allow the use of tracking dogs once the shooting stops. Be sure to dress your dog in blaze as well, an important safety aspect this hunter neglected.

If you miss, the deer may stand still or take a few bounds and then wait to try to pinpoint any further sign or movement, giving you a chance to shoot again. Even if you don't get another shot, follow up your first one. Many a hunter has been surprised to find a dead deer just over the ridge after what he or she assumed was a sure miss.

If you hit the deer and it runs off, stay put—a few minutes for gun hunters, perhaps 60 for bowhunters. Many deer are lost because the hunter follows too quickly. Frantic, unplanned pursuits blot out tracks and blood sign that could lead you to the deer. Or you could spook the deer and cause it to run again.

Despite many claims to the contrary, you can't predict the behavior of wounded deer. It's not true that deer always run uphill, or go to water or run a straight course. Do your trailing based on the sign you find, not where you think the deer should go.

Some states allow the use of trailing dogs, which can be a great help in recovering wounded deer.

HAIR AND BLOOD CLUES

Look for hair around the shot site. Lots of hair most likely means a grazing shot; only a little hair, a body shot. You'll find mostly brown hair if the shot was high; white if it was low. Noticing bone fragments, signifying a leg hit, can also be helpful.

Carefully studying blood at the scene of the shot can provide some valuable clues as to where the deer was hit and how you should proceed in tracking it. Don't disturb the site; mark it in case you need to reexamine it later.

Once you start trailing the deer, move as quickly as possible. If you proceed too slowly, the blood trail will dry and become much less obvious.

The blood trail is your best link to the deer. Always walk beside it, not on it, so you don't destroy clues. If you lose the blood trail, mark the last blood found, then look for overturned leaves, scuff marks, or bent plants that may indicate the animal's direction. Deer tend to bleed more when they exert themselves, so you're more likely to pick up the blood trail where a deer has crossed a gully, ditch, or fence. If you still can't pick up the blood trail, systematically search heavy cover nearby. Make every effort to retrieve a wounded animal before resuming the hunt, even if it takes the rest of the day.

It's really not possible to tell where a deer was hit by the color of the blood. Some people maintain that pink blood means a lung hit; dark blood, a liver hit, etc. But even blood experts can tell little about the wound's location based on color.

Don't jump to conclusions based on the first blood sign. The initial blood pattern may be misleading because any wound causes immediate surface bleeding. Look for one of the following patterns to develop:

- Fine droplets sprayed on both sides of the trail for the first 50 to 100 yards. Droplets may be several feet up on tree trunks and brush as well as on the ground. Small bubbles in the blood that burst when you touch them indicates a hit in the heart, lungs, or large blood vessels in the neck. The chances are good that you'll find your deer dead within 200 yards.

- Large splotches of blood at the spot where the animal was hit, turning to continuous drops that diminish within 100 to 200 yards. You may find some clots along the trail. Bleeding continues as long as the deer is moving but stops when the animal lies down. This pattern indicates a hit in the leg, back muscles or neck muscles, or, rarely, in the body cavity. Eventually, these wounds will stop bleeding, so you'll have to trail the deer based on other clues.

- Blood trail is difficult to find at first, then large splotches appear between 20 and 50 yards. Blood sign steadily decreases until only scattered specks are found after 100 yards. This pattern is typical of gut-shot deer. Food particles in the area where you hit the deer and putrid-smelling blood confirm a gut shot.

The volume of blood circulating through the digestive system diminishes as the muscles of a moving deer demand more blood. This, together with clotting, explains why the blood trail thins out after about 50 yards.

Gut-shot deer are the most difficult to recover. If you suspect a gut shot, wait at least 2 hours before trailing, even if you fear the deer will spoil or rain will wash away the blood trail. When a deer beds, the blood flow to muscles decreases and flow to the gut increases. The deer will bleed to death in its bed and will be found within 200 to 500 yards, if you don't chase it. But if you follow too soon and spook the deer from its bed, the trail will then have little, if any, blood.

ETIQUETTE AND SAFETY

No matter what type of trail you're following, ask your partners for help if you need it. Be sure to tell them exactly what to do. Be quiet, stay together, and designate shooters for safety's sake. Someone should stay near the last blood spot and look ahead for the deer while the others search for more blood or tracks.

Always get permission before trailing onto any private land you don't have permission to hunt. Keep track of your location and use a compass or GPS unit—it's easy to get lost when you're concentrating on a blood trail.

Sooner or later you'll come upon the animal. If it's standing or bedded with its head up, shoot it again.

Approach a downed deer slowly and quietly from behind, watching for signs of life. If it doesn't move, jab it with a stick. If it does, kill it with a rifle shot in the neck or an arrow in the chest cavity.

PREPARATION IS KEY

A little homework before a deer hunt can save a lot of time and effort once you've bagged your animal. And it will ensure that the meat you bring home will be in prime condition for the table.

Familiarize yourself with state and local regulations. Some states prohibit quartering and skinning in the field; others require that you turn in certain parts for biological study. Be sure to check the regulations booklet available with your license. For more information, contact state or federal wildlife-management agencies.

If you are hunting for a trophy, consult in advance with a reliable taxidermist. He or she can give you advice on the best ways to handle the head and antlers in the field. There are also several good do-it-yourself kits for antler mounting and hide tanning.

The hides of deer make excellent leather. Many tanneries will buy raw hides directly from hunters. If you plan on selling the hide, find out how the buyer wants it prepared. Some tanneries will exchange a raw hide for a pair of finished leather gloves (or you may prefer to have the hide tanned and returned to you).

In the Field

Before you shoot, consider the location and body position of the animal. Remember that you'll have to get it out of the area after it's down. If you spot an animal across a canyon, consider possible drag routes before shooting. A trophy buck standing in a bog may be a tempting target, but you may need an extra helper to move it to dry land for field dressing and quartering.

Shot placement affects both the quality and quantity of the meat you bring home. A study at Texas A&M University showed that game killed instantly with a clean shot produces meat more tender and flavorful than game only wounded with the first shot. Game

The blood trail is your number one path to the deer. Wounded deer often seek sheltered areas to bed, so if you lose the blood trail, retrace your steps to your last sighting of it and look nearby—there may be a buck in the heavy undergrowth.

animals, like humans, produce adrenalin and other chemicals when frightened or stressed; these chemicals make the meat tough and gamey. A poorly placed shot may also damage choice cuts, or rupture the stomach or intestines, tainting the meat.

If possible, shoot an animal that's standing still rather than running. A shot in the heart or neck will drop it instantly, and you'll lose little meat.

Approach a downed animal with caution, keeping your gun loaded and staying away from the hooves and antlers. Nudge the animal with your foot, or gently touch your gun barrel to its eye. If there's any reaction, shoot it in the head or heart. When certain the animal is dead, unload your gun and place it safely out of the way.

Field-dress the animal immediately to drain off the blood and dissipate the body heat. Wear rubber gloves to protect you from any parasites or blood-borne diseases the animal may be carrying, and to make cleanup easier.

The step-by-step instructions on the following pages will guide you through a field-dressing procedure that produces a clean carcass. Splitting the pelvis is optional with this method. In warm weather, you may wish to split the pelvis, because the hams cool faster when separated. However, an animal with a split pelvis is more difficult to drag. The separated hind legs flog around, and the cavity may get dirty.

If you elect to split the pelvis, cut between the hams as described. Then, locate the natural seam between the two halves of the pelvic bone, and cut through it with your knife. On a large or old animal, you may need to use a game saw or hatchet. Some hunters stand their knife upright with its tip on the seam, then strike the knife with their palm to split the pelvis. Do not attempt this unless you have a sturdy knife; you could damage the blade.

Be sure to follow state regulations requiring evidence of the sex left on the carcass. Antlers are usually adequate to identify a buck; in some states antlers must be a certain length for the animal to be legal.

Where the law allows, attach the registration tag after field dressing, rather than before. The tag may get ripped off during the dressing procedure.

There's nothing easy about hanging a large animal from a tree. Be sure to have the proper gear, like a strong rope or even a compound pulley (inset). Hanging facilitates cooling the carcass and also helps protect it from ground scavengers. Equipment for field-dressing whitetails includes a folding lock-back knife and a spare; small whetstone or sharpening stick; several foot-long pieces of kitchen string; two clean sponges; zip-lock plastic bags; rubber gloves; block and tackle; and nylon rope. Other useful items include cloth bags for carrying out the quarters if skinned, and a hatchet or folding saw for immediate quartering. Hooks can be used to help split the ribcage or hang the deer. The best part about these tools is they all fit comfortably in a small pack or backpack.

FIELD-DRESSING WHITETAILS

Proper care of wild game in the field ensures that the meat you bring home will be in prime condition for the table. Immediate dressing drains blood and dissipates body heat. Always wear rubber gloves to protect yourself from any parasites or blood-borne diseases the animal may be carrying, and to make your cleanup easier.

Follow state regulations requiring evidence of the sex on the carcass. Where the law allows, attach the registration tag after field-dressing so it doesn't get torn off during the dressing procedure.

There are many ways to field-dress a deer. The following step-by-step instructions show one method we've found to get the job done.

How to Field-dress Big Game (Right-handed)

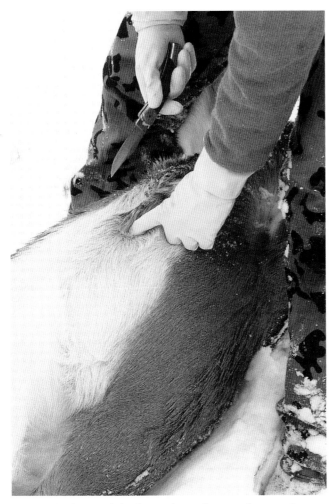

Locate the base of the breastbone by pressing on the center of the ribcage until you feel its end. Make a shallow cut that is long enough to insert the first two fingers of your left hand. Be careful not to puncture the intestines when cutting.

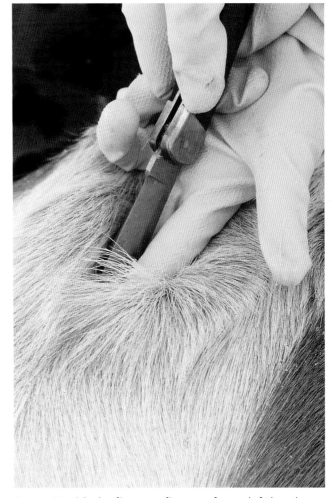

Form a V with the first two fingers of your left hand. Hold the knife between your fingers with the cutting edge up, as shown. Cut through the abdominal wall to the pelvic area. Your fingers prevent you from puncturing the intestines.

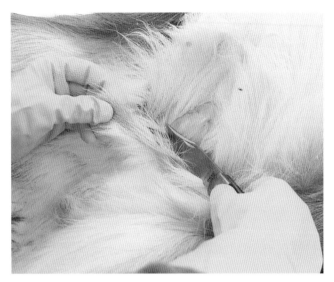

Separate the external reproductive organs of a buck from the abdominal wall, but do not cut them off completely. Remove the udder of a doe if it was still nursing. The milk sours rapidly and could give the meat an unpleasant flavor.

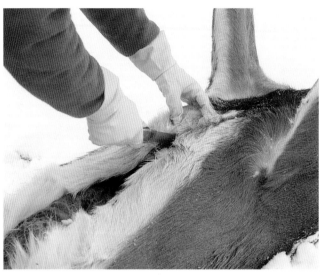

Straddle the animal, facing its head. Unless you plan to mount the head, cut the skin from the base of the breastbone to the jaw, with the cutting edge of the knife up. If you plan to mount the head, follow your taxidermist's instructions.

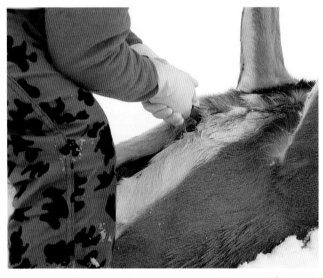

Brace your elbows against your legs, with your left hand supporting your right. Cut through the center of the breastbone, using your knees to provide leverage. If the animal is old or very large, you may need to use a game saw or small axe.

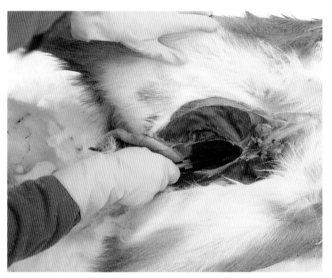

Slice between the hams to free a buck's urethra, or if you elect to split the pelvic bone on either a buck or a doe. Make careful cuts around the urethra until it is freed to a point just above the anus. Be careful not to sever the urethra.

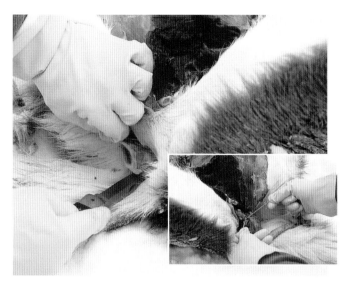

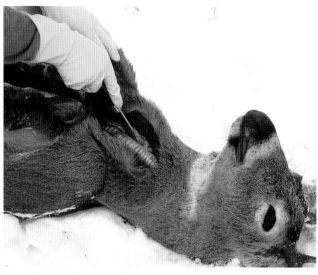

Cut around the anus; on a doe, the cut should also include the reproductive opening (above the anus). Free the rectum and urethra by loosening the connective tissue with your knife. Tie off the rectum and urethra with kitchen string (inset).

Free the windpipe and esophagus by cutting the connective tissue, severing both organs at the jaw. Grasp them firmly and pull down, continuing to cut where necessary, until freed to the point where the windpipe branches out into the lung.

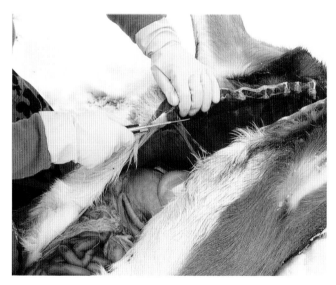

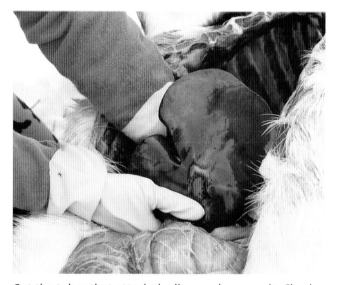

Hold the ribcage open on one side with your left hand. Cut the diaphragm, from the rib opening down to the backbone. Stay as close to the ribcage as possible; do not puncture the stomach. Repeat on the opposite side so the cuts meet over the backbone.

Cut the tubes that attach the liver and remove it. Check the liver for spots, cysts, or scarring, which could indicate parasites or disease. If you see any, discard the liver. If the liver is clean, place it into the same plastic bag as the heart. Place both on ice as soon as possible.

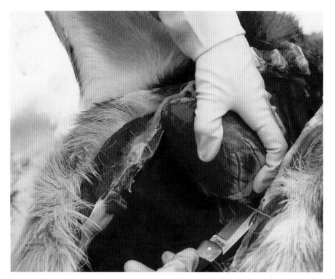

Remove the heart by severing the connecting blood vessels. Hold the heart upside down for a few moments to drain excess blood. Place the heart in a plastic bag. Some hunters find it easier to remove the entrails first, then take the heart and liver from the gut pile.

Pull the tied-off rectum and urethra underneath the pelvic bone and into the body cavity, unless you have split the pelvic bone (if you have, this is unnecessary). Roll the animal onto its side so the entrails begin to spill out the side of the body cavity.

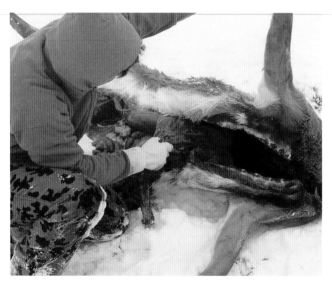

Grasp the windpipe and esophagus firmly. Pull down and away from the animal's body. If the organs do not pull away freely, the diaphragm may still be partially attached. Scoop from both ends toward the middle to finish rolling out the entrails.

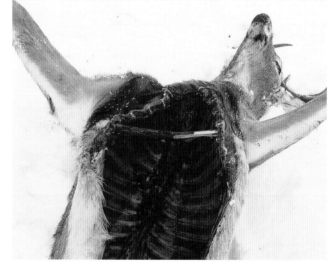

Sponge the cavity clean, and prop it open with a stick. If the urinary tract or intestines have been severed, wash the meat with snow or clean water. If you must leave the animal, drape it over brush or logs with the cavity down, or hang it from a tree to speed cooling.

Tips for Safely Handling Wild Game

Sources such as the Chronic Wasting Disease Alliance, Wisconsin Department of Natural Resources, and other wildlife officials have suggested precautions for hunters field-dressing animals and handling deer in areas where CWD is found. The following are good tips to remember:

- Wear rubber or latex gloves when field-dressing carcasses.
- Avoid the use of saws. Do not cut through spine or skull.
- Bone out the meat from your animal.
- Remove all internal organs.
- Minimize the handling of brain, spinal cord, spleen, and lymph nodes (lumps of tissue next to organs or in fat).

- Use equipment dedicated to field-dressing only; do not use household knives or utensils.
- Thoroughly clean knives and equipment, and sanitize by soaking in a mixture of equal parts chlorine bleach and water for 1 hour.
- If you will be using a professional processor, request that your animal be butchered individually and not combined with meat from other animals.
- Do not eat the eyes, brain, spinal cord, spleen, tonsils, or lymph nodes of any deer.
- Do not eat any part of a deer that appears sick.
- If your deer is sampled for CWD testing, wait for test results before eating the meat.

TRANSPORTING WHITETAILS

After field dressing, move the animal to camp as soon as possible. Leave the hide on to protect the meat from dirt and flies. The hide will also prevent the surface from drying too much during aging. In hot weather, however, you may want to remove the hide in the field to help cool the carcass.

If you plan to skin the animal in the field, bring along a large cloth bag or sheet to keep the meat clean during transport. Never put the carcass or quarters in plastic bags unless the meat is thoroughly chilled. The plastic traps the body heat, and the meat may be ruined. Avoid plastic garbage bags; they may be treated with a toxic disinfectant.

Wear blaze-orange clothing and make lots of noise when you move an animal in the field. Hunters have been known to mistakenly shoot at animals being dragged or carried. For this reason, the traditional method of carrying a deer by lashing it to a pole between two hunters is not recommended. If you must carry an animal in this way, drape it completely with blaze-orange cloth.

Once in camp, hang the animal up. Hanging aids cooling and blood drainage, and the stretching helps

Drag a deer with each front leg tied to an antler to keep from snagging brush. If the deer is antlerless, tie a rope around the neck. Snow makes dragging easier. If the terrain is dusty, sew the carcass shut with a cord after punching a hole in each side of the rib cage.

tenderize the meat. Clean the clots and excess blood from the heart and liver, then place them in plastic bags on ice.

Ideally, the carcass should be cooled to 40 degrees Fahrenheit within 24 hours. Cool it as rapidly as possible, but don't allow it to freeze. The meat loses moisture if frozen and thawed, and the carcass is difficult to skin when frozen even partially. If the days are warm and the nights cool, keep the carcass covered with a sleeping bag during the day. If the nights are warm as well, store the carcass at a locker plant.

The best way to transport an animal home is in a closed trailer or covered pickup. In cool, dry weather, you can carry an animal on top of your car, with the head forward. Do not carry an animal on the hood, because heat from the engine will spoil the meat. If your trip is long and hot, pack bags of dry ice around the carcass. Or, quarter the animal, wrap well in plastic, and pack it into coolers in ice. Be sure to check state laws regarding transport of whitetails.

HANGING, AGING, AND SKINNING WHITETAILS

How should I hang my animal—from the head or by the hind legs? And what about aging—does it improve the meat or spoil it? If I'm going to age the animal, should I leave the hide on during aging or take it off? These questions cause a great deal of debate among hunters.

If you want the head for a trophy, the first question is answered for you: The animal must be hung by the hind legs. Many hunters hang all big game this way—not just whitetails—and the U.S. Department of Agriculture recommends this method for butchering beef. Hanging by the hind legs allows the blood to drain from the choice hindquarters. If your animal must be hung outdoors, however, it's better to hang it from the head because of the direction of hair growth. Otherwise, the upturned hair traps rain and snow.

Many laboratory and taste tests have demonstrated that aging will definitely tenderize the meat. The special tenderness and flavor of beef prime rib results from

extended aging; whitetails can benefit in the same way. It's a matter of personal taste; some prefer the aged flavor and tenderness, others don't. Aging is unnecessary if all the meat will be ground into venison or sausage.

To prevent unwanted bacterial growth during the aging process, the carcass temperature must be stabilized between 35 degrees and 40 degrees Fahrenheit. If it fluctuates widely, condensation may form. Temperatures above 40 degrees promote excess bacterial growth and cause the fat to turn rancid. If you age the animal outdoors or in a shed, be prepared to butcher it immediately or take it to a locker should the weather turn warm.

Leave the hide on during aging, if possible. It helps stabilize the temperature of the meat, and also reduces dehydration. In a study at the University of Wyoming, an elk carcass was cut in half down the backbone; one half was skinned, the other was not. After two weeks of aging, the skinned side lost over 20 percent more moisture. Animals aged without the hide will have a great deal of dried, dark meat to be trimmed, further reducing your yield.

Some people prefer to quarter their meat, wrap the quarters in cloth, then age them in a refrigerator or old chest-style pop cooler. The effects are almost the same as hanging a whole carcass. The meat may be slightly less tender, because it doesn't get stretched as much.

If you prefer not to age the animal, delay butchering for at least 24 hours, until the carcass has cooled and the muscles have relaxed. The cuts will be ragged and unappealing if you start before cooling is complete, and the meat will be tough if butchered while the muscles are still contracted.

SKINNING WHITETAILS

Skinning is easiest while the animal is still warm. If you age the meat, however, it's best to leave the skin on until butchering.

Most hunters skin their animals by hand. The task isn't difficult, requiring only a knife and a saw. For easiest skinning, hang the animal from a pulley. Then you can raise or lower the carcass, so the area you're working on will always be at eye level. Or, hoist the animal on a rope running through a heavy-duty screw eye fastened to a solid ceiling beam.

Try to keep hair off the meat during skinning. Keep your knife sharp, touching it up as necessary with a steel or stone. Cut through the skin from the inside out, so your knife slips between the hairs. This way, you avoid cutting hairs in half or riving them into the meat, and your knife won't dull as quickly.

After skinning, lay the hide out on a piece of plywood, skin side up. If you take a few moments to scrape off any bits of meat or fat, you will get a better piece of leather.

Most tanneries prefer to receive a hide salted and rolled. To protect it from rain and animals during the salting process, find a sheltered spot like a shed or garage. Sprinkle the skin side liberally with salt, and rub some into the edges, cuffs, and neck area. Tilt the plywood slightly so the hide will drain.

After a day, add more salt and fold the hide in half, skin side in. Roll the folded hide into a bundle and tie it with twine. Don't put the rolled hide in plastic, except for shipping, because it may rot. Keep it cold, and get it to the tannery as soon as possible.

If you have a deer hide, save the tail. It can be used for jig and fly tying, and hide buyers may pay several dollars for it.

If you're not going to butcher the animal yourself, deliver the carcass to the butcher with the hide still on, and let him skin it.

How to Hang a Whitetail by the Hind Legs

Make a gambrel out of a 3-foot-long 2x2. Cut a shallow notch all around the wood an inch from each end, and another in the middle.

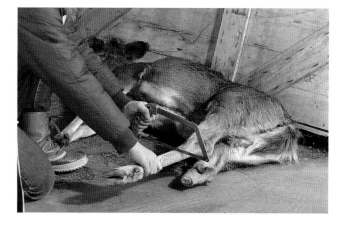

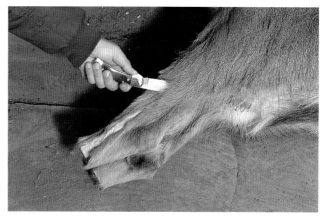

Saw off the bottom of each hind leg several inches below the knee. Cutting from inside the skin, slit the skin on each leg to a point about 4 inches above the knee.

How to Hang a Whitetail by the Hind Legs *continued*

Peel the skin over the leg to uncover the large tendon at the back of the leg. Then slit any tissue between the bone and the large tendon. The tendon is needed for hanging the animal, so be careful not to sever it.

Insert the gambrel in the slits. Tie each leg to the wood, wrapping the rope in the notch. Tie 6 feet of rope to the center notch, then loop it over a sturdy beam or through a pulley. Hoist the deer completely off the ground.

How to Skin a Whitetail Hanging by the Hind Legs

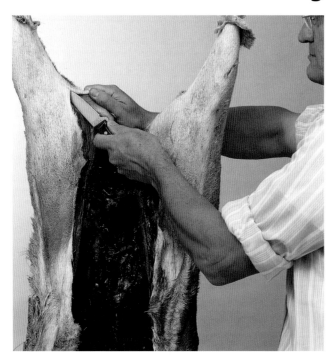

Cut the hide along the inner side of each hind leg. Note that the cut is made from the inside of the skin.

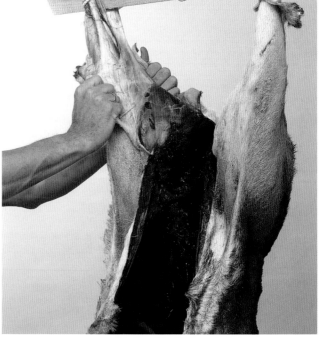

Peel the hide away from the legs. Continue peeling until both legs are skinned and you reach the tail.

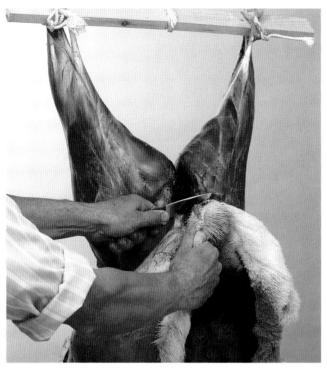

Sever the tailbone close to the animal's rump. Leave the tailbone inside the skin.

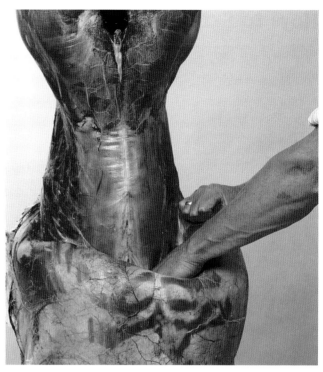

Continue peeling, using your fist to free the hide along the back. Use a knife only where necessary; take care not to cut a hole in the skin.

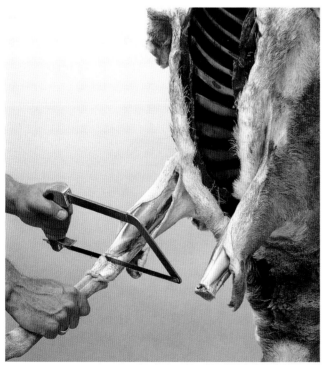

Saw off the front legs just above the joint after cutting along the inside of each leg and peeling the hide. Keep skinning until you reach the head.

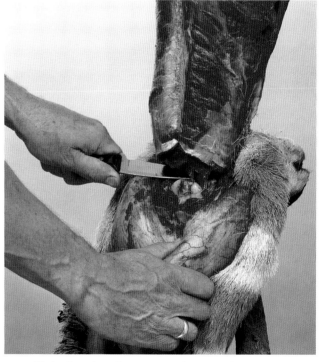

Cut off the head at the center Atlas joint (center). First, make a deep cut around the neck at the base of the skull. Twist the head to pop the Atlas joint.

How to Skin a Whitetail Hanging from the Head

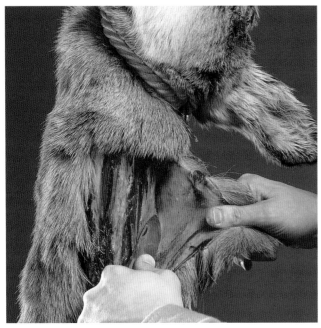

Cut the skin around the base of the head. Then peel the hide away from the neck with your fingers, using a knife only where necessary.

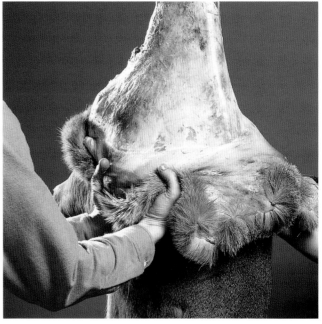

Peel the hide over the shoulders. Saw off the front legs above the joint, as described on the prior page. Pull the hide off the front legs.

Keep skinning down to the rump. Sever the tailbone; cut off the hind legs above the knee. Cut the hide along the inside of each leg. Pull the hide completely off.

If you prefer more tender meat, hanging and aging your whitetail at the butcher shop is not a bad idea. Many butcher shops offer this service at very little cost.

CAPING-OUT YOUR TROPHY

If you wish to mount the head of your deer, but have no caping experience, the job is best left to an expert. Though not particularly difficult, caping is time-consuming, and a slip of the knife could mean a less-than-perfect trophy.

Most taxidermists prefer that you bring the entire deer to them, so that they can skin and cape it to their own satisfaction.

If you cannot take the carcass to a taxidermist, the next-best option is to take the entire hide with head attached. To skin the deer; hang it by the hind legs and peel the hide down to the head before severing the

neck. From brisket to head, the hide should be free of cuts. The taxidermist can then determine how much of the hide he needs for the mount and do the intricate work of skinning out the head himself.

Should circumstances dictate that you cape the deer yourself, follow the instructions on these pages. Also be sure to follow the precautions listed at left for safely handling wild game. Maintain a shaving edge on your knife and work slowly and carefully because any mistake means extra work for the taxidermist.

If you'll be hunting a few more days, hang the cape or hide with head attached in the shade where air can circulate freely. Never place it in any type of container. Trapped air will warm quickly, causing the hide to spoil. Once home, get it to a taxidermist immediately. If you can't, store the hide in a freezer.

FIELD-JUDGING ANTLERS

Whether you're specifically targeting trophy-class bucks or not, you must be able to quickly recognize a true trophy from a slightly smaller buck. Easier said than done, because fully mature bucks usually don't stand still for long. Some monster bucks may not expose themselves to human eyes for more than 60 seconds in their entire lives.

At the same time, he who acts hastily finds himself dragging the wrong buck out of the woods. A buck that looks wide and heavy from the front might have just a few short tines when viewed from the side.

This is a job best left to an expert, but most hunters agree, one worth waiting (and paying) for. Few wall-mounts garner as much bragging rights as a trophy buck.

RECORD BOOKS

The most widely accepted scoring system for whitetails is that of the Boone and Crockett Club (B&C), official record keepers for all North American big game. To be eligible for the B&C record book, bucks must be found dead or taken in fair chase by either gun or bow. The Pope and Young Club (P&Y), which maintains records for animals shot with bow and arrow only, also uses the B&C scoring system.

Both clubs maintain records in typical and nontypical categories. In the typical category, the more closely the two antlers match, the better the net score. Under the scoring system for typicals, deductions are made for asymmetry, meaning that unbalanced racks don't score as well as perfectly balanced ones of the same general dimensions. The minimum net score for a buck to qualify as a B&C typical is 170 points; P&Y, 125 points.

Many hunters prefer the rough-and-ready character of nontypical racks with odd-shaped sticker points and drop tines. As far as these sportsmen are concerned, any antler the buck manages to grow atop its head is just fine. Under the B&C scoring system, nontypical antlers are scored the same as typicals, with the usual deductions for asymmetry, but all abnormal points are then added to the final score. Minimum entry score for a B&C nontypical is 195 points; P&Y, 150 points.

DEER ANATOMY

Estimating antler size in the field is done by comparing the features of the antlers against other anatomical features of known dimension.

For example, the ears of a mature buck are generally 6 to 8 inches long; the spread between the tips of the ears, 16 to 18 inches. The nose-to-eye distance on most

Monster of the Forest. King of the Prairie. Whatever you call him, a trophy buck is a majestic animal indeed. Trophy bucks can be found anywhere, but taking one is easier said than done!

mature bucks is 7 to 8 inches, and the circumference of the eye is about 4 inches.

Knowing these dimensions lets you estimate the pertinent antler measurements of the B&C scoring system: the length of the main beam and each tine; the circumference of the main beam, measured at the base and between the tines; and the inside spread between the antlers. But you'll need to do these calculations as quickly as possible; you often have little time to judge these measurements and add them for a rough estimate of the buck's score.

The best training for field-judging antlers is to study photographs and, more important, mounted heads of known score. Practice by studying mounted heads from different angles, estimating the antler measurements by comparing them to the anatomical features. Use a tape measure to check your guess.

Memorize how a 22-inch-wide rack looks from the front compared to an 18-inch rack. Notice how a long main beam reaches back, swings wide, then curls forward toward the deer's nose, while a shorter beam usually remains straight at the tips. If you find a set of antlers that curls in at the tips, measure them for beam length—you'll be surprised to discover these curved antlers are much longer than they first appear.

After a little practice, you'll soon develop a knack for estimating a buck's general score at a glance. That's the key for quickly and accurately field-judging live bucks.

SCORING BASICS

It is relatively easy to learn how to estimate a buck's general score—for instance, a 110-class typical verses a 150. But if you're hoping to take a buck that qualifies for either record book, you'll need to learn how to score more precisely.

Here are five easy steps:

1. Count the tines on one antler, guess the length of each, and add these measurements.

2. Estimate the length of the main beam, plus its circumference at the base and between the tines; add these numbers to your score.

3. Double this number, assuming the other antler is relatively symmetrical to the first.

4. Estimate the inside spread between the antlers and add this number to get the total rough score.

5. If time permits, you can subtract points for any broken or missing tines.

Practice Example

Let's assume you're stand hunting with a rifle and you see a deer trot through an opening in the brush. You see the rack—it's heavy, tall, and wider than the distance between the tips of the ears. These features

Field-judging antler scores is a fun way to enhance the hunting experience. Using known measurements of the deer's anatomy, savvy hunters can quickly estimate the relative score of a buck.

alone place it roughly in the 130- to 150-class, and if you sense the buck is about to bolt, you might take a shot based only on this glance.

But the buck is in no hurry. He stops, presenting himself broadside, and you quickly focus his head in your binoculars. You see three tall tines sticking up from the main beam, so he's probably a 10-pointer. You can't yet see the brow tine, but the next tine up (the G-2 tine in the scoring system) looks about 2 inches longer than the ear (which you know is about 8 inches long), making this tine close to 10 inches. The next tine is shorter, about 6 inches; the third is about half as long as the ear; call it 4 inches. Add 10, 6, and 4 for 20 points. (You'll add in the length of the brow tine when the buck turns to expose it.)

You see that the main beam stretches forward to halfway between the buck's eye and nose and reaches pretty high above his head. You decide that the main beam looks to be about three times longer than the 8-inch eye-to-nose distance, giving you 24 inches. Add this number to the previous score, for a total of 44.

While waiting for the buck to present a front-on view, you can score the antler mass by estimating the circumference of the main beam. The base of the antler looks considerably larger than the circumference of the buck's eye, which is about 4 inches, so you guess the antler is about 6 inches around. That's thick! The beam stays thick past the first and second points before beginning to taper off, so you add 6 plus 6 plus 5 plus 4 to arrive at 21. Added to the previous 44 points, you've now scored a total of 65. Double this score for the other antler and you're already up to 130—and you haven't yet added in the spread between antlers or the length of the brow tines.

Finally the deer turns and looks right at you, revealing antlers that extend about 1 inch beyond the tip of each ear. You know the distance between the tips of his ears is about 18 inches, so that means the antler spread must be about 20 inches. You're up to 150 points. Now you see the brow tines; they are surprisingly short, only about 4 inches long. Double this number for 8 inches, and add this in for a total score of 158!

Do you take this buck? Although its score falls below Boone & Crockett minimums, this animal is a fantastic trophy. Ultimately, it's up to each hunter to set his or her own criteria for what qualifies as a "shooter."

The antler patterns of nontypical bucks are helter-skelter and topsy-turvy. A perfectly healthy buck can bear a nontypical set of antlers, and nontypicals are quirky and fun animals to behold.

WHITETAIL CONSERVATION

Over the 300 years between the arrival of Columbus and the virtual colonization of the United States from coast to coast, whitetail numbers fluctuated repeatedly. Indian and white hunters killed large numbers for meat and hides to send to market. Settlers often depended heavily upon native game while they cleared the forest for their farms. When these farms would fail, as they often did, and the settlers would move even farther west, depleted deer populations rebounded temporarily as nature reclaimed the clearings, providing prime whitetail habitat. This cycle repeated itself many times in the settling of North America.

In the late 1800s, once the continent was laced with roads and railroads that could carry both settlers west and white-tailed deer parts to market, the extermination of the white-tailed deer began. Venison was a popular staple of city dwellers and could be found on the menu of many fine restaurants and for sale in markets. In order to feed this demand, market hunters took to the woods. At the same time, residents of burgeoning rural communities went afield to hunt whitetails. With no hunting seasons or bag limits, a growing human population took a heavy toll on not only white-tailed deer, but many other native species. Although this era's unregulated sport hunting contributed to the whitetail's decline, the larger blame can be laid upon an insatiable appetite for venison in the cities and a desire for the supple leather created from the deer's hide.

From a pre-Columbus population of somewhere between 23 and 33 million, the whitetail's numbers crashed to an estimated low of 350,000 to 500,000 by 1900. The pressure on white-tailed deer only diminished when they became so difficult to find that it was no longer profitable to go afield. In many parts of the U.S., whitetails were virtually extinct or only remnant populations remained.

It's hard to believe today, but at the turn of the twentieth century over 100 years ago, whitetail numbers were alarmingly low, well beneath one million animals. Responsible hunting practices and a newfound appreciation for the whitetail has made its recovery one of North America's most successful animal population recovery stories.

Early hunter-conservationists grew alarmed and were instrumental in seeking laws to protect this highly esteemed and beautiful animal—the very root of wildlife management in this country. With the advent of controlled hunting seasons and bag limits, combined with this new science of wildlife management, whitetails climbed back from the brink of extinction.

Boy, how times have changed.

In many parts of North America, deer populations are so abundant, whitetails are considered a nuisance. The incidence of vehicle-deer collisions has increased dramatically in the last decade, and suburbanites, as they build their starter-mansions in what once was wild land, bump nose to nose with the adaptable whitetail and curse this animal's taste for their shrubbery.

It seems strange then to even talk about whitetail conservation. After all, they are doing quite well, aren't they?

Yes, they are, but there remains concern at several levels.

One such concern could be summed up by the term "habitat fragmentation." Whitetails do well in places where there are lots of edges and variety of habitats, so simply carving up habitat isn't always a problem. The concern arises when the use of this habitat is incompatible with hunting. Without hunting, whitetail populations skyrocket, and there is no other effective means of controlling them. Dot the woods with homes, though, and hunting becomes not only more difficult, but is often frowned upon, and sometimes outlawed.

In several parts of the U.S., the whitetail is already semi-privatized, particularly in Texas. There, and elsewhere, "high fences" have gone up, enclosing large areas of land. Within are trapped the public's deer. It makes little difference that you couldn't have gotten permission to hunt this land anyway because without the fences, deer were free to leave that land (where you might then bag one), and to complete their natural cycle, which includes roaming to breed, thus benefiting the species, including those you harvest down the road.

With the advent of high fences, natural movement stops, and public ownership is essentially moot. In fact, many landowners perceive that they own the deer, and in the state of Texas, as this book was going to press, a bill had been introduced that indeed would make deer private property. Inside many of these high-fence compounds, individuals are also manipulating whitetail genetics for the sake of larger antlers.

Whitetails have also become a commodity to buy and sell, even over the Internet. Canned hunts for large-racked, semi-domesticated whitetails are offered in

From the edge of extinction, whitetails like this flourish once more. In fact, whitetail populations are so abundant in some communities that they are considered a nuisance and a hazard. In the late 2000s, Wisconsin offered unlimited doe permits for $1 each to quell the rising herd and curb the spread of CWD.

This conflict is becoming more evident every day, and the only way to deal with it is for today's hunter-conservationist to become involved in land-use planning issues, so that unfragmented blocks of huntable habitat are preserved.

The second great concern arises from the privatization and commercialization of whitetails. North American hunting tradition and conservation is based on the simple principal that wildlife belongs to the state, not the individual on whose land it may spend time. This system has led to the creation of the most successful wildlife management system in the world. Without the public ownership of wildlife—whitetails included—the system will collapse because no one wants to pay for something from which they derive no benefit.

Whitetail hunting is a lifelong pursuit. By respecting the sport and respecting the animals, the legacy of whitetail hunting will burst in the twenty-first century and beyond.

In North America, wildlife belongs to the state, and not the individuals whose land the wildlife call home. This system of conservation is the most successful in the world, and the more hunters who get involved with conservation and understand what's at stake, the more whitetails will flourish and enrich future generations of hunting tradition.

many parts of the country. An insult to both the animal and to our hunting traditions, these canned killings risk raising the ire of nonhunters, and casting all hunting in a very dim light.

Finally, there is the very real threat of disease, the most serious of which is known as chronic wasting disease (CWD). Essentially the wild counterpart of the now infamous mad cow disease of Great Britain, CWD has now been found in wild deer in a half-dozen states. It is a particularly troubling disease, not only because it devastates the deer population, but because whitetails live in close proximity to people—and are also eaten by people—and there remains the real risk that, like mad cow disease, it may be transmissible to people.

Whitetails have been around a long time. No doubt,

they'll be around a lot longer. They are remarkable creatures and seem well suited to adapt to most of the changes we throw at them.

But not all.

What nonhunters don't understand about those of us who hunt is that we love and respect our quarry. We appreciate the gift they are to us and value the time we spend in pursuit. But because they give us so much, we also owe it to the wildlife we hunt to work for the betterment of its habitat and health.

Not all hunters are conservationists. They should be. Consider joining an organization that works to preserve wild places and advance sound wildlife management practices. It is the least we can do for the animals we hunt.

TIPS FROM THE PROS

PRO TIPS FOR OPENING DAY

In most states, more bucks are taken on the first day than at any other time during the season. One reason for this is that the deer, not having been hunted all summer, are not feeling pressured, and are not on full alert for hunters. That changes once gunshots begin to go off and human scent permeates the woods. To give you your best shot at the best time, we asked eight seasoned hunters what they do on the opener.

Scout for Food Sources

Ronnie Strickland, *Haas Outdoors/Mossy Oak*

"Scouting in many parts of the country, especially down South, mostly revolves around food sources. I begin long-distance scouting in late August, while crops are still in the field, using binoculars or spotting scopes from a good vantage point—many times, a vehicle. The whole purpose is to leave the deer undisturbed. Even the bigger bucks seem to show themselves around agricultural fields then. It may be right at dark, but they will show. Pick out landmarks where bucks continually enter fields; then move in and scout the area for precise stand locations.

"Scouting is an ongoing part of hunting. Once crops are gone, I focus on acorns. A knowledge of where the trees are is valuable. If you're in a new area, nothing beats legwork. You can't find those great out-of-the-way spots unless you're on your feet. I hunt the acorns until the bitter end, checking trees and moving to the freshest sign. Even when the rut kicks in, I stay on acorns if they're still available. Does will be eating them and the bucks will find the does. When acorns are gone, keep walking and find the current food source. It may be winter wheat or rye planted by farmers, but continue scouting the food."

From Mississippi, Strickland, 42, has been deer hunting 30 years. His favorite deer rifle is a 50-caliber in-line muzzleloader. His bow is a compound with graphite arrows, Simmons Landshark broadheads, no release.

Use the Right Scents

Terry Rohm, *Wellington/Tinks*

"Opening day here in Georgia is usually pretty warm. You need to reduce your body odor as much as possible because a deer's nose is his number-one defense. Use unscented soap, shampoo, and laundry detergent. Don't use perfumes at all. When you get into your stand, spray exposed skin and rub your face and hair with an odor neutralizer, such as Non-Stink®. If it's really hot, you need to wash off your sweat with a cloth; I then put that cloth into a plastic bag because there's lots of odor and bacteria on it.

"It also helps to use a cover scent when you get to your tree stand. Early in the year I like to use buck urine. Because the rut is not on, the deer are not interested in rutting, but are interested in the social group communication. If a buck smells buck urine and thinks it's another buck, he comes in to get to know that buck. Tarsal gland [scent] works great, and it's something you can use for weeks if you take proper care of it. A lot of people try to use rut scent like Tink's 69® too early. The rut is not on, and it's just not right. Early in the season I don't use a lure to actually draw the deer in but to get them to stop, especially in bow season. I put lure on both sides of the trail, and when a buck comes down the trail and gets to that scent, he's going to smell it. When he stops, you need to shoot him, as that's your best opportunity."

Rohm, from Buckhead, Georgia, is 41, and has been hunting since he was 12 years old. His favorite bow is a Jennings Buckmaster with aluminum arrows; his favorite gun a Remington 25-06.

Decoy Them into Range

Dave Berkley, *Feather Flex Decoys*
"Last year we discovered that although deer will approach a single decoy cautiously, when you put multiples out, caution is thrown to the wind and they just barge right in. I had only one old doe get cautious last year on approaching a multiple set. Bucks just absolutely, tail-down, head-up, come right on in."

Berkley has also been experimenting with using turkey decoys as confidence decoys for bowhunting whitetails. "I carry five or six and make a little flock. A deer will not move or feed through a flock of feeding turkeys, because the birds will chase him off. They do pay attention to the turkeys, but will always skirt around them. I steer deer with my flock, making them go the way I want, right by my stand."

Berkley, 50, has been deer hunting since he was 16. He lives in Louisiana, and is primarily a bowhunter. He hunts with a High Country bow, Beman arrows, Elk Country broadheads, and a Pro release.

Call Them In

David Hale, *Knight & Hale Game Calls*
"You need to match your calling on opening day to the timing and geographical region you're hunting. If it's bow season, in most places that's the first of October. You're basically looking at feeding and bedding periods, with the rest of the day wasted. Get as close to those areas as you can, then use contact sounds. They're not a lot different from the grunting sounds you'll use in the rut, except you're more aggressive during the rut. Here you're trying to get their attention and say 'I'm a deer, I'm over here,' and they come out of curiosity. As the season progresses and the deer become more mobile, do more calling. There's also more opportunities during the course of the day.

"In those areas where the peak of the rut occurs on opening day of gun season, you need to do as much calling as possible because those deer are in a search mode and they're likely to walk into your realm of calling any hour of the day.

"For those states that open gun season during the post-rut, as do many northern states, you need to spend your time calling around areas where you've seen a lot of sign. Bucks are often easier to call during this time because they're searching for does again. It may be the best time to call."

David Hale is from Kentucky, 51 years old, and has been hunting whitetails since age 14. He uses a 30-06 deer rifle and a PSE Whitetail Hunter bow, Simmons broadheads, ACC carbon arrows, and shoots with a release. "I've got to have every advantage in the world," he says.

Stay All Day

Peter J. Fiduccia, *Outdoorsman's Edge Book Club*
"We hunt about 55 minutes outside the heart of Manhattan, in New York. It's basically farm country—cows, apples, and corn—and we have a fair amount of pressure. We have a lot of people coming up out of the city as well as lots of people who live in the area and hunt. You have the occasional buck that's killed the first hour or two in the morning, but we find that on opening day, most of the deer are killed around 9:30 a.m. and 1:30 p.m. My basic advice is to go into the woods with enough clothes, food, and drink so you don't have to leave your stand or come out during the midday period.

"It used to be a guy could go into the woods on opening day and there were only a few archers who had been chasing deer around before that. Nowadays there are so many archers, especially in this area, that by the time firearms season opens the deer already know they're being hunted hard. So opening day isn't the magic time that it used to be, when you might catch a buck off guard as he's sneaking back to his bed. We find that if you stay in the woods, and in that one stand, the entire day, eventually a deer moved by somebody winds up coming by your stand."

Fiduccia, from New York, just turned 50. His favorite gun is a 280 Remington, his bow is a Golden Eagle with aluminum arrows and Satellite Titan broadheads, and he uses a release.

Learn the New Patterns

Tony Knight, *Knight Rifles*

"Make sure all your equipment is in shape, your rifle is sighted in, you've worked up the correct load, and you have the accessories needed. One thing you need to remember is, on opening day of gun season, the bucks won't follow the same pattern they did earlier during archery season. All of a sudden, all those flashlights start coming through the woods on opening morning and it's a shock to them. But if you're lucky, somebody is going to drive one by your stand. Although I'm sure it's more efficient to stay in your stand, I like to hunt the first couple of hours or so from a tree, then get down about 10:00 a.m. and do some still-hunting. I take a cushion and walk a bit, then sit quite a while.

"There's often another opening day, the special muzzleloader season in many states, and it's usually after the normal gun season. Hunting is usually a lot tougher because of the pressure the deer have seen. During that time, still-hunting, and watching food sources early and late in the morning, will be productive. You will have to do a lot of walking, looking, and some stirring up with drives."

Knight, from Iowa, is 51 and has been hunting for 30 years. His favorite gun? A Knight in-line muzzleloader.

Hunt Escape Routes

Brad Harris, *Lohman Game Calls*

"On opening day of gun season, I like to position myself where I can see a long way so I can cover as much property as possible. I try to set up where several fingers, or two or three ridges, might meet in a saddle, places where I can get as much deer traffic as possible. But I won't hunt those areas after the first couple of days, because they're too open.

"If I'm hunting public land and I know pressure is going to come from different parking areas, then I'll set up along escape routes from those areas. I'll get into the thickest spots where deer will try to seek refuge when they feel pressure from other hunters that morning. I'll set up in places where it's necked-down—again, saddles—but thick lines of edge or timber where they travel when spooked."

Harris, from Missouri, is 40 years old and has been deer hunting since 1970. His favorite rifle is a 270,

favorite bow a Golden Eagle Pro Revolution. He likes Easton arrows and Satellite Titan broadheads, and he doesn't use a release. Harris used to bowhunt on opening day of the gun season, but for the past few years he's used a gun so he can hunt with his teenaged son, who took a record whitetail buck scoring 192K gross last season.

Take a Smart Stand

Jay Cassell, *Contributing Editor at Outdoor Life magazine*

"Where you place your tree stand is critical. I look for a tree that overlooks a deer runway, or where a couple of trails cross. I scout during the preseason to make sure those runways are being used, then place my tree stand 10 or 15 yards back from the intersection of the trails. I try to place it in, or in front of, a hemlock so my silhouette is broken up. With dense cover behind me, deer probably won't see me draw my bow or raise my rifle. If I have to hang my tree stand in a tree that's out in the open, I try to put it on the side of the tree opposite the trails. I never go so high that I feel queasy, but I do like to be at least 15 feet up. You really need to set up your tree stand and then see what the view is like. You may not want to go too high because in some situations deer will be able to see you from far away. For instance, on one hill that I hunt, I put my tree stand too high and deer were seeing me from 200 yards away. Last year I moved the seat down about 2 feet and now they can't see me until they're right up on me.

"Always use a safety belt when you go into a tree stand. Climbing trees is serious stuff; I've heard and read about too many people either killed or injured from falling out of stands. It can happen to you."

Cassell, from New York, is 45, and has been deer hunting for 20 years. He has used a 30-06 Browning BAR for the past 10 years, but is switching to an Ultra Light Arms 30-06 this year. For bowhunting he uses a Golden Eagle Evolution bow, Easton 2117 aluminum arrows, Satellite Titan broadheads, and Scott release.

INFORMATION SOURCES

The following are a few organizations and agencies that offer data concerning CWD, among other wildlife-related topics. Contact them for more information.

Boone and Crockett Club
406-542-1888
www.boone-crockett.org/news/news_
cwd

Colorado Division of Wildlife
303-297-1192
http://wildlife.state.co.us

Chronic Wasting Disease Alliance
www.cwd-info.org

Kansas Department of Wildlife & Parks
620-342-0658
www.kdwp.state.ks.us

Minnesota Department of Natural Resources
651-296 6157
www.dnr.state.mn.us/mammals/deer/
cwd.html

Montana Fish, Wildlife & Parks
406-751-4564
www.fwp.state.mt.us

Mule Deer Foundation
www.muledeer.org/cwd.htm
888-375-3337

Nebraska Game & Parks Commission
402-471-0641
www.ngpc.state.ne.us/homepage.html

New Mexico Department of Game and Fish
800-862-9310
www.gmfsh.state.nm.us

Oklahoma Conservation Commission
405-521-6787
www.okcc.state.ok.us

Pope and Young Club
507-867-4144
www.pope-young.org

Rocky Mountain Elk Foundation
800-225-5355
www.rmef.org

South Dakota Department of Game, Fish & Parks
605-394-2391
www.state.sd.us/gfp

The Wildlife Management Institute
202-371-1808

Wisconsin Department of Natural Resources
608-266-2621
www.dnr.state.wi.us

Whitetails Unlimited
800-274-5471
www.whitetailsunlimited.org

Wyoming Game and Fish Department
307-745-4046
http://gf.state.wy.us

Alberta Sustainable Resource Development
780-944-0313
http://www3.gov.ab.ca/srd/fw/index.
html

Saskatchewan Environment & Resources
800-567-4224
www.serm.gov.sk.ca/fishwild/CWD-
survey.htm

MANUFACTURERS
Barrie Archery, LLC
P.O. Box 482
Waseca, MN 56093
507-835-3859
507-835-5097
www.rockymtbroadheads.com

Browning
One Browning Place
Morgan, UT 84050
800-333-3504
801-876-3331
www.browning.com

Cabela's, Inc.
One Cabela Drive
Sidney, NE 69160
800-237-4444
800-496-6329
www.cabelas.com

Carl Zeiss Sports Optics
13005 N. Kingston Ave.
Chester, VA 23836
800-441-3005
804-530-8481
www.zeiss.com/sports

Gerber Legendary Blades
P.O. Box 23088
Portland, OR 97281
800-950-6161
www.gerberblades.com

HHA Sports
7222 Townline Road
Wisconsin Rapids, WI 54494
800-548-7812
www.hhasports.com

Hunter's Specialties
6000 Huntington Court NE
Cedar Rapids, IA 52402
319-395-0321
319-395-0326
www.hunterspec.com

Primos Hunting Calls, Inc.
604 First Street
Flora, MS 39071
601-879-9323
601-879-9324
www.primos.com

Scent-Lok
1731 Wierengo Drive
Muskegon, MI 49442
800-315-5799
231-767-2824
www.scentlok.com

Sightron, Inc.
100 Jeffrey Way, Suite A
Youngsville, NC 27596
919-562-3000
919-562-7129
www.sightron.com

Tink's
P.O. Box 244
Madison, GA 30650
800-713-7278
706-342-8993
www.tinks69.com

INDEX